D0065443

MENTAL TERRITORIES

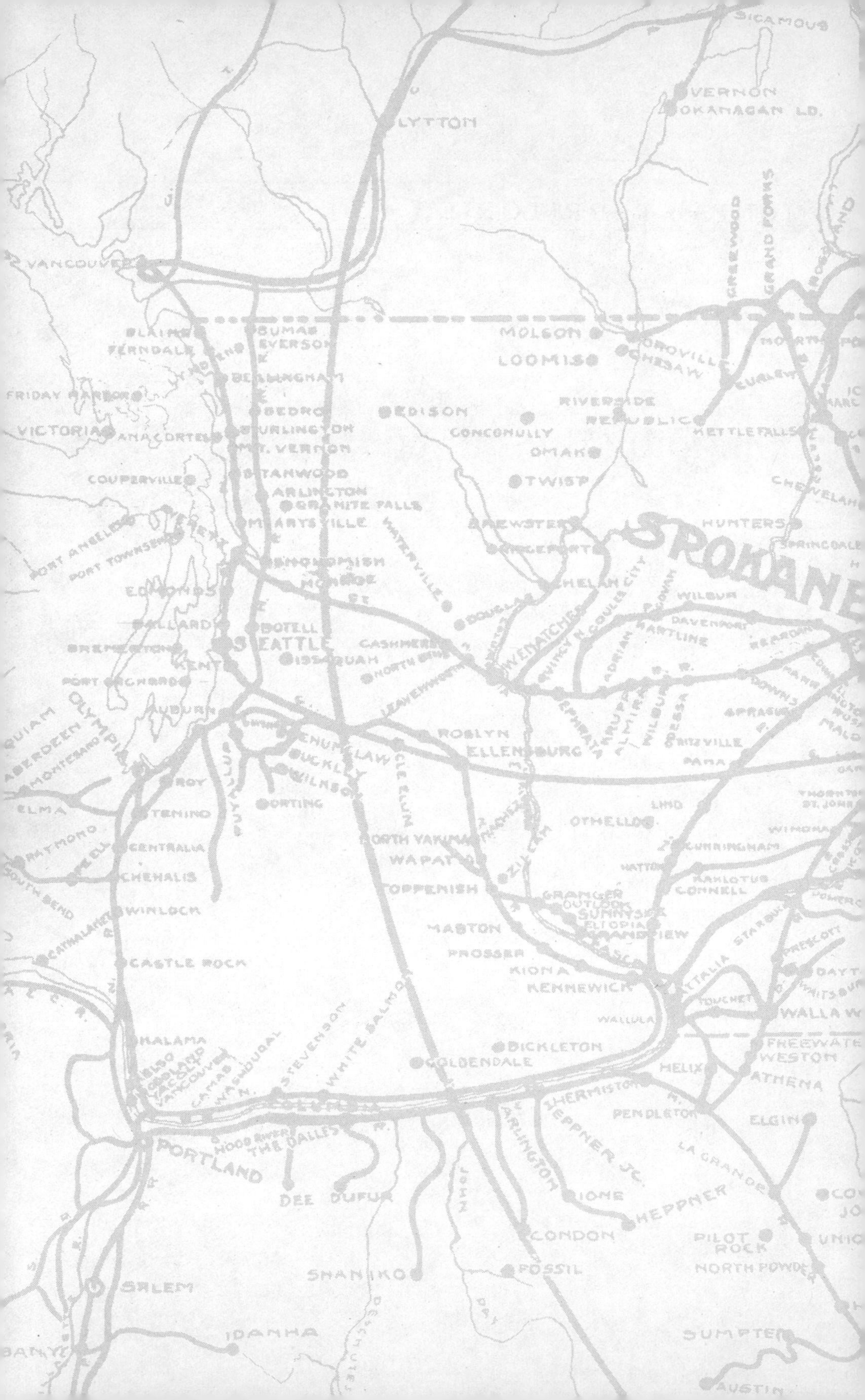
SICAMOUS
VERNON
OKANAGAN LD.
LYTTON
GREENWOOD
GRAND FORKS
VANCOUVER
BLAINE
SUMAS
EVERSON
FERNDALE
BELLINGHAM
MOLSON
OROVILLE
LOOMIS
CHESAW
FRIDAY HARBOR
SEDRO
EDISON
RIVERSIDE
REPUBLIC
KETTLE FALLS
VICTORIA
ANACORTES
BURLINGTON
MT. VERNON
CONCONULLY
OMAK
COUPERVILLE
STANWOOD
TWISP
ARLINGTON
GRANITE FALLS
MARYSVILLE
BREWSTER
HUNTERS
PORT ANGELES
PORT TOWNSEND
SNOHOMISH
MONROE
BRIDGEPORT
SPOKANE
WATERVILLE
CHELAN
EDMONDS
BALLARD
BOTELL
SEATTLE
DOUGLAS
WENATCHEE
WILBUR
DAVENPORT
HARTLINE
BREMERTON
CASHMERE
ISSAQUAH
KENT
NORTH BEND
PORT ORCHARD
OLYMPIA
AUBURN
ABERDEEN
MONTESANO
ROSLYN
ELLENSBURG
ENUMCLAW
BUCKLEY
WILKSON
CLE ELUM
EPHRATA
ODESSA
RITZVILLE
SPRAGUE
ROY
ELMA
TENINO
ORTING
PUYALLUP
OTHELLO
CENTRALIA
CHEHALIS
NORTH YAKIMA
WAPATO
CUNNINGHAM
KAHLOTUS
CONNELL
TOPPENISH
GRANGER
OUTLOOK
SUNNYSIDE
WINLOCK
MABTON
GRANDVIEW
PROSSER
CASTLE ROCK
KIONA
KENNEWICK
PRESCOTT
WALLULA
TOUCHET
WALLA W
KALAMA
BICKLETON
FREEWATE
WESTON
GOLDENDALE
STEVENSON
WHITE SALMON
HELIX
ATHENA
HERMISTON
PENDLETON
ELGIN
ARLINGTON
HEPPNER JC.
PORTLAND
HOOD RIVER
THE DALLES
LA GRANDE
DEE
DUFUR
IONE
HEPPNER
CONDON
PILOT ROCK
NORTH POWDER
SHANIKO
FOSSIL
SALEM
IDANHA
SUMPTER
AUSTIN

MENTAL TERRITORIES

Mapping the Inland Empire

KATHERINE G. MORRISSEY

CORNELL UNIVERSITY PRESS

ITHACA AND LONDON

First published 1997 by Cornell University Press.
First printing, Cornell Paperbacks, 1997.

Library of Congress Cataloging-in-Publication Data

Morrissey, Katherine G.
   Mental territories : mapping the Inland Empire / Katherine G.
Morrissey.
     p. cm.
   Includes bibliographical references (p.) and index.
   ISBN 0-8014-3250-2 (cloth : alk paper).—ISBN 0-8014-8326-3
(pbk. : alk. paper)
   1. Inland Empire—Historical geography. 2. Inland Empire—
History—Psychological aspects. 3. Spokane Region (Wash.)—
Historical geography. 4. Spokane Region (Wash.)—History—
Psychological aspects. 5. Regionalism—Inland
Empire. 6. Regionalism—Washington (State)—Spokane Region.
7. Human geography—Inland Empire. 8. Human geography—
Washington (State)—Spokane Region. 9. Culture conflict—Inland
Empire—History. 10. Culture conflict—Washington (State)—
Spokane Region—History. I. Title.
F852.M67 1997
979.7'37—dc21   97-23223

Printed in the United States of America

Cornell University Press strives to utilize environmentally responsible suppliers and materials to the fullest extent possible in the publishing of its books. Such materials include vegetable-based, low-VOC inks and acid-free papers that are also either recycled, totally chlorine-free, or partly composed of nonwood fibers.

Cloth printing   10 9 8 7 6 5 4 3 2 1

Paperback printing   10 9 8 7 6 5 4 3 2 1

CONTENTS

ACKNOWLEDGMENTS

In the time I have spent on this project I have accumulated many debts to a wide variety of people and institutions. My first thanks go to Howard R. Lamar, whose patient guidance and open-minded intellectual generosity gave me the space to explore mental territories. I am grateful for his assistance and support. Kai Ericson contributed significantly to my understanding of the social sciences and offered encouragement along with cogent advice. My early forays into regional studies were guided by a talented and inspiring set of teachers: John Mack Faragher, Patricia Nelson Limerick, George Miles, and Charles S. Peterson. These historians of the United States West, each of whom defines the region in his or her own distinctive way, provided examples of ways to interpret the western past. My thanks as well to the faculty of the American Studies Program, Yale University, and to my colleagues in the Departments of History at Williams College and the University of Arizona for their support and encouragement.

The residents of the Inland Empire have been remarkably tolerant of this often misguided outsider. In particular, I would like to thank the Dirks family of Sprague, Washington, and the Charters family of Castlegar, British Columbia, for their interest in my project and their hospitality. I appreciated and benefited from the time that Susan Armitage, John Fahey, Joe Franklin, Keith Petersen, and Carlos Schwantes took from their busy schedules to share their understanding of the region and to discuss certain aspects of this work.

Archivists and librarians, both within and outside of the region, provided valuable assistance and suggestions as I gathered the materials. Terry Abraham of the University of Idaho, Judy Austin of the Idaho State Historical Society, Peter Blodgett of the Huntington Library, Jim Cromwell of Selkirk College, Helen Crysler of the Pend Oreille County Historical Society, Karen DeSeve and Doug Olsen of the Eastern Washington State Historical Society, Marian Garvey of the Stevens County Historical Society, Chris Kull of the Monroe County Historical Society, Shawn Lamb of the Nelson Museum, Meredith Melnick of the Cranbrook Archives, Museum, and Landmark Foundation, Nadene Miller and Nancy Compau of the Spokane Public Library, Charles V. Mutschler of Eastern Washington University, Edward Nolan, formerly of the Eastern Washington State Historical Society and now at the Washington State Historical Society, Frances O'Conner of the Kimberely Museum, Bill Quaile of the Fernie Museum, Mary Reed of the Latah County Historical Society, Rosemary Santopinto of the Greenwood Museum, Derryll White of the Fort Steele Provincial Heritage Park, W. Thomas White and Bob Frame of the James J. Hill Reference Library, and Tania Yakimowich of the Glenbow-Alberta Institute were especially helpful. I also thank family, friends, and colleagues who helped me track down sources and offered suggestions, including Barbara Chamberlain, Adrienne Donaldson, Agnes Koch, Stephen Lassonde, Deborah Marlow, Eileen, Ellen, John, Patricia, and Richard Morrissey, Kathryn Morse, Ian Robinson, Karen Swann, and David Yoo.

The work has benefited materially from a National Endowment for the Humanities Fellowship for College Teachers and Independent Scholars, a W. M. Keck Foundation Fellowship at the Huntington Library, research grants from the James J. Hill Reference Library and the Yale University American Studies Program, and a Provost's Authors' Support Fund Award from the University of Arizona. The Feminist Studies Focused Research Activity at the University of California, Santa Cruz, the Department of History at Stanford University, and the Center for the Humanities at Williams College provided facilities that fostered the work. Peter Agree and Cornell University Press have patiently attended to its completion.

Intellectual debts are difficult to acknowledge specifically. Conversations, and arguments, with generous colleagues, students, and friends over the years have helped me define my own ideas and come to understand other perspectives. As an interdisciplinary scholar I have found these mutual efforts in intellectual inquiry crucial to my work as well as rewarding. Among those in this community of scholars to whom I am indebted are Karen Anderson, Jacqueline Dirks, Dana Frank, Maureen Fitzgerald, Jay Gitlin, Gail Hershatter, Regina Kunzel, Richard Lowry, Roger Nichols, Kathryn Oberdeck, Kimberly Phillips, Elizabeth Raymond, Mary Renda, Jennifer Robertson, Karen Sawislak, Tom Smith, Catherine Stock, Tamara Plakins Thornton, Linda Watts, and the students at the University of Arizona who have patiently listened to Inland Empire tales. I would especially like to thank those who have read parts of this work: Gail Bernstein, William Cronon, David Dinwoodie, Ann Fabian, Alison Futrell, Valerie Hartouni, Frederick Hoxie, A. Yvette Huginnie, Susan Johnson, Patricia Nelson Limerick, Peter Mancall, Jean Pederson, William Robbins, Thomas Spear, Michael Steiner, and Laura Tabili. I have been fortunate to have the support, sharp reading, and wise counsel of an interdisciplinary faculty writing group at the University of Arizona; Laura Berry, Jehanne Gheith, Janet Jakobsen, and Beth Mitchneck have my warm thanks. While I may not have been able to respond to all the readers' suggestions, the work as a whole has benefited from their comments and criticisms.

Finally, my deepest appreciation goes to my parents, John and Eileen Morrissey, for their love and support.

K. G. M.

INTRODUCTION

MENTAL TERRITORIES

Walking through the hills above Pullman, Washington, one summer, I came across a series of broken granite blocks amid the underbrush. As I searched further, a pattern emerged: the outline of a forgotten cemetery appeared in the scattered remnants of headstones, mounds, and fences; the vegetation alternated from dry bunchgrass to tangled bushes and wild-flowers covering the neglected graves. Here, just off a trail wandering be-tween the Sunnyside City Park and a new subdivision under construction, I had found it—the old Pullman cemetery where Oscar Amos spent so much of his life.

I had looked unsuccessfully for this place. A few weeks before, when I had asked a local historian, Keith Petersen, about the sites of Pullman graveyards, he had directed me to the city cemetery on the bluffs south of town and to the iron-gated Independent Order of Odd Fellows plots to the west. Then he had remembered a third, unmarked cemetery he had once literally stumbled across as a student—a few headstones in a farmer's field. "I haven't been there in years," he recalled. "There's been a lot of construction up there since then; I'm not sure anyone could find the place today."

My queries and subsequent wanderings in the hills were attempts to satisfy my curiosity about the life of a particular man, Oscar Amos. His papers—scattered notes and rambling essays that filled the backs of old posters and barbershop calendars—were kept largely uncataloged in the local university archives. The collection was unusual, located among the papers of university presidents and professors, the financial records of local ranches and businesses, and the manuscripts of prominent settlers.

Oscar Amos lived and worked in Pullman at the turn of the century. He was a grave-digger, sewer cleaner, and handyman in this southeastern Washington town; he was also the town drunk and a self-styled philosopher.

"19 years is up today at noon sense i came to Pullman there has been meny changes taken place."[1] In his stream-of-consciousness writings, marked by creative spelling and colloquial grammar, Amos recorded these changes along with descriptions of his work, thoughts, and dreams. It is a nightmarish collection of papers, in part because of its subject matter. On relocating bodies, he noted, "i was barehanded the Box was fillt of water i scraped around feeling for bones . . . some flesh was left on one of them." On the consequences of drinking, he wrote, "the afterBirth is filled with horrow and unhappiness whatever that monster is it has trapped meny poor creature in its grip this is Hell on earth." But it is also foreboding for historians because of its form—two manuscript boxes stuffed with odds and ends of paper, including his notes on books of ancient history, religion, and philosophy and his frequently undated journal entries. A single page often has three separate entries scrawled sideways or upside down in smeared pencil, making it difficult to discern the order and, at times, the content of the entries. The sources of his inconsistent philosophies are also wildly mixed; he makes reference to the Masons, a fraternal order; the Rosicrucian fellowship, an occult research society; Christian preachers; a socialist newspaper; politician Robert LaFollette; the American Institute of Psychology; Swami Bhakta Vishita, a Hindu teacher; the Grangers; and Annie Besant among others.

Little is known about Oscar Amos apart from this collection of papers. He arrived in the southeastern Washington town of Pullman from Vincennes, Indiana, either along with or following a group of families from the same midwestern town. He claimed a poorhouse upbringing in rural Scott County, Indiana: "my mother was a clergley daughter my father was a labor and drinker Grand Pa would not let his daughter step in side of home no more." He appears in Pullman's public record only a few times; his periodic lockups for drunkenness were noted on the police blotter and, toward the end of his life, an article in the local paper celebrated this "colorful character." Oscar Amos, the author declared, was "the champion ditch digger of the Inland Empire," who had, figuratively at least, "dug his way with pick and shovel from Pullman to Spokane."[2]

The words used to describe Oscar Amos and his ditch are significant. As the Inland Empire champion, Amos had dug his way not to China or to the West but north to the city of Spokane. At the turn of the century, as railroad and chamber of commerce pamphlets were quick to point out, "all roads lead to Spokane." The eastern Washington city was more than simply a transportation hub, however; it was the "Heart of the Inland Empire."

The Inland Empire

What was the Inland Empire? Where was it? If you ask most Spokane residents today some recall, perhaps after some thought, the words on the masthead of the *Spokesman-Review;* the city's newspaper proclaims daily to be "the voice of the Inland Empire." Other locals describe a region that extends beyond the circulation of the paper to cover all of eastern Washington and northern Idaho. Still other boosters claim it stretches even farther west and south into Montana and Oregon. Their definitions, couched in seemingly concrete references to state boundaries, deal with an abstract historical concept. For those who demarcate the place, the Inland Empire is a Pacific Northwest region imbued with particular meanings, forged through a set of historical circumstances.

Yet even as one listens to those who live within the region, it is clear that the evocative power and contested nature of the Inland Empire persist alongside a contemporary obscurity. As Donald W. Meinig, a native son and historical geographer, explains, "The Inland Empire and Spokane are among the clearest examples we have of a region and its capital, yet Spokane and the Inland Empire are also among the least known cities and regions in all of America."[3] At an academic conference a few years ago, I presented a paper based on my research concerning the area of eastern Washington, northern Idaho, and southeastern British Columbia once celebrated as the Inland Empire. After I had finished my talk, a member of the audience got to her feet to add some comments of her own. "I am from Spokane, Washington," the white-haired woman explained. "I'm from the Inland Empire and I want to tell you that regardless of what you say, we are not invisible." Referring to the area and its inhabitants, she declared, "We are an important region." She spoke with considerable emotion about her attachment to the place. Both her words and the passion of her response may have surprised many in the audience; few had heard the term "Inland Empire" or its application to a specific region before that morning.

Less than one hundred years ago this was not the case, according to those who identified with the place. "It is a singular fact," wrote one Spokane committee in 1909, "that the people of the Inland Empire center their pride in the term 'Inland Empire' and hold the Inland Empire in their affections above their affections for their state."[4] Those who boasted about and boosted the Inland Empire emphasized the cohesiveness of the place and its people. "Heart," "affections," and "pride"—the words used to define the Inland Empire—suggest the emotional attachments that supplemented the economic and political regional ties. These intangibles were difficult to describe or explain. As one pamphlet written for outsiders pointed out, "Residents of the Pacific northwest are inclined to take it for

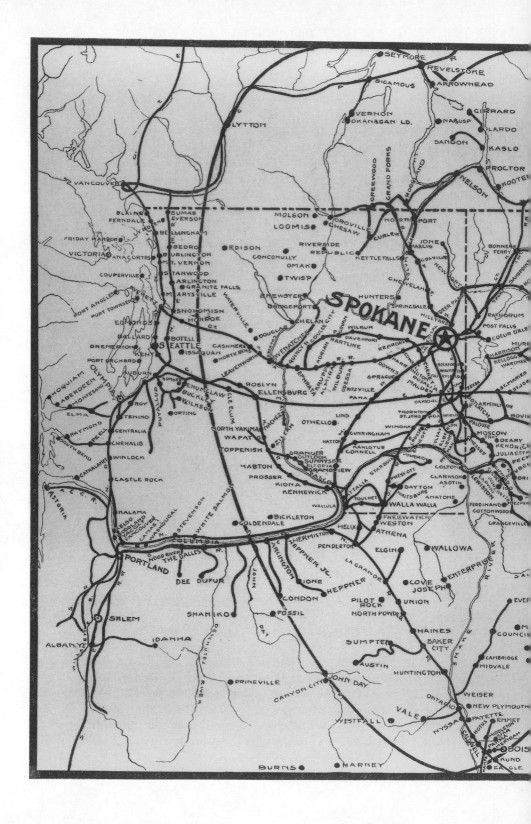

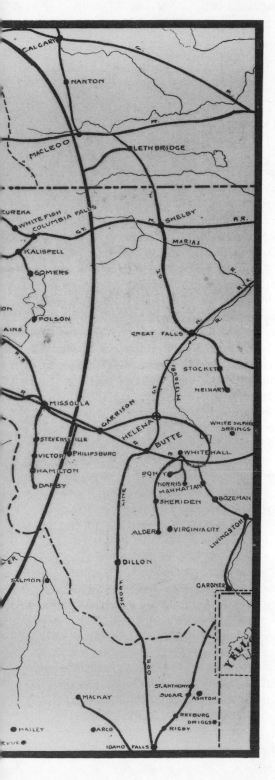

"The Inland Empire" The Heart of the Inland Empire, in this 1910 version, stretched from British Columbia down to Boise, Idaho, and from the western side of the Cascades to beyond the eastern slope of the Bitterroot Mountains. Railroad lines and river systems link the region's towns to its capital, Spokane. Oscar Amos's town, Pullman, Washington, is located south of Spokane, just to the west of Moscow, Idaho. By permission of the Geography and Map Division, Library of Congress.

granted that their eastern friends understand exactly what is comprehended by the words 'Inland Empire.' "[5]

When asked to explain to such disbelievers, the turn-of-the-century inhabitants who wrote about the region used "natural" and symbolic evidence of coherence. Referring to environmental landmarks, they defined the region by geographic rather than human boundaries: "It is . . . separated from the great prairies by the Rocky mountains, from the Pacific Coast region by the Cascades, on the north by the Selkirk mountains and extending south as far as the Blue mountains in Oregon."[6] They drew a mental image of a round bowl, emphasizing the mountains that rim the region. A circle, the symbol of perfection in the Christian tradition, contained and protected the various interrelated sections of the region. At its implied center, the city of Spokane served as the "hub" around which radiated "the smaller and equally enterprising cities and towns which are the spokes in the wheel." The empire was a "natural division."[7]

In reality, of course, the boundaries are not so clear-cut or symmetrical. On a map, the area inhabitants described as the Inland Empire appears more like an amorphous blob than a circle. Ecologically and geographically, Spokane could not be considered a center, situated as it is on the edge of the volcanic Columbia Basin. To the west these basalt plains, covered with sagebrush and bunchgrass, are marked by arid channeled scablands; "it is the 'Big Bend' country, treeless, shadeless, leafless, featureless," wrote the disgruntled traveler Owen Wister in 1892.[8] To the south, the basin, well watered by streams, breaks into the rolling hills of the Palouse, a fertile area once covered by rich native grasses. Spokane, located at the falls of the Spokane River and amid the ponderosa pines that fringe the basin, faces a different terrain to the north. North-south valleys, visual reminders of the glacial fingers of the Cordilleran Ice Sheet, stretch down from British Columbia; they are divided by the Okanagan, Kootenay, and Selkirk mountain ranges where the ponderosa pines merge into forests of white pine, fir, tamarack, spruce, and cedar. Mixed forests and higher elevations mark the land to the east of the city as well; the Pend Oreille and Coeur d'Alene are among the many lakes that break up this mountainous country.[9]

Literate residents of this ecologically diverse area frequently characterized themselves in their public and private writings as a united, settled people with shared goals. Echoing each other's prose, they described "homesteaders" and "homebuilders," businessmen and boosters who were industrious, energetic, and future-oriented. In letters and diaries they used words such as "liveliest," "progressive," "busy," and "enthusiastic" to characterize the people and their activities. The region's promotional literature spoke of "the very best kind of immigrants . . . people with brains, money and enterprise." Just as these residents of the Inland Empire defined their diverse environment as a single unit, they perceived the peoples within the region, themselves and their neighbors, as a harmonious community of like-minded settlers, working together to create a future home.[10]

In reality, of course, the population was not so homogeneous. Although census materials are not complete or entirely accurate for this period, federal records indicate that Inland Empire settlers came from more than thirty-three countries, thirty states, and ten provinces. The Scandinavian countries, Germany, Russia, and Italy contributed the largest number of foreign-born residents, but China, Switzerland, and the British Isles were also well represented. The settlers spoke different languages, frequently lived in ethnic or religious enclaves, and belonged to a variety of organizations.[11]

In the region-focused rhetoric, these relative newcomers rarely counted the area's native inhabitants—the Yakima, Nez Perce, Spokane, Colville, Okanagan, Kootenai, Coeur d'Alene, and other Salish peoples—as residents. Eager to sustain their own visions of place, they equally ignored conflicts and confrontations between and among class, cultural, and racial groups. This rhetoric of unity, though false in these ways, reflects the hegemonic nature of discourse. In part, the contests among social groups, which threatened to undermine regional identity, also served to foster it. To a remarkable extent, new settlers subsumed these differences into a single self-definition, especially when speaking or writing to an outside audience.

The rhetoric of unity accelerated the development of a regional identity; it also influenced to a certain extent the character of subsequent settlers. There was "a kind of cultural imprinting of the values of the people already there on later immigrants," suggests the historian Otis Pease about the Pacific Northwest as a whole, "a kind of unconscious screening, partly self-selective, resulting in a degree of homogeneity between old-timers and newcomers . . . because they had been predisposed to go where it was culturally congenial for them."[12] A belief in their united future, in the concept of the Inland Empire, tied these "old-timers" and newcomers together. They shared a sense of self grounded in place, engaged with the environment of the Inland Empire as a physical space and as a mental landscape. Although he speaks of a different time and place, the anthropologist Anthony Cohen's remarks on the relationship of people and place in contemporary rural Britain equally apply to the Inland Empire: "The ethnography of locality," he writes, "is an account of how people experience and express their differences from others, and of how their sense of differences becomes incorporated into and informs the nature of their social organization and process. The sense of difference thus lies at the heart of people's awareness of their culture."[13] Equally revealing are the ways people use the visible differences to create a cohesive unit. To elaborate the sense of difference

that identified the Inland Empire, to explore the perceptions of environment and community that defined the place, is the task of this book. In
tracing the creation and maintenance of this region from the 1870s to the
1910s through the words, actions, and objects of its settlers, I seek to
uncover the ideas and dreams that have tied people and place together in
the American West.

What, then, is the Inland Empire? It is a perceptual region composed
of a series of settlements tied together by mental concepts. Regions are
constructed entities, ways of organizing people and place. While territorial
politicians and environmental circumstances influence the shape of regions, the boundaries that govern the residents are those they draw for
themselves. Perceptual regions are created and developed in people's
minds. They are vague, shifting ideas, but they engender strong loyalties.
They are as much psychological as geographical, political, or economic
divisions. The pervasive identification of the Inland Empire reflected in the
rhetoric of its turn-of-the-century inhabitants as well as the persistent
contestations over its meanings illustrate the power of mental territories.[14]

Frontier/Region

When new settlers of the inland Northwest sought to define their region,
they called on their everyday experiences and on contemporary nineteenth-
century language and ideas such as those about frontier, settlements, and
the West. Although the meanings of the term "Inland Empire" and regional
identification underwent continual reassessment, the Inland Empire came
to be associated with characteristics that drew upon these ideas, especially
as they were linked to the experiences of residents. Traditional terms such
as "frontier" and "settlement," for example, do not entirely correspond to
what residents meant by the Inland Empire. The words inhabitants used
served as a shorthand for meaning. But while individually notions of settlement and notions of frontier were inadequate, residents formed new meanings by using these potentially conflicting terms concurrently. How these
westerners defined themselves and their place in the context of traditional
terms thus helps to illuminate a part of the region's identity.[15]

Ideas about the West as a frontier influenced the late nineteenth-century
settlers. The history of the United States West tells of the interactions
among different peoples in particular environments. Western historians
have recounted a story of successive frontiers, of the creation of American
character at "the meeting point between savagery and civilization." The
creation of the Inland Empire is not a frontier saga, but the concept of the
frontier strongly influenced its story, especially as that story was told by
turn-of-the-century immigrants. In many ways residents perceived the In-

land Empire as a frontier. According to the census definition of a settled area reiterated by the historian Frederick Jackson Turner—a population "density of two or more [persons] to the square mile"—parts of the Inland Empire remained a frontier beyond 1920.[16] Residents, often self-consciously, used frontier rhetoric to describe their regional identity. The concept of frontier as a force that transformed diverse peoples in diverse environments into Americans appealed to Inland Empire inhabitants as they tried to reconcile the inherent strains and conflicts within their regional community.[17]

Yet at the same time Inland Empire residents embraced characteristics contradictory to the frontier image. They referred to themselves as "settlers," rather than "frontiersmen" or "pioneers," preferring to avoid the pejorative connotations of "frontiersmen," which conjured up visions of backward wilderness dwellers. ("Pioneer" was a term used only retroactively when settlers joined the Inland Empire Pioneer Association.)[18] Likewise, the Turnerian definition of "frontier" differentiates between a moving frontier—"the edge of settlement"—and settlement behind this line. Those who settled in the interior Pacific Northwest, even after 1890, the date associated with the end of the frontier, rarely recognized this distinction; they accepted potentially conflicting ideas associated with the terms "frontier" and "settlement" in their perceptions of place. In their minds the Inland Empire was simultaneously a frontier and a settlement.

The well-known language and tradition of the American settlement process helped shape the immigrants' experiences in the inland Northwest; their experiences also reinforced their self-definitions. Consider, for example, the interactions of settlers with their physical environments. Between 1870 and 1910, the number of people entering and establishing themselves in the territory east of the Cascades and west of the Bitterroot Mountains grew dramatically. The increasing population, in different configurations, significantly changed the face of the land. At the same time, the land significantly influenced the minds of the settlers. The visible elements of the region's physical environment—both natural phenomena, such as buttes, coulees, rolling hills, and mountain valleys, and human alterations, such as wheat fields, irrigation canals, and orchards—came to be identified as signs of the region's essence. Although ecological changes—the gradual disappearance of native grasses in the Palouse owing to the introduction of livestock, for example—had started years earlier, they were not linked to the identity of the region until they occurred with a rapidity for which individuals could take credit. The Inland Empire grew along with the changing environment, and growth was defined as a frontier process. Settlers took pride in both ecological diversity and ecological change.[19]

This optimistic vision of a particular territory had roots in accepted ideas about the West as a frontier of opportunity. Drawing on the persistent myth of the West as a land of plenty, the peoples of the Inland Empire considered theirs a place of abundance. The intersection of different ecological zones had long provided ample resources for the region's inhabitants.[20] The diverse ecology contributed to the development of flexible mental and physical responses to the environment. Consider, for example, the late nineteenth-century settlers' economic use of natural resources. Seasonal work drew farm owners into the mining areas. Miners hired on at farms, ranches, and lumber mills. Such economically diverse activities as cutting railroad ties and hauling freight, promoting land sales and constructing roads, and selling goods and clearing land were perceived as part of the settlement process. Even if in reality individuals spent their entire work lives affiliated with one occupation, such as farming, they did not identify themselves solely as farmers. May Arkwright Hutton, for example, a woman, a suffrage activist, a writer, and a participant in a successful mining venture, was typical of those who identified with a multiplicity of roles. Individual self-conception, like regional self-conception, was flexible. Washington Grange members, most of whom were eastern Washington (Inland Empire) residents, often found themselves at odds with the national chapter because of their inclusive outlook. As William Bouck, master of the Washington Grange, pointed out, the membership was diverse: "Farmer and industrial worker stand together in this Northwest, as nowhere else in the world. They have had the same experiences, the same background. . . . I know them by the thousands. They are in every grange in the state." Despite the hyperbole, Bouck knew whereof what he spoke. His own checkered background as farmer, hard-rock miner, timber cruiser, store owner, and postmaster made him aware of the typical patterns and influenced his thoughts and ideas.[21]

Like Hutton and Bouck, other late nineteenth-century immigrants interpreted their experiences within the context of a settled frontier. While "frontier" implies a transient population and "settlement" a static or rooted one, neither implication accurately reflected the situation in the Inland Empire. Although population shifted greatly during this period, people generally moved within the area, and residents perceived no inconsistency between this mobility and their conceptions of their settled society. They traveled both physically and mentally in a known world. As the imagery of the newspaper article about Amos suggests, certain directions and types of travel made more sense than others. For a young man to travel 350 miles from his home near Wenatchee, Washington, to the Slocan in British Columbia was not perceived as a dramatic migration, but his brother's 100-mile move to Seattle was a major upheaval, tantamount to desertion.[22]

Catharine Burgess Carr, for another example, traveled frequently; her job as a hosiery and undergarments saleswoman in northern Idaho demanded it. In her letters written in 1914 to her husband, William, in Elk

River, Idaho, Catharine displays an acceptance of mobility as a part of her own life and also of those of her customers. Historians rarely recognize traveling saleswomen in relation to frontiers or settlements. In fact, until recently, frontier scholars infrequently acknowledged women's work, whether inside or outside the home. The term "frontier" implies an individualistic male population. "Settlement" implies a family population. But the people who came to or moved within the region, even within the mining districts, were never all male; women and men shared in the creation of the Inland Empire. In their self-definitions they were both individuals and community builders. Kinship, community, and other social ties connected individuals and served to reinforce regional awareness.[23]

What drew residents of the Inland Empire together and shaped their regional identity was not so much a consensus of opinion; it was not that everyone agreed. Rather they held in common ways of thinking, a stake in the meanings associated with their place, and a vision of the future. Their ways of thinking, shaped by nineteenth-century ideas of frontier, settlements, and the West and by their experiences in a particular place and time, distinguished their region.[24]

Regionalism and Regional Identity

Regionalism and regional studies have resurfaced in recent years in a variety of academic disciplines. Shaped by the understandings developed through the emerging field of cultural studies about the contested, unstable, and multiply constituted categories of "culture" and "identity" and the ways in which power resonates through language, discourse, and representations, these new works contribute to a reconceptualization of ethnographic, sociological, and historical studies.[25] The resurgence of "locality studies" in geography, "new regionalism" in literature, "regional studies" interdisciplinary programs, "new localism" in anthropology, and "new western history" reflect the influence of interdisciplinary approaches. David Jordan summarizes the trend: "It has become clear that regionalism is more than just nostalgic 'local color,' but that it comprises a dynamic interplay of political, cultural, and psychological forces. As notions of cultural homogeneity become increasingly outdated, and as humanity's tenuous place in the natural world seems in peril, regionalists have begun to speak out."[26] Regionalists do not, however, speak in one voice. Some scholars, for example, have substituted regions for nation-states as units of analysis. In the face of the destabilization of "nations" into "imagined communities," regions retain the taint of wholeness as natural definable divisions. Other scholars, however, embrace regions as representations of diversity. Responding to the critique of nationalism as hegemonic and colonialist, regionalism allows for marginal voices, multiple identities, and transnational examinations. The appeal of regionalism as an intellectual construct lies, in part, in its malleability.[27]

Scholarly examinations of regions are further complicated by the ways people identify with places. Regionalism and regional identity are vexed issues. The attachments that individuals create to a particular place, the ways people identify with one location over another, are often difficult to fathom or to explain. What defines a region? What are its boundaries? Certain regional boundaries are easier to define than others. One might distinguish between those elements that may be represented on a map and those that cannot be reduced to a cartographic form. Physiographic features, which serve to unify, isolate, or otherwise characterize the land-scape, for example, are significant elements of any region, seen as "natural" boundaries. Political boundaries are another set of lines demarcating counties, states, or federal administrative units. More elusive, but still representable, are economic and social features such as reliance on particular markets or membership in a religious or ethnic group. These environmental, political, social, and economic features are among the central elements commonly used by scholars and writers to define regions.

Another, less tangible, feature is also acknowledged by most scholars who study regionalism. As the historian William Robbins notes, "Regionalism by definition—with its many hues and shades of meaning—is largely a mental construction." Whether they define this characteristic as "a broadly based common perception of social reality which, while not simply and lucidly defined, directs attention to the shared particularism of one's roots, values, and sense of purpose," or simply as "a state of mind," scholars more frequently note than explain its existence.[28]

This book examines this elusive feature of regionalism. How do perceptions influence the creation of a region? How do individual ideas about a particular place come to be shared by groups of people? What mental boundaries do people draw around their place? What do the debates over what constitutes appropriate boundaries tell us about a region and its residents? How do these contests over meaning work to define individuals as a people? And, in particular, how was it that the inhabitants of eastern Washington, northern Idaho, and southeastern British Columbia came to define themselves during the late nineteenth and early twentieth centuries as members of the Inland Empire? To explore these questions, this historical case study investigates the formation of a particular "mental territory" at a particular period of time. While environmental, economic, political, and social factors all contribute to regional identity, the focus here also includes cognitive factors.

Today, the Inland Empire still retains meaning for some of its residents; the region is a conceptual place. But it is one whose meaning has changed over time and has been contested. As Edwin Bingham and Glen Love note, "A sense of regional cohesion and identity is a subjective and protean matter depending on angle of vision and changing circumstance."[29] Just as residents disagreed over their regional definition, so too have historians presented differing conceptions of this interior Pacific Northwest region.

At the turn of the century, regional historians writing about the recent past recognized the existence of the Inland Empire but rarely defined its characteristics.[30] In 1912, a Spokane publisher released the first history of the region, a three-volume work that focused on the eastern Washington city and its "country." Written by a local author, Nelson W. Durham, *Spokane and the Inland Empire* covers the events and people of this region from the days of the explorers "up to the present." Typical of the countless subscription histories of western United States cities, counties, and states published in the late nineteenth and early twentieth centuries, the work is not a synthesis or an analytical interpretation. Durham assumed that his audience shared his understanding of the integrity of the region about which he wrote.[31]

Outside of the Pacific Northwest the terminology needed explication. George W. Fuller, librarian of the Spokane Public Library, too penned a three-volume history, *The Inland Empire of the Pacific Northwest, A History,* in 1928, published by the Spokane publishing house of H. G. Linderman. Fuller defined his subject as "that section of the Pacific Northwest which has long been regarded as a social and economic unit—the Inland Empire." He went on to explain that "just when this natural subdivision became aware of its existence can not be positively determined, but the name has long been accepted." When the New York publishing house of Alfred A. Knopf reprinted a one-volume version of the same work in 1931, however, although its subject had not changed, it appeared under a new title, *A History of the Pacific Northwest,* and the first chapter, "The Inland Empire," was dropped.[32]

When another local historian sat down to write about the region more than seventy-five years later, he followed the accepted New York–based associations, and did not share Durham's assumption. Carlos Schwantes, a professor at the University of Idaho, does not associate the term "Inland Empire" with the region in which he lives. His region is the larger Pacific Northwest, encompassing the states of Oregon, Washington, and Idaho. In *Pacific Northwest: An Interpretive History,* Schwantes acknowledges the influence of geographic features and defines the region as a hinterland. "No matter how valuable its natural resources were to succeeding generations of entrepreneurs, the Pacific Northwest remained geographically remote from the continent's centers of economic and political power," Schwantes argues. "That remoteness, combined with its historic role as supplier of raw materials, defined the Pacific Northwest as a colonial hinterland."[33]

Schwantes's regional definition is widely accepted. Most scholars, if they acknowledge the Inland Empire at all, identify it as part of the larger region known as the Pacific Northwest.[34] As their descriptive language suggests, they define this "hinterland," "remote corner," or "colony" in relation to the country as a whole. Not surprisingly, it is mainly local historians and geographers who recognize the Inland Empire as a region. In his 1965 book, *Inland Empire: D. C. Corbin and Spokane*, and his more recent *The Inland Empire: Unfolding Years, 1879–1919*, John Fahey chronicles the region's economic and institutional history. For Fahey, the Inland Empire is defined predominantly by environmental determinants: "Although politically it embraces parts of four states and one province, much of this region's history reflects the unity imposed by its geography." He explains that economic developments such as the construction of railroads and the introduction of industrial mining reinforce these physiographic boundaries. Joining Fahey, Donald Meinig, too, starts with the land. As a historical geographer and native of the Palouse, Meinig uses formations beneath the earth's surface—ancient lava flows—to define his environmental region and in *The Great Columbia Plain* explores the changing human relationships with this physical environment.[35]

These scholars—whether they are insiders who identify with the region or outsiders who do not—define the parameters of their studies in similar ways. State lines and physiographic features mark the boundaries of their regions. Even Schwantes, Fahey, and Meinig, each of whom writes from an insider's perspective, use economic, geographical, or political language and, in some sense, employ terms and ideas external to the region to define its boundaries.[36] Like many scholars who investigate regionalism, they emphasize what draws a region together, that is, the shared set of factors that defines one place and sets it apart from others. Regional studies are traditionally characterized by their focus on agreement and consensus.

Yet to stop at the homogeneous characteristics of a place and its people or to define a region heuristically tells only part of the story of regional identity. What intrigues me most about the ongoing creation of regions— and I would argue that regions are always in the process of formation—is the persistence of conflict and contestation. Indeed, in most cases conflict and contestation characterize regions more than consensus does. Regions are made up of different individuals and groups who are engaged in conflicts over meanings of places, over the relations of peoples in and with places, and over their often competing visions of the future. These struggles are both material and representational. And they take place not only in the world of writers and historians but also in the world of the everyday.

As a historian of the American West, I am intrigued by the ways in which nineteenth- and twentieth-century peoples bounded their lands and created regional identities. As an interdisciplinary scholar, I am influenced by theoretical perspectives drawn from the social sciences and literature. Reflecting these concerns, my book is both a history of a particular place and time and an illustration of a particular way of studying the past. As I trace the creation and maintenance of the Inland Empire during the late nineteenth and early twentieth centuries, I employ a methodology based on the "semiotics of culture," one that is concerned with the intellectual representations and behavioral components of identity formation. The phrase, variously defined, refers to an emerging field of interdisciplinary study, connected principally to the disciplines of anthropology, psychology, literature, and linguistics. I use the term to refer to my own historical cross-disciplinary approach that draws on theoretical work in cultural anthropology, cognitive psychology, and literature. In this interdisciplinary approach, using the theoretical works of social science and literature and applying them to historical questions, I seek to contribute not only to the work of historians but also to the work of scholars engaged in cultural studies.[37]

The story of the Inland Empire is distinctive in its particulars; through conflicts and debates, its inhabitants created a particular set of regional bonds and a particular way of thinking about those bonds. Its sustained coherent vision was remarkable. Nonetheless, throughout the West other regions formed in similar ways. The story of the West is of the countless creations and destructions of regions, communities, settlements, and places, of lost visions and forgotten dreams. Ghost regions exist throughout the West and help define its essence today.

It may not seem so odd by now to have started a study of the creation, the birth of a region in a place of death, to have started a study of the perceptions of environment and community with the words of a sewer cleaner and town drunk. It is time to return for another look at what cemeteries and the words of Oscar Amos have to tell about the creation of the Inland Empire, about regions, communities, and places.

Semiotics of Culture

Cemeteries have long been noted by historians, sociologists, and geographers as places that reveal as much about the living as the dead.[38] Whether considered "expressions of religious ideologies on land," an "idealized microcosm of the . . . landscape," or a "visual memorial to our collective past," graveyards have fascinated scholars.[39] As cultural institutions, cemeteries both reflect and order "residents' perception of the land"; they give "identity to every neighborhood."[40] They contain some of a society's most enduring cultural symbols and beliefs. The city cemetery of Pullman, for example, with its hillside location, traditional plantings, family organization, and east-facing plots, reflects the persistence of Old World ideas, while its parklike setting, shaded walks, compass orientation, and grid pattern reveal nineteenth-century American adaptations. Cemeteries also express more local concerns. The log-shaped headstones in the separate Odd Fellows graveyard testify to the importance of the Idaho timber industry in the self-identification of former Pullman residents.

For a new territory, the existence of a cemetery marks the presence of a settlement rather than a frontier. To set aside a piece of land dedicated to funerary rites is not the act of transient people. Survivors erect headstones not only to mark the dead but also to enable the living to find the site, to visit, to remember. In a literal way, to create a graveyard is to sink roots into the soil. For followers of Euro-American cultural traditions, a new settlement's cemetery serves both psychic and physical needs. In confrontation with the unknown, whether a new territory or the hereafter, the ritual of establishing sacred space enables individuals and groups to create a place. Place is more than simply a location; it is also a "center of meaning" or an "organized world of meaning." Selecting land on which to construct monuments, to demarcate their connection to the past, the settlers enact particular understandings about the need to exert control over nature and time. The cycle of birth, death, and rebirth expressed in this tradition-bound place anchors them in a changing world.[41]

Cemeteries are an easily recognizable piece of sacred space; but similar psychic needs for both individuals and groups are fulfilled by other aspects of the built environment. Reading the landscape—such as the Pullman cemetery—to reveal cultural patterns is an important part of this book.[42] Material objects, as Richard Poulsen points out, contain "the language of symbols": "Symbols are ultimate form: they embody cultural meanings by assuming shapes and configurations dictated by the culture. They are timeless storehouses for anything a culture produces of enduring significance."[43]

Sketch maps, promotional maps, and other spatial orienting forms, for example, reveal subjective worldviews along with objective information. As outward signs of internal mental maps they represent knowledge about spatial orientation (that is, they help get you from here to there), but they are also representations of, on one level, the self (that is, the creator of the map), reflecting personal knowledge and experience and, on another level, culture. Embedded in these cognitive maps are culture-specific (emic) symbols.[44] The environmental description of the Inland Empire discussed earlier related more to internal than external maps. Descriptions of a location, of an area, whether in map form or prose, reflect the inner cognitive map of the describer.

Folklorists such as Poulsen and cultural geographers find evidence of regional identity in maps, objects created by humans, and alterations of the natural environment.[45] But even as these nineteenth-century signs continue to mark the landscape of the twentieth century, their meanings have changed. Over time, as the Inland Empire has taken on different resonances, the visibility of earlier markers has faded from view. To comprehend with new eyes what the settlers saw when they entered the territory, it is important to investigate the nineteenth-century values of these signs.[46]

What were the residents' perceptions of place? Perceptions, as defined here, refer to the conscious and unconscious collaborations of the mind and the senses. Environmental perceptions are the responses of an individual to the external world that result when a person sees, hears, smells, tastes, and feels a specific environment within the context of his or her expectations, knowledge, and experiences. They serve as a basis of regional identity. By definition, then, perceptions are almost intangible. They exert a pervasive influence over an individual's thoughts and actions but are difficult to unearth. Perceptions of the Inland Empire reveal themselves most readily during periods of change and at points of conflict. As the cultural geographer Yi-Fu Tuan notes, "place" can be made visible by "rivalry or conflict with other places."[47]

To reveal the organized world of meaning, the value of the signs, the perceptions of place that defined the Inland Empire as a region, I examine the words, material objects, and mental maps that emerge at these points of conflict and during these periods of change. Since the meaning of words or objects is determined by contrastive relations to other signs in the system, it is important to look at all manner of signs. That is, the context is essential in understanding the text. In the relationship of actions and language, in the space between the context and the text, are the signs that reveal meaning.[48] As Cohen points out, "The simplified identity which a collectivity presents to the outside world (as opposed to a label which may be imposed upon it from outside) is informed by its internal intricacies."[49]

The entire process, the context of the formative years of the Inland Empire, is lost to history. All that is left are clues, fragments in the language of its inhabitants, in the layout of cemeteries, and in the promotional maps and letters home. Reading these diverse clues in concert with each other helps materialize that ghost region, the Inland Empire. In essence, the position from which I am arguing here is based in the "semiotics of culture": that encoded in words, maps, objects, and landforms are perceptions and that perceptions hold a key to the system of meanings that is the essence of the Inland Empire.[50] Although not all perceptions can be altered (some are innate, others are limited by the physiology of the sense organs), I am concerned with those that are learned.[51] These learned perceptions are both individual and shared. How do individuals come to create and share culture-specific perceptions? What shapes the transition of individual private signs into group or public symbolic signs?[52]

To identify the shared "mental territory," the perceptual region known as the Inland Empire, my analysis focuses on internal or indigenous texts—letters and diaries of settlers, government documents, other personal and public papers, real estate promotional pamphlets, maps, buildings, and townplans. I examine the words, actions, and objects produced by people living within self-defined regional boundaries to uncover mental perceptions, to read the cultural "signs" of this particular place and time, to reveal the codes of meaning through which late nineteenth-century inhabitants created a cognitive region.[53]

Examining indigenous evidence to uncover mental perceptions, I argue that ongoing debates among different groups of people seeking to control the region's identity and direction worked to define the place. During times of private or public crises and confrontations, such contests are especially visible and reveal perceptions normally hidden from view. The book examines a variety of crises and confrontations: "moments" of disruption, periods of change, points of contact, or events of signification. Each of these "moments," identified through a comparative examination of the available words, actions, and objects created by residents during this period, serves as an entry into the mental world of the Inland Empire.[54]

Chapter 1 explores the cognitive process of mapping the Inland Empire from the perspective of individuals and communities. Two types of "moments"—the personal disruption experienced by new settlers and the collective disruption experienced by the rebuilders of Spokane Falls after its 1889 fire—reveal one emerging vision of the Inland Empire. Characterized by its future orientation, distinct social boundaries, and notions of control, this vision, especially as represented by the rebuilt city, came to influence perceptions held not only by Spokane residents but also by those outside the city's limits.

Not everyone, however, agreed with this version of the Inland Empire. In fact, the creation of the mental territory relied on the ongoing debates over its boundaries, its identity, its meaning, and its future. While the Inland Empire remained, as do all regions, an ongoing creation and an elusive mental concept, the debates reveal particular cultural categories that regional residents contested. Ideas about the acceptable parameters of change, control, and variety, for example, infuse these public discussions. What one group regarded as change, another group saw as instability. What one group embraced as variety, another group perceived as unacceptable difference. And actions one group defined as necessary for control, another group experienced as repression. In the public debates over the Coeur d'Alene reservation and the Coeur d'Alene mining conflicts, for example, disagreements over the emerging regional definitions are clearly visible. Chapters 2 and 3 examine these moments of collectively experienced change refracted through the prisms of race and class.

The creation of the Inland Empire—the physical and mental establishment of a new place and space that various groups attempted to define as their own—helps illustrate the changing dynamics of power. This book traces the process of becoming, a process that occurred through the struggles among various interests; the definition of the Inland Empire emerged from this struggle. Yet even as local groups operated with a definition grounded in their experiences, they were continually confronted by different visions of the region. Chapter 4 explores moments of self-presentation from the perspective of the region as a whole. Public celebrations and promotional literature mark such cultural concerns. As the region expanded its boundaries in physical and cognitive ways, it underwent profound transformations. Outsiders' versions of the region came to dominate public perceptions of it and to reshape insiders' accounts of themselves. By the 1910s both local residents and contemporary observers acknowledged emerging tensions between private and public and between insiders' and outsiders' understandings of the region. The contestations among these perspectives shape the moments analyzed in Chapter 5, especially those contestations centered around the region's involvement in national and international trends and events.

Each of these types of moments, whether individual, collective, or regional, reveals certain aspects of the mental territory known as the Inland Empire. Relying as it does on indigenous words, actions, and objects created by individuals, this book is structured around certain representative characters. And it is fitting that people remain at the center. From Oscar Amos to Luvina Buchanan to Andrew Seltice to Charles Clarke, it was the people who came together in this western place and their ideas, dreams, and visions that created the region. Today, not all residents of eastern Washington, northern Idaho, and southeastern British Columbia claim membership in the Inland Empire. But as the final words of the woman who spoke up at the regional conference vividly illustrate, the legacy of the turn-of-the-century mental territory remains. "We," she concluded, referring to those who share her attachment to place, "we are not dead."

In brief, the Inland Empire I am exploring is inland—the inner world of people's minds—and an empire—based on an aggressive, forward-looking, futuristic policy of control. Like the pattern of the old cemetery that emerged on the Pullman hillside, it is hidden in the underbrush that has grown up since then; only fragments remain, but they are enduring granite fragments that have much to tell us.

One final story:

A couple of months after I had visited the Pullman cemeteries, I was walking through another graveyard some 150 miles away. It could not have been more different. On flat, dry ground, almost devoid of vegetation and surrounded by a wire mesh fence, rows of white crosses composed the St.

Eugene Mission Indian Cemetery. Torn ribbons of red, white, black, and yellow fluttered on sticks marking the corners of the grave sites. Interspersed amid the wooden crosses were carved headstones of granite. Most of the people buried here outside Cranbrook in southeastern British Columbia had been members of the Kootenai tribes. Looking at the mixture of Indian tradition, Catholic crosses, and syncretistic markers I was struck both by the creation of new forms and the persistence of difference.

This introduction ends, then, with the idea of difference. The Inland Empire was not a homogeneous community. It thrived on diversity and difference. In its balance between coherence and chaos, it represents a search for meaning. In the words of Oscar Amos: "a community of people what are they and what is ment by the word law or social function does it mean that each unit which is part of the whole is equeal to the other. no. it does not. desires and fancyes of the human destney is so rampat in most ever emotion of activity that humans are kept apart." Oscar Amos spent much of his life seeking the meaning of existence. He sought answers in Near Eastern philosophy, ancient history, Masonic ritual, alcohol, socialism, and Christian doctrine. In the end, however, he was largely defined by his place within a region. He was the champion ditch digger of the Inland Empire.

INSET

Spokane

Spokane, Queen of Inland Empire,
T'was not man but Judgement higher,
That chose this beauty spot for thee,
On which to build thy destiny.

He who planned this great upheavel
Long ago in times primeval,
Paused here and with prophetic hand,
Did pour the lava o'er this land.

He planned of thee and of thy fame
Here on the river of thy name,
These mighty falls he gave to man
To lend assistance to His plan.

And these fair streets with flowers strewn,
Once out of solid rock were hewn,
And now tall buildings skyward rise
In tribute to man's enterprise.

And with the Empire's wealth arrayed,
The steel-shod caravans of trade,
Across the continent are whirled
Into the markets of the world.

Long live thy Subjects as they strive
And may thy Empire always thrive,
But in thy progress bear in mind,
To thee the Master was most kind.

—Le Roy Benson

Washington Magazine, May 1906, p. 197.

CHAPTER 1

MAPPING THE INLAND EMPIRE

In 1870 the Inland Empire did not appear on maps. Eastern United States mapmakers, who drew maps of the territory west of the Rocky Mountains, of the Pacific states and territories, and of Oregon and Washington territory, did not label the interior Pacific Northwest as a distinct region. Located in cities such as New York, Philadelphia, or Washington, D.C., these cartographers, engravers, and compilers based their representations on "authorities"—primarily published reports and maps of earlier explorers and route finders. Most relied on U.S. government sources, culling details, at times erroneous, from expeditions such as those led by Meriwether Lewis and William Clark or Captain John C. Frémont and from such surveys as Governor Isaac Stevens's 1850s railroad route surveys and Captain John Mullan's 1860s military road survey. Some incorporated information gathered by Hudson Bay Company fur traders.

Despite these efforts, on-location map users found the maps lacking. As one military observer complained about existing Pacific Northwest maps in 1881, "I could not help being struck with the great lack of information concerning certain portions of the country which it is intended to represent. There are large areas containing many hundreds of square miles which are comparatively unknown, and what little is known is of the most inaccurate and untrustworthy character, and that which is put upon the maps is largely hypothetical." Western U.S. mapmakers, usually associated with the offices of territorial surveyors general or mining engineers located near the Pacific coast in Olympia, Portland, or San Francisco, relied on these same authorities along with more local sources of information. In contrast to their eastern U.S. counterparts, these cartographers marked additional geographical features on their maps; they included general descriptive labels drawn from oral and written sources. Stretching over otherwise blank sections of the map, words and phrases defined spaces by their landscape features—the Spokane Plains, Bunch Grass Prairies, Great Basaltic Section, Great Plain of the Columbia, and Great Plateau of Spokane. Although the western cartographers used more descriptive terms and included more relief details than their eastern counterparts, the Inland Empire was not among those terms.[1]

Not until the late 1880s did western mapmakers start to represent the interior Pacific Northwest as a regional unit. And initially such a designation remained a peculiarity of maps produced in western U.S. locales. The mapmakers most inclined to designate an interior region were those based in the town of Spokane Falls. Their maps reflected the views and definitions of the local residents and promoters of "that vast extent of territory, now being rapidly peopled, known and suggestively spoken of as the 'Inland Empire.' "[2]

"Known and suggestively spoken of as the Inland Empire"—such written references to the region predate the published maps, and as the phrasing indicates, the term and idea of the Inland Empire predate its predicted realization. The published cartographic record only partially reveals the mapping of the Inland Empire. The development of meanings, ideas, views, and definitions by peoples in a particular place—the cognitive process of mapping the Inland Empire—was a gradual formation. While traditional maps, as cartographic representations, offer a formalized understanding of place still accessible to people of a different time, mental maps are less tangible and available. The ways that individuals or communities perceived their places in a new region, that is, the cognitive maps they created, are visible to only a limited extent through the words and objects left behind. This chapter examines such linguistic and physical remnants created by two overlapping groups of newcomers to the interior Pacific Northwest during the late nineteenth century in an effort to uncover the world of meanings that shaped the Inland Empire maps. "Homesteaders" and "town builders"—the appellations with which these predominantly Anglo newcomers identified themselves—altered the visible landscape as they plowed up the land, constructed sawmills, laid out town sites, erected buildings, and established businesses. They also, as the maps indicate, affected its interior landscape as they dreamed their dreams, planned for the future, strategized to avoid setbacks, rationalized their circumstances, and worked to enforce their visions. Together these material efforts and mental constructions shaped the place that came to be known as the Inland Empire.[3]

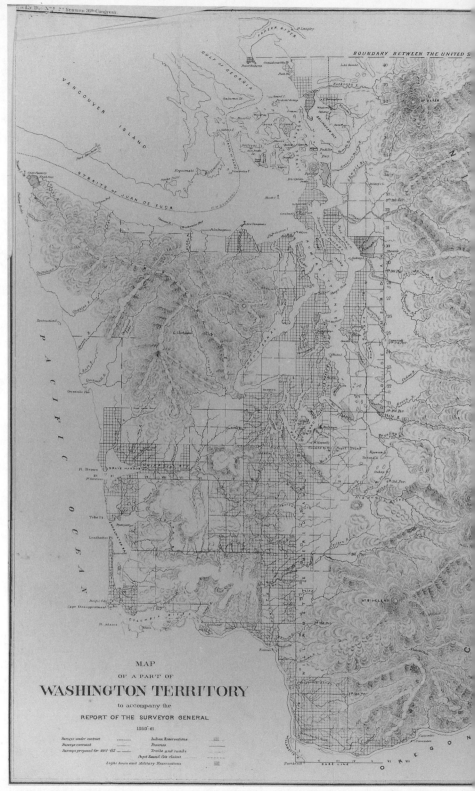

Before the Inland Empire Unsurveyed lands of the "Great Plateau of Spokane" are divided by the Columbia Guide Meridian on this 1865 General Land Office Map of the Public Surveys in the the Territory of Washington. The Washington territorial governor Isaac Stevens's proposed railroad route bypasses the Spokane ferry near the river's falls, where a town site would be established six years later. Courtesy of Map Collection, Yale University Library.

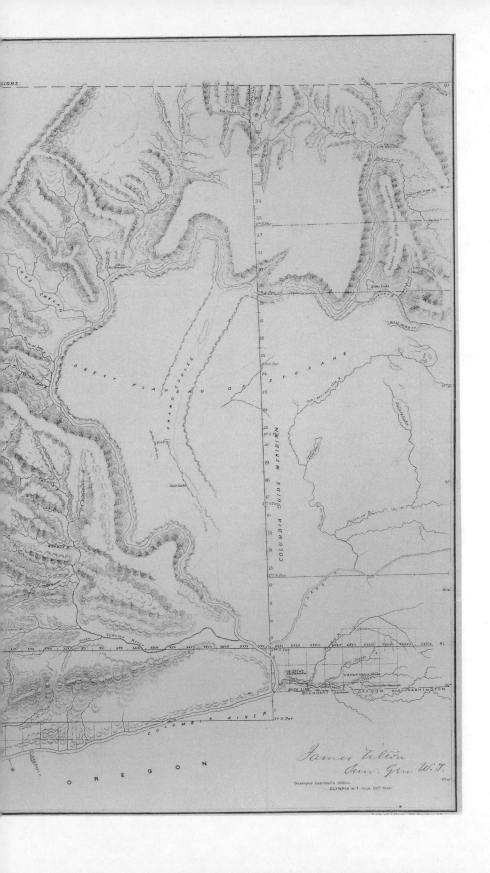

OREGON

Surveyor General's Office.
OLYMPIA W.T. Sept 29th 1860

Envisioning a "New Country"

On May 4, 1877, Luvina Buchanan wrote to her sister Nan, who was back home on their Missouri family farm, to describe her life in Paradise Valley, Idaho Territory. "This is a new country, only settled six years," she explained. "It is very healthy and the best soil I ever seen anywhere much better than the soil in Oregon." She described the variety of potential crops and continued, "Beckie is living one mile from me. They have a nice place . . . but the country is being settled up very fast and I would like to see you coming to take up a claim. It is the best place in the world for a poor man."[4]

Paradise Valley, the site of present-day Moscow, Idaho, and only ten short miles from Oscar Amos's town of Pullman, Washington, enticed the Buchanans and other settlers with rich farming lands along the tributaries of the Snake River. The southeastern corner of Washington Territory was indeed "being settled up very fast" during the 1870s. According to the federal census, population increased at least 400 percent during the decade. Settlers and visitors remarked on the number of new homesteads that spread out from the nucleated settlement of Walla Walla, the market and military center established since the 1830s on the Oregon Trail, and along the Columbia River passageway.[5] Newly arrived farm families from the western states of California and Oregon and midwestern states such as Indiana, Iowa, Missouri, and Wisconsin filled the streets of Lewiston, Dayton, Colfax, and other smaller towns outlying Walla Walla. Drawn to the area by favorable reports from earlier settlers and fueled by a search for an idealized "better life," this flood of new immigrants overflowed onto the prairie lands and along the river valleys adjoining these communities. Day laborers, domestic servants and cooks, prostitutes, mule and horse packers, speculators, real estate agents, merchants, hotel and rooming house keepers, blacksmiths, and others offered services to support, and be supported by, the "influx of strangers."[6]

Many of the "strangers," like Luvina Buchanan, attempted to decipher their "new country" to those familiar with their "old" country through letters written to absent family and friends. While they took up homestead claims, planted crops, and engaged in the myriad activities required for reestablishing themselves, they also wrote letters that created in words what they strove to create through their actions. The letters map out their plans and, less intentionally, mark the process of reidentification. Through the act of writing they participated in the simultaneous transformations of the "new country" into a home and of themselves from "strangers" into residents. From the vantage point of the 1870s immigrants, this interior part of the Pacific Northwest seemed like a "new country," an unsettled place where they could create a future for themselves. Available maps, which portrayed a largely unsurveyed land with only a few scattered settlements, reinforced this perspective. Such descriptions, however, tended to ignore not only the ways in which newcomers brought the past with them but also preexisting settlers.[7]

Though at times uncharted, this interior part of the Pacific Northwest was far from uninhabited. A variety of communities, some defined by national, racial, or ethnic origins, occupied the landscape. For the members of these communities, the interior Pacific Northwest was not the "new country" envisioned by settlers like Luvina Buchanan. Often longtime residents, they pursued various economic activities—ranching, trapping, soldiering, mining, and lumbering, as well as farming. Reaching farther north from the lower Columbia River where homesteaders staked their claims, ranchers summered cattle and sheep over the Big Bend range. Along the upper Columbia River a different, racially mixed community engaged in ranching as well as other economic pursuits. Clustered around Fort Colville, former Hudson Bay Company employees held small farms, hunted and trapped a diminishing supply of animals, and ran cattle. The census taker noted roughly equal numbers of whites and "half-breeds" or Indians outside of the garrison. Soldiers and officers stationed at Fort Colville, like those at other regional posts such as Forts Lapwai, Walla Walla, and Simcoe, supported by accompanying laundresses, sutlers, and laborers, represented U.S. government interests.[8]

Camps of prospectors and miners, dwindled in size since the peak of the area's 1860s gold rush boom, eked out a seasonal living in the surrounding mountain hills and valleys. Many of these remaining miners were Chinese men who congregated in racially segregated camps such as those along the Columbia River in Washington and along Oro Fino Creek in Idaho.[9] These male enclaves relied on merchants and packers who traveled between Walla Walla and Fort Colville with supplies. The packers often stopped along the trail near the falls of the Spokane River, where a sawmill and ferry operation shared space with bands of Spokane and other Salish-speaking native peoples, who wintered along the banks. There too Enoch Mills, one of the "civilized" Lower Spokanes, ran a farm on fertile bottom lands. Jesuit Fathers Joseph Cataldo and Joseph Joset and other Catholic clergy assigned to the Rocky Mountain missions also passed through the small river settlement. The Jesuits tended to avoid contact with the Protestant clergy who maintained separate, and rival, missions in the area.

Native peoples lived both on and off several established reservations; the U.S. government set aside lands for the Yakimas in 1855, the Nez Perces in 1863, and the Coeur d'Alenes in 1867.[10] Most of the Columbia Plateau peoples, who numbered around thirty thousand according to government and missionary sources, followed their traditional seasonal pattern of migration dependent on the changing natural resources. Others, such as those living near Fort Colville, participated in the metis culture associated with the fur trade. Some, such as the Enoch Mills family, established homesteads under federal laws or missionary supervision.

The federal manuscript census recorded these interlinked yet segregated communities of people, whether U.S. soldiers, reservation Indians, Chinese miners, metis ranchers, or Christian missionaries. Uncounted and even less visible were any number of transient and mobile peoples: packers and prospectors, government employees such as the Corps of Engineers team sent to survey Spokane Falls, and a substantial percentage of native peoples.[11]

As this description makes clear, a diverse set of groups and individuals constituted the population base of the future Inland Empire region. Although they often lived in separate communities and followed different interests, their lives overlapped along a limited number of social and economic lines. Travel routes marked the physical manifestations of these sometimes tenuous connections. Miners and missionaries, soldiers and packers, natives and federal government employees encountered each other on the well-used trail stretching north and south between Walla Walla and Fort Colville, the government's Mullan Road, which linked an east-west route over the Bitterroots to the Columbia River, and other routes. Former fur trader Stephen Liberty, for example, first met the Coeur d'Alene leader Andrew Seltice while Liberty carried U.S. mail in northern Idaho Territory. Despite these personal, economic, and physical connections, such residents did not share a collective perspective of the interior Pacific Northwest.[12]

Surveying Chains

The process of envisioning a new country, of developing a regional consciousness, of mapping the Inland Empire took place on a variety of levels. The physical creation of maps—dividing the landscape into property—mirrored, and at times distorted, the creation of internal maps. Luvina Buchanan's mental map of her new country depended upon cartographic representations but also derived from collective and individual experiences, ideas, and views. We need to read both external and internal nineteenth-century maps.

Among the transient peoples who used the interior Pacific Northwest routes were individuals actively involved in creating even more lines on the maps. Federal government and railroad surveyors, the latter usually followed by construction teams of Chinese work crews, traversed the lands of eastern Washington and northern Idaho throughout the 1870s and 1880s. As the surveyors moved their measurement chains, noted types of soil and vegetation, and calculated distances, they mapped out routes for two transcontinental railroads, the Northern Pacific (completed in 1883) and the Great Northern Railway (completed in 1893), along with hundreds of branch lines. They also divided the diverse landscape into the sections on which homesteaders such as the Buchanans would establish their claims.[13]

Usual surveying techniques involved use of a measurement chain physically laid across the land and instruments such as the transit, level, and clinometer. When the surveyors reached an obstacle around which they could not lay their chains, they employed a different method of calculating the distance—triangulation. They measured a baseline at right angles to the survey line alongside the river, lake, or other obstacle. Then they selected a prominent point on the other side of the obstacle to use as the top of their imaginary triangle. By measuring the angles of the triangle from the ends of their baseline, they calculated the distance with trigonometry.[14]

Families such as the Buchanans used the maps these government surveyors created to locate and file on their homesteads. For their nineteenth-century users, the maps guided their understanding of the land, placing the "new country" in often familiar contexts. Relying on cartographic conventions, descriptive terms, cultural categories, and shared assumptions, the mapmakers provided a decipherable manual for the newcomers.

As texts, the maps employed a system of representational codes to present visible landmarks—routes, topographical features, and physical structures, for example—symbolically in two-dimensional space. Keys translated dotted lines as trails, blue lines as rivers, and circles as towns. The maps also identified other land markers—political boundaries, lines of longitude and latitude, and place names, for example—that to the uninitiated were invisible on the physical landscape. In giving these abstract markers the same symbolic importance on the maps as the visible landmarks, mapmakers shared with the map users an implicit understanding of the "natural" order of the landscape. Representing land as state-regulated property, accessible for private individual ownership, a commodity to be bought and sold on the market, the maps connected their users to national, economic, legal, and political systems. As government maps, for example, the land survey maps extended state authority over the land and the map users.[15]

The social vision embedded in the maps subordinated the natural environment to both individual and state use. The surveyors ran their principal measurement lines—"Colville Base Line" or "Columbia Meridian Line," for example—north and south or east and west, regardless of environmental barriers. Dividing a variegated landscape of hills, circuitous streams, bluffs, and coulees into uniform, numbered, and definable township units, six miles by six miles square, the maps emphasized order, control, and utility over natural variation. Even the language of the survey maps—

terms such as "townships" or "reserved school sections"—presented reassuring words of implied future use that supported the settlers' own plans.[16]

As this discussion of the material and symbolic components of land survey maps suggests, in addition to such external maps, the Buchanans and other newcomers used and created internal maps to help them locate their place and their future. Such internal or mental maps have their own set of symbols and codes. But the explanatory keys, like the maps themselves, are missing. To enter the world of Luvina Buchanan and her fellow settlers, to recreate and understand their mental maps, is a daunting task. Luvina's letter to her sister Nan offers one obstacle-laden passageway for historians. The language she uses and the meanings she infers were bound by her personal, cultural, and temporal frames of reference about which we have only fragmentary evidence. Some of the "lines" may have needed no explanation for the nineteenth-century audience, but they do need explication for a twentieth-century audience.

If we know too little about the nineteenth-century world, we also know too much. We know the future. The Buchanans and others like them only imagined their future. Their perceptions of the future—their plans, their mental maps—exerted a powerful influence on their lives and actions. What we see, what is visible to us, are the surviving representations of that influence. We can pinpoint the appearance of the words "Inland Empire" on published maps, for example, but not its precise development as a meaningful term. We can identify the role of the state in dividing land into townships but not the reasons why individual newcomers elected to settle in one place over another. The obstacles created by time and knowledge prevent us from directly recreating nineteenth-century mental maps, from laying our measuring chains. Although we cannot reconstruct their internal maps, we can develop our own extrapolation of their world, a way of interpreting prominent points that helps reveal not only the connections among them but also the connections between their world and ours. And it is here that the government surveyors' technique is useful. The letters home offer an opportunity for historians to enter the nineteenth-century world through a similar process of triangulation.

The letters home are a point of contact that helps open up the mental world of the nineteenth-century correspondents. They are letters written between people who shared the same background and who once shared the same experiences, correspondence that strives to interpret a new experience—that of living in the Inland Empire—in the language of these previously shared experiences. The writer and the receiver stand at different points of a triangle with their letters creating a baseline between the two. From our vantage point at the vertex we can use the baseline—the letters—to calculate the angles, to measure the distance, to construct our representations of their mental maps. As evidence of threshold moments, situated in the doorway between these two sets of experiences, the letters are particularly revealing. In watching the correspondence, in reading their words within context at this moment where the two worlds are revealed, we can create an understanding of that world.

Luvina Buchanan's letter belongs to a particular genre: letters written by settlers—individuals entering a new area consciously to create (or recreate) a home and future—to the folks back home. An intertwined set of concerns informs this correspondence. For the writers, the letters maintain connections to the known past, even as this past becomes increasingly remote. Before relinquishing the old, the settlers hang on to it through the written word. In some ways the settlers use these links to the past as an aid in formulating a future. The scrawled sheets, representing connections to people, to place, and to time, exist as talismans, charms that protect the writers while they venture into an alien environment. Reporting on activities and plans, describing personal changes, chronicling the oddities of new encounters, justifying their move away from home, in short, transcribing their experiences into language, the settlers, through their letters, engage in the gradual process of reshaping themselves.[17]

The character of these letters varies. Letters between separated married couples, letters by women to extended family members, and letters by single men to friends differ in tone from each other. The writers' socioeconomic class and educational experiences influenced the letters' style and level of adherence to rules of grammar. The character of the relationships between the letter writers and letter receivers, the individual sets of experiences discussed, and the motivations for writing also shaped the content and form of the correspondence.

Women and men wrote letters home. But when both were part of a household, women, the caretakers of kinship ties, wrote more frequently than men. And women and men expressed themselves differently in their prose. Joint letters by married couples, in particular, reveal the gendered character of these letters. Commonly such letters included several pages written by the wife, followed by an addendum by the husband. As Elizabeth Hampsten, who has examined the letters and private writings of midwestern women during this same period, argues, women "placed" themselves in relation to their connections to people and their immediate circumstances. In these joint letters, husbands relied on their wives to communicate general news; their words, echoing as a chorus, tended to focus on concrete details and their own activities.[18]

Although various factors distinguished the content and form of the letters, male and female letter writers employed a common language within the nineteenth-century letter-writing genre. In this most personal form of written expression, individuals use the same words as they describe the experience of entering a new area to create a home and a future. Specific phrases occur and recur in these letters home. Luvina Buchanan's 1877 letter to her sister Nan, for example, includes clichés: "the best I ever seen . . . settled up very fast . . . I would like to see you . . . the best place in the world for a poor man."

The phrases are not unique to the settlers of the Inland Empire. Certain expressions, such as "the best poor man's country," as James Lemon points out in his historical geography of southeastern Pennsylvania, have a long history of use in reference to promising agricultural land. People persisted in using them because the terms were shortcuts to a world of meaning. Within the context of nineteenth-century language, ideas, and meanings, such phrases had distinct resonances. They both marked and contributed to a shared linguistic community. These recurring phrases present a way of decoding the language, of interpreting the keys to the mental maps created by the committed settlers of the Inland Empire.[19]

"Best Poor Man's Country"

To nineteenth-century Americans, a "good poor man's country" referred to land that required more "strength, understanding and perseverance" than wealth to yield a rich harvest. The editor of the *Spokane Falls Review* explained the local application of the term during the 1880s: "This is the poor man's country in the sense that it pays a larger reward to industry than almost any other."[20] New settlers in eastern Washington such as John Cady, from Nevada, discovered "a good poor man's country and for farming it cannot be excelled." On a tour of inspection in 1879 he reported that "the country through which we traveled is the finest body of agricultural land I ever saw in any country."[21] For nineteenth-century users, the term "a poor man's country" suggested that the natural resources of the area could be transformed, through hard work and knowledge, into products for economic gain. While the words themselves refer to individual masculine effort, men and women habitually used the phrase within the context of family and community efforts. For Luvina Buchanan, writing to her sister, women as well as men were potential beneficiaries of the "poor man's country." And as references in the letters to prices and wages reveal, even a single man working alone relied on the workings of the market.

Examining the phrase within its ninteenth-century context points to its meanings for the new settlers. Yet not all the implications of "a good poor man's country," or the other clichés used in the letters home, are decipherable. Some individuals, embittered by the limitations of other "good poor man's" countries, may have intended a bit of irony in their references. When men and women each used the phrase, they may have envisioned the efforts needed to transform the country in gendered terms. The collective and widespread use of the cliché, however, does reveal the development of a particular mind-set shared by the new settlers.[22]

Superlatives abound in the descriptions these settlers sent back to their families and neighbors; it was not only a good poor man's country, it was the *best* poor man's country. William Henry Stoneman, for example, found "Spokane growing fast" in 1881: "Emigrant families having a hard time as prices are high, as well as wages, but think this is the best poor man's country in the world. . . . Potatoes and turnips best I ever saw."[23] Letter after letter included phrases such as "the best," "the finest," or "it cannot be excelled." When writers qualified these phrases, they struck a personal note; things are the "best *I* ever saw." Stoneman's description of root vegetables and Cady's evaluation of farmland echo Luvina Buchanan's description of the soil, crops, and scenery in Paradise Valley. These laudatory accounts would not seem out of place in promotional pamphlets written by town site speculators or railroad land office agents. The personal qualifications, however, added validity for the readers of the private writings. That Spokane Valley potatoes, for example, are the ultimate in the writer's experience is or would be irrelevant to the reader unless he or she had some knowledge of the extent and content of that experience. The words imply shared experiences, a shared known world. They imply trust, a connection between the sender and the receiver that extends beyond the superficial. When the boosters and speculators relied on this same hyperbolic prose, they consciously echoed these personal communications to create an illusion of similar trust.

The letters are replete with even more specific references to the shared known world. "The weather," wrote R. Hurlburt to a woman named Rhoda, "has been hot and uncomfortable, not Kansas hot, but hot nevertheless."[24] With these shortcuts of language that compare the unfamiliar with the familiar, that appeal to a shared sense of humor and irony, settlers tried to communicate across what they acknowledged was a widening gulf of understanding. The desire to share their experiences was strong. "I wish you could see that road," Annie Gordon wrote to her sister. "It is the highest road that ever I was on. . . . And the lovely fresh feel of the air, you can't imagine anything like it in N.S. [Nova Scotia]." Whether the immigrants hailed from physical environments as diverse as Nova Scotia or Kansas, they persisted in identifying points of commonality between some aspect of the environment of the Pacific Northwest and their previous homes.[25]

Not everyone was impressed by the same aspects of the area. Different expectations, coming from a variety of backgrounds and experiences, shaped visions of the place and its future. David Robert McGinnis, a native of Illinois, for example, came to Spokane in 1883 at the age of twenty-seven to see the country for himself. Anthony M. Cannon showed him around, but each man saw the same eighty-acre tract with different eyes. For Cannon, one of the early investors in the town site, the north-side tract "would rapidly come into use for home building and it could be bought for $40 per acre." "To me," reported the amazed McGinnis, who thought of home-steads, not town sites, "it seemed that it would take many a year before that 80 acres could be in demand. In addition, I was a black-soil, deep-mud product of central Illinois and I could not conceive of that gravelly thin-grassed soil ever becoming of any value for farming purposes. There also were myriads of large black beetles all over the ground and that increased my pessimism about that land." Eyes and minds trained by their previous homes, some travelers like McGinnis rejected the rampant enthusiasm. And some wide-eyed settlers like Samuel McCrosky found their vision tem-pered by thoughts of home or, at least, suggested as much when writing to those back home. "I am not dissatisfied with the prospects in this country," McCrosky hastened to explain to his fiancée, Maggie Cochran, "and I have passed through many lovelier countries elsewhere, but I have found none to compare with old Tenn in its many qualities of goodness."[26]

Most settlers, however, kept quiet about their disappointments; perhaps they were predisposed to finding the best of everything. Their superlatives served to justify the momentous decision to leave home, their known world. Optimism surrounded even their grudgingly made negative descriptions. "This is a fine country," declared Calvin E. Wilson from Palouse in 1883; "but it was fearful could this winter—46 below zero but it is fine weather now as ever I have seen."[27]

Embedded in the phrase "the best poor man's country" are sets of as-sumptions that underlay this optimism. The phrase implies a belief in the potential to improve one's economic position and a faith in individual effort. Equally important, it suggests that in transforming nature, one could transform oneself. Given these assumptions, nineteenth-century settlers identified themselves not with the physical environment as it existed but with the human-made changes to the environment. As they transformed the countryside, as it became more familiar, they seized upon these changes—real or imagined—as reflections of themselves. Entering with such an understanding, newcomers emphasized potential and saw the world through such a prism.

The "newness" of the surroundings, as evidenced in freshly sawed plank buildings and the unfamiliar environment, bespoke potential for the set-tlers. "This is a very promising section of the Country," explained Thomas W. Symons, sent by the Army Corps of Engineers to survey for a bridge at Spokane Falls, to his brother in Saginaw, Michigan, in 1879, "and the one of all others that I have seen where I would settle if I wanted to lose myself from the civilization of the East and grow up with a new community."[28] When Symons, focused on his assigned task, looked at the river, he saw a bridge; at the falls, he envisioned a dam. Through settlers' eyes, focused on self-assigned homesteading tasks, grasslands turned into fields of crops. Merchants and real estate promoters saw towns as bustling cities. These often different visions shared a preoccupation with the potential of the region and a utilitarian view of its natural resources.

In Symons's official report on the Columbia River, he remarked on these shared knowledges and the ways they influenced language. As a somewhat detached observer who had no plans to stake his future to this nonetheless "very promising section," he explained the local terminology with a tinge of skepticism: " 'Bunch grass' has become the synonym for things good, strong, rich, and great; bunch-grass country is the best and finest country on earth; bunch-grass cattle and horses are the sweetest, fleetest, and strongest in the world; and a bunch-grass man is the most superb being in the universe." In contrast, "sage-brush has become almost a synonym for worthlessness, and to say that a piece of land is sage-brush land condemns it at once in the minds of many people." Learning the distinctions between bunchgrass and sagebrush, the newcomers came to share not only a vocabulary but also a vision of the future.[29]

The clichés in the letters home are concerned as much, or more, with the future as with the present. As they created an ideal world in prose, telling a story of success to the folks back home, the letter writers contributed to the formation of the region. Even the skeptical Symons, encapsulating the usual narrative, projected a prosperous settled future, "when the whole land shall be a waving field of grain, with here and there a village or a city with railroads traversing the country in every direction, and a vast commerce being carried on between the sea and the interior." These visions of the future were constricted by the past. Or, to make the same point in a different way, the past made the future possible. Through their connections to the past, as evidenced in the letters home, settlers conceptualized a new place. Their desire to recreate the known world was not only a way to hold onto the past and to adjust to the new but also a way to move into the future. As they created the future they sought to preserve the past.[30]

"I would like to see you"

Letters not only described and interpreted the "new country," they also attracted emigrants to the region. Their evocations of place contributed in tangible ways to the process of settlement. One Kansas-born emigrant described the procedure: "Letters came occasionally from father's father and brother who had arrived in Washington Territory in the fall of '78. . . . They told of the climate and everything *as they saw it.* 'A great opportunity for a man to get a start—bunch-grass knee high, and a great future for anyone who got in in time to get government land.' . . . They kept writing trying to get us to come." Finally, in 1882, after a doctor recommended that a family member should seek a change in climate for health reasons, the family left for Washington with a neighboring family.[31]

Prospective settlers relied on family ties and social networks, perhaps more than published sources, to acquire firsthand information about the new country. Twenty-eight-year-old Albert Keats, who reached Spokane in June 1880 and was employed as a clerk in a general merchandise store, felt burdened by the chore. As he complained to his cousin Julia in a letter of January 11, 1883, "I received a letter yesterday from P. Brown Brother to Walter, asking Information about this country, this is the 2nd one I answered the last one the best I knew how and I hate to say anything that would induce them to come but would much rather that they would hunt their own location as I have had to do and then if things don't go just right they have nobody to blame but themselves."[32] Readers and writers, as Keats knew all too well, attached responsibility to this kind of information exchange. Recognizing the exaggerated claims of promotional pamphlets, prospective settlers looked to the words of acquaintances, friends, or kin for validation and support.

In an effort to avoid repetitive work and to speed the region's promotion, many sent descriptive letters to hometown newspapers. John Cady wrote home to the *Silver State,* a Winnemucca, Nevada, newspaper from his new home in Colfax. As he explained, "On leaving Humboldt, I promised at least a hundred persons that I would write and give my opinion of this Territory. After writing a dozen or more letters on the same subject, the job became monotonous, and I have concluded, with your permission, to give them a column in the *Silver State.*" Acknowledging these requests, local newspapers such as the *Spokane Times* regularly published columns such as "How to Reach this Country," which provided information for their readers to send to friends contemplating a move. Such use of the media broke down the sometimes artificial distinction between public and private writings. Letters, newspaper articles, and promotional literature shared claims of authenticity, optimistic descriptions, and enthusiastic projections. Railroad promotional pamphlets, for example, often included testimonials and letters by successful settlers as a means to authorize their claims.[33]

The letter writers, like other promoters, pursued their own ends as they sought to recreate the emotional and economic support of their past world by encouraging friends and family to join them in the new place. "I am very sorry to hear that you are changing your mind about coming out here," wrote a disappointed J. Fred Hume to his friend R. Bellamy in New Brunswick. "Come and see this great country of ours. It will do you good *and* will improve your health very much."[34] Settlers strove to surround themselves with the known—whether terms or objects or people. They retained ties to the past world and tried to recreate it in the ways they organized their new world and tried to encourage parts of that old world to join them in the new. Ideally that recreation included people, such as family members and neighbors, but it might also include familiar vegetation and material objects. Seeds and plants reminded one of home through the senses of sight, smell, and touch. "I wish you'd send me a bunch of yellow primroses," wrote Maudie Craig to her daughter. "There isn't such a thing here, and I'm sure that if the people would only take the time to make gardens they'd grow."[35]

Settlers replanted people as well as primroses in the local soil. "There is plenty of vacant land here yet, but it is hard for strangers to find it," explained Cady. "Most of the settlers are holding land for their friends, will tell you positively, the land around there is all taken up and give you glowing descriptions of localities twenty miles from there." He went on to locate his own area precisely for interested readers and potential settlers; "Myself and fellow Humboldters have located on Crab Creek, 60 miles northwest of Colfax, four miles from the N.P.R.R., and 50 miles above where the road is now being graded." Cady, particularly from the perspective of pre-1870s inhabitants, might be considered one of the "strangers" new to the area, but he clearly did not classify himself or his friends as such.[36]

For another example of chain migration, consider the experiences of a group of Wisconsin settlers. In 1871, Dr. W. W. Day moved to Dayton, a small agricultural settlement in southeastern Washington Territory, and established a homestead along with a private practice. A letter from Day to his friends the Hunters, in Mondovi, Wisconsin, validated reports they had received from elsewhere: "The soil is rich, deep and very productive. It is capable of producing more grains per acre than any soil that I have ever seen. . . . We raise the finest quality of potatoes, turnips, carrots, parsnips, beets and onions that I ever saw grow in any country." Day's descriptions impressed the Hunters and many others in Mondovi. Although the exact number of emigrants who left Mondovi for Washington Territory is not known, at least one hundred people made the move. When the Hunters left for Dayton in 1878 they were joined by four or five other Mondovi families and some individual travelers, creating a group of over forty. These emigrants, some of whom had been members of the Mondovi Baptist church choir, shared similar hopes for their move.[37]

After the group arrived in Washington Territory, they wrote home echoing Day's sentiments. D. C. Gardner informed his wife, "I think this is the best country for a poor man that is willing to work that I ever saw. . . . We have the finest beef here that I ever saw, and the finest fruit, grain, and potatoes. . . . I know you will like it here. You cannot help it. There is some of the finest scenery here that I ever saw in any country." James Hunter wrote to Otis Warren of Mondovi: "Tell your father there are plenty of fish in the North Palouse, ten or fifteen miles from here—the largest I ever saw, and plenty of game on the mountains. . . . Apples are raised here that weigh over two pounds. One man raised five apples which weighed eleven pounds. How is that? And the best I ever saw in my life. Mr. Day, at Dayton, has the best orchard I ever saw. . . . It is the best country to raise horses I ever saw. . . . This is the easiest country to farm in that I ever saw. . . . All kinds of vegetables are raised here, such as cabbage, turnips, beets, onions, carrots, etc., the largest and best I ever saw. . . . I believe this to be the best country for a poor man to come to that I know of." Not all of the Mondovi group settled in Dayton, or if they did, they did not stay there very long. But they did remain in the region. The forty-one people in the Hunter group scattered throughout the area. E. B. Gifford moved his family east to the Pullman/Moscow area. George Hunter also established a farm there, and his sisters Elma and Luella lived nearby. Gifford's sons Chester and Charles went north to Spokane County, where the Ide family named their small town Mondovi. Lena and Cushman Hunter and the Christian family also lived in Spokane Valley. The Eager family, who had split off en route to settle in Boise, Idaho, eventually rejoined their friends. The year 1880 found them boarding with another Wisconsin family near Dayton. In the Dayton area alone twenty Wisconsin-related families, including the Henry Hunter family, established farms at the start of the decade. During the succeeding years the Mondovi group continued to live in the region.[38]

The networks that drew settlers such as the Mondovi emigrants to the region helped sustain them in their new location. The former Wisconsin residents, for example, with their friends scattered over several hundred square miles, developed an understanding of a broad area beyond the Dayton locale. These linguistic, emotional, and physical connections contributed simultaneously to the development of a collective understanding of the new country.

"Settling up very fast"

The letters home not only served to attract settlers and maintain connections to the past, they also reveal the gradual reconciliation with a new place, a new home. The correspondence of a New York State couple exemplifies the process of reidentification. Charles B. Dunning and Josephine Hiller Dunning arrived in Washington Territory in 1880. Over the next twelve years they kept in touch with their New York relatives by mail. "We are away off here in W.T.," opened Josephine, who keenly felt the physical and psychological distance, in her first letter from Washington to her aunt and uncle on April 20, 1880. "We think it is a very nice country much better to make money in than N.Y." She described "some of the best apples I ever saw and nice potatoes." Charles explained their initial ambivalence toward the move to Uncle Singleton and Aunt Mary: "I have never had any regrets that I left there for I know this is a far better country than that—but it is new and at present we have to put up with some inconviences, but we will soon overcome them." Their letters home served as a way to take stock and to reflect. The emotional ties between Washington Territory and New York transcended the lack of physical connections. "And dont you know Auntie Heaven is just as near W.T. as N.Y.," commented Josephine on the death of one of their New York relatives. The optimistic tone of their reassuring notes continued over the years, but the contexts of their qualifications changed. At first the letters made constant references to New York as the Dunnings bridged the gap between their new world and the old: "I don't know of a family in here but what are satisfyed with the country & five years will do for this country what it took 25 to do for N.Y.," Josephine wrote in 1881. She was also pleased to identify tangible connections to her eastern birthplace: "Two of the people I am acquainted with here are natives of N.Y. and are splendid people." The letters repeatedly reassured both readers and writers of the wisdom of their choice. "I like the country & the people better & better the longer I stay & the more I get acquainted," noted one letter. "The longer we stay here the better we like and we know we can make something here," repeated Josephine the following year. "It is a better climate than N.Y. and we are glad we came Only I wish I could see you once more." As the Dunnings gradually adapted to the new surroundings, they ceased referring to New York. By 1884 there were no doubts: "We are better satisfied with country this spring than ever before. Any one could not help like a country that looks as this does now." [39]

The letters of other settlers echoed this phenomenon of liking the country "better and better the longer I stay." Alice Roberts, for example, wrote longingly to her sister Rhoda in 1883: "I received your last [letter] on Friday. I was getting very anxious to hear from home. It had been a long time since I heard. It is *home* to me. I often dream of being there." Six years later, Alice had become convinced of her new country's future. "We were at Mr. Harris's not very long ago and he wants to go back to Kansas. She likes it here. He is very foolish for this is a much better country to make a living in than Kansas and he is like most of the rest of us, he is not over burdened with wealth." [40] Helmer Steenberg tried to explain his feelings to his friend Helen Munson of Virginia, Wisconsin: "It is two years next month since I left the old town and really it does not seem half that long. There are so many Virginia [Wisconsin] people out here that it seems just like home to me and I could not get homesick if I tried. I like the west better every day and don't know when I will see Wisconsin again." [41]

As they became acquainted with their new surroundings and neighbors, settlers forged new bonds of attachment. At first, as Steenberg's experience suggests, a shared past helped create bonds. Just as Josephine Dunning found other New York natives, a former Oregon resident, R. K. Skaife, delighted in meeting other transplanted Oregonians.[42] Eventually, however, a shared present as well as a shared perception of the future drew people together. Growing social networks supported other moves within the region. As strangers became neighbors, they linked their futures together. A group of railroad workers in Cheney took up adjoining lands in Latah County, Idaho, in 1880. As Kate Price Grannis tells the story,

> They found out this land was thrown open for settlement there and a great bunch of people from there [Cheney] that had gotten acquainted, they'd come from different parts of the east and my folks were from California, my father, and my mother's folks were from Kansas. . . . And when this land was thrown open, then a bunch of them went up and located there, and they were acquainted with each other. Now the Hawkins' and the Lundsfords and some of those people, and that's how Avon country got started, or, Latah county.[43]

While the settlers created new attachments to people and place, they faced increasing problems in communicating with their old friends, neighbors, and kinfolk. The letters reveal the frustrations inherent in bridging the distance of understanding. As an exasperated Tommy Norbury complained to his sister in response to his family's correspondence, "Mother does not quite seem to have 'grasped' the country yet."[44] The only solution Maudie Craig, who earlier had yearned for home and its yellow primroses, could suggest to her daughter was, "You and George must visit this country and get your ideas enlarged." Through the correspondence, settlers like Norbury and Craig could mark the ways their own ideas and "grasp" of the country had shifted. From their perspective, the people back home had needlessly narrowed their horizons. No longer "strangers" in a "new country," Craig, Norbury, Roberts, and other letter writers presented themselves as residents.[45]

Perhaps the last word on letters home should go to sixty-year-old W. B. Field. Writing in 1888 from "my land" at Loon Lake, some forty miles north of Spokane Falls, he described the extensive forest land and then hastened to explain,

> They are putting in saw mills and settling it up very fast they are about to build a railroad . . . we Shall go into Stock I never saw such a place for horses and cattle as this is . . . in the months July August we have the most delightful weather you ever saw I think there is the best chances for a man of enterprise one who has sand enough to do something and dont get homesick . . . I think if Roy and Clare were here they would be delighted there is the grandest scenery here you ever saw I would like to see you all very much but never expect to see that country again.[46]

Field's use of the usual superlatives and clichés—"settling it up very fast," "the most delightful weather you ever saw," "the best chances for a man of enterprise," "I would like to see you"—echoes that of Luvina Buchanan. As an older man who chose to settle on ranching land, Field had different experiences than those of the younger woman, who, with her husband, established a farm more than two hundred miles away. Yet as their language reveals, they shared more than we might recognize. Field and Buchanan, like other newcomers to the interior Pacific Northwest, faced a period of personal disorientation as they attempted to amend their mental maps. While the settlers who came together in Paradise Valley, at Fort Colville, or along the Spokane River, brought distinctive ways of seeing, they shared a set of experiences and the language to describe those experiences. As economic, social, and political interests united the interior Pacific Northwest homesteaders with other residents, they enlarged their fields of vision. Joining others as members of emerging communities, they built upon these commonalities as they participated in reshaping or constructing collective identities.

Those people who chose to settle on homesteads and ranches, such as Buchanan and Field, maintained a set of shared experiences and language. As self-described homesteaders, they mapped their surroundings with attention to those natural and human-made surroundings that would contribute to their planned agricultural-based future. Yet they did not create a sense of themselves and their future in a rural vacuum. Connections to the world outside the homestead remained inherent in their letters, plans, and maps. They located themselves, as did the former Humboldter John Cady, with references to roads, railroad routes, and towns. Their anticipated and realized participation in the market economy depended on those lines and dots. Increasingly, their lived experiences—economic and social—as well as their mental constructions—cultural and emotional—intertwined with those of the people who chose to settle in cities and towns, especially with those who identified themselves as town builders.

Spokane Falls

The letters home written by settlers in eastern Washington, northern Idaho, and southeastern British Columbia occasionally refer to a growing settlement at the falls of the Spokane River. Some writers recognized the site's potential as an urban center. "If you will look at a map of Washington Territory, along the projected route of the North Pacific R.R., you will see a spot marked Spokane Falls," wrote the Baptist minister of Moscow, Idaho Territory, in 1879: "Perhaps there is no better water-power in the world. The impression is that this place will become the Lowell and the metropolis of all this upper country. A nice little village is now springing up where the future city will be."[47]

The "nice little village" consisted of fewer than fifty wooden buildings, including two mills, located on three blocks. The town site had been established the previous year by James N. Glover. Glover, owner of a store and sawmill, was a six-year resident at the falls. Arriving in 1873 as a speculator, he and two partners bought up squatters' rights in the unsurveyed land in anticipation of future development. Rumors of the arrival of the Northern Pacific Railroad, along with the promotional activities of Glover, J. J. Browne, and Anthony Cannon, drew a growing population to the site. Another Spokane booster was W. H. Merrick, an attorney. This was his prophetic vision: "I see nothing in the way of the town continuing to thrive as it is the natural outlet of a large tract of country to the west and northwest to say nothing of the East and southeast, is one of the handsomest sites for a town in the world, has the best water power west of Minneapolis which is already well improved and is already a town of 3000 inhabitants there or thereabouts." Like the visiting Baptist minister, Merrick drew connections between the natural environment and the "natural" industrial and commercial use of that environment. His clichés echoed those of the homesteaders when he claimed, "For scenic beauty [Spokane Falls] excel anything I have ever seen."[48]

Most diarists and letter writers of the early 1880s, however, wasted few words on the settlement. Their individual concerns took precedence over the potential urban center envisioned by Glover and other early boosters. In the same year that Merrick cataloged Spokane Falls's advantages, John Truax came to town. The day after Truax arrived, the newcomer noted in his diary, "This is a very nice place and growing verey fast But i cant se what there is to kep it up." Even Merrick combined his boosterism with some skepticism: "I say *if* because I have seen so many inland towns spring up with excellent prospects and for a time thrive luxuriously and afterwards go to decay that I view them all sceptically." As Truax and Merrick acknowledged, believers in Spokane Falls needed "to see" the place through future-oriented dreams.[49]

In their memoirs early visitors to Spokane recalled, often ruefully, their own skepticism and myopia. As one pointed out, the hamlet located at the falls was not particularly impressive: "We passed through Spokane Falls which was a little settlement with only two or three hundred people. Father could have homesteaded the land on the north side of the river where the courthouse is now but he didn't think it would be wise to waste his homestead rights on that barren gravel."[50] Another remembered, "My first visit to Spokane did not impress me to any extent. A single unpaved street ran the length of the humble village that was destined to be the future metropolis of the Inland Empire. At that time there must have been a half dozen scattered towns throughout the region that could have equalled Spokane in size."[51] For homesteaders and even potential town dwellers, Spokane Falls gained value in retrospect. Their stories of lost opportunities underscored the eventual success of the "humble village." As a ferry site, milling location, and supply center for the growing population attracted to the region by mining booms or open agricultural lands, Spokane Falls grew steadily. In the town known as "the Falls" the population jumped from 350 in 1880 to "nearly 3000" five years later. By the end of the decade 12,000 people called Spokane Falls home.[52]

In its years of rapid expansion during the 1880s, particularly after the completion of the Northern Pacific Railroad in 1883, Spokane Falls was predominantly a city of wood. As in other rapidly growing nineteenth-century towns or "instant cities" in the American West, wooden houses, stores, sheds, sidewalks, fences, and poles crowded the town site of Spokane Falls. Even the recently constructed block buildings of stone and brick relied on a wooden substructure. Visitors confronted a conglomeration of stores, homes, boardinghouses, lunch counters, restaurants, hotels, saddleries, manufacturing establishments, saloons, and other structures jumbled on the land between the river and the railroad tracks. The settlement's location along the edge of great forests of ponderosa pines and hardwood trees made wood the cheapest and most available construction material. Although settlers cut down most of the trees within the established town site as the city grew, scattered ponderosa pines remained within its limits to tower above the one- and two-story frame structures. Sheds and stables peppered the open spaces within the interiors of city blocks. In addition to the wooden buildings, stacks of drying lumber awaiting shipment by the Northern Pacific Railroad filled whole blocks of downtown Spokane Falls. The wood even reached into the river itself in the form of platforms extending from the milling operations located along the banks or on one of the three small islands above the falls. In the south channel, created as the river flowed around these islands, log booms contained groups of fresh-cut logs, while plank walkways reached out from the shore. Wooden bridges stretched across the river connecting the islands with the north and south banks.[53]

During the dry summer of 1889 this city of wood caught fire. A German-born carpenter, Jacob Klein, was an eyewitness to the start of the blaze: "One Sunday evening, about 7 p.m. on the 4th of August, 1889, I took a lunch in one little restaurant close to the N.P. depot, and the cook spilled some lard on the stove, and the wallpaper back of the stove caught fire. They could have put it out easy but the cook said to let the old shack go, and it went up in smoke, also the one near by. By that time, a breeze came up from the S.W. and within five hours, 31 blocks of the heart of the city went up in smoke. I never saw such a fire in my life as that one."[54] The

Lost in the Debris This eerie photograph captures the destruction caused by the Spokane Falls fire of August 1889. By permission of Cheney Cowles Museum/Eastern Washington State Historical Society, Spokane, Washington.

"great fire" of Spokane decimated the entire downtown area. Although not as familiar as the great fires of London, Chicago, or even Seattle, the blaze dramatically disrupted the lives of many residents. For the transient population and downtown lodgers who lost their worldly possessions in the blaze and for the businessmen, shopkeepers, and merchants whose business assets, often uninsured, went up in smoke, the fire was traumatic. The conflagration also had larger ramifications for those it did not directly damage.

The Spokane Falls fire of 1889 and the rebuilding of the city in its aftermath open up a window onto people's mental conceptions of place. As a disruptive experience for individuals and for the community as a whole, the fire marked time in a powerful way. People often identified life experiences or events as happening before or after the destruction of downtown Spokane Falls. In another way, the fire served as an immediate, drastic form of "defamiliarization"; it forced residents of Spokane Falls and its surrounding area to look at what they took for granted and, rather than rebuild, to build anew. The reshaping of the city constituted an opportunity to construct a particular future which, though predicated on the past and bound by the limitations of existing materials, focused on the transformation of the city into a regional center. Here in this period of change, this moment of defamiliarization, we can enter into the nineteenth-century world through another version of triangulation. In this version, the Spokane Falls fire of 1889—as experienced in time and through collective memory—marks one point of the triangle, while the rebuilt and reenvisioned city of Spokane marks another. From our vantage point at the vertex, it is possible to use the process of rebuilding the city as a baseline to measure the imaginative and material transformations that took place over time, as the destruction of the city led to the creation of a particular vision of the city and the Inland Empire. Examining the words and actions of residents and visitors, the noises and sights of the city in the aftermath of the fire, opens up a space for us to recreate the nineteenth-century mental world.[55]

Dismay and dislocation characterized the initial reaction to the drastic changes in the visual landscape. "How sad and desolate the City looks," lamented the mother-in-law of one of the leading city businessmen in her diary.[56] In their private descriptions, residents particularly recorded their sensual disruptions—especially those related to sight—immediately after the fire. "Such a sight as I never saw before," reflected the businessman Daniel Dwight, "Men, Women, Children and whole families without food or shelter. And a sad sight to see such fine blocks in ruin in such a short time." Joseph Boyd's hardware store in the Hyde block was destroyed. As he wrote to his wife a week after "our dreadful disaster," "It is enough to break almost anybody's heart to see the terrible destruction of our beautiful city—every noble brick and stone building that once looked so fine and handsome layed in dust and ashes. In fact every way we turn there appears to be nothing but desolation." The city residents had lost their physical and mental landmarks. "It was only by counting the streets," explained Dwight as he tried to locate himself among the ruins, "that we could tell in what locality we were, everything was so changed."[57]

The fire created a new space. Only charred boards and rubble remained to cover the flat lands along the south bank of the Spokane River between the river and the railroad tracks. "We were lost in the debris," recounted a former Spokane Falls resident, Martha Gay Masterson, who came to visit the burned city. "With the landmarks gone, we were strangers in our old home."[58] The newly created physical space opened up a mental space where residents, particularly those of a certain class, income, and power, worked to reconceptualize the city, its relationship to the region, and their futures. In telling the story of the fire and its aftermath, town boosters developed a narrative of success which emphasized control over elements defined as wild and untamed—a narrative familiar to late nineteenth-century Americans. In rebuilding the city, bankers and businessmen sought to solidify their status—to articulate it in brick and stone. In contests over the use and regulation of the burned-out district, residents expressed their concerns about appropriate behavior, social acceptability, and civic membership along lines of racial and economic class differences. The vision eventually captured in the rebuilt city extended its influence beyond the city limits to those who visited Spokane Falls and those who looked to Spokane Falls as the center of their region.[59]

In confronting the results of the blaze, the people of Spokane Falls drew upon the known experiences of other similar disasters. In many respects the "great fire" was not unexpected; during that dry summer of 1889, fires were common. From the streets of Spokane Falls and other settlements, residents could see smoke from numerous forest fires raging in the mountains. From nearby Coeur d'Alene, the day after the Spokane Falls fire, M. Gilbert described "a dense smoke from fires all over northwest. . . . I don't know but before we are through we shall all burn up. It has been a year of disasters by flood & fire surely." Other cities and towns in the territory experienced damaging fires. In June "a conflagration that has no equal in the history of fires on the Pacific Coast" ravaged Seattle's downtown. Less than a month later, fire devastated the business portion of Ellensburgh, the major urban settlement of central Washington. Spokane Falls residents, along with other Washington and Idaho territory settlers, had contributed to the relief of their sister cities. These recent reminders of nature's destructive power framed the responses to Spokane's disaster.[60]

In understanding and describing their own experiences, residents, newspaper writers, and promotional writers also relied on a familiar narrative of nineteenth-century city development. Because of the many fires in nineteenth-century cities and towns, tales of destruction and rebirth had long been incorporated into progressive stories of urban growth. By the late nineteenth century, fires had become defined as part of a maturation process for a "young city." Central to these narratives was the devastating Chicago fire of 1871 and the dramatic rebuilding of that city. In their private and public writings, Spokane Falls residents compared their situation to this nationally identified disaster. The well-known story of the Great City rising from the ashes fostered a sense of confidence in an eventual rebirth. In some senses, the blaze validated Spokane Falls—other great cities had experienced great fires, therefore Spokane, which had now experienced a great fire, would emerge as a great city. It had been "tested by fire."[61]

Memoirs, oral histories, and autobiographies reveal how pivotal an event the fire was for those who aligned their interests with the Inland Empire. It became a shared memory. Many personal accounts use the fire as a community reference point, telling and retelling the story in similar words with different particulars. "My personal experience upon that eventful Sunday night in 1889," recalled Albert A. Kelly, "is as vivid to me tonight as if it were last Sunday night." In memory, the fire of 1889 came to symbolize the emergence of the Inland Empire. "Rising Phoenix like from the great fire of 1889," according to many, the city of Spokane and its tributary country entered a grand age. In reality, of course, the region changed gradually, but the fire became the event around which discussion of that change clustered. Jennie Boughton described the fire in her memoir: "The fire of 1889 was the beginning of a new Spokane. It grew and spread out. Business houses changed quarters, and it was altogether different from the old Spokane. It grew more rapidly and although it was still a western city, it grew to be more cosmopolitan. Mines were developed, saw mills built; every business grew. Spokane became the second city in the state." Memoirs such as Boughton's capture the fire in its most positive sense, as seen in retrospect. Centering the city within a regional space, the narratives of Spokane's emergence after the fire reflect the success of a particular vision.[62]

This narrative of success triumphing over adversity, of a united populace facing tragedy and working together to achieve a collective rebirth, developed quickly in the public press. Newspapermen, claiming that a revitalized belief in the future characterized the residents of the city, promoted this perspective of a shared disaster and united civic optimism. As the *Spokane Falls Review* reflected in the week after the blaze: "From the millionaire to Chinaman no exception has been made, all are on a common level of grief, the only difference being that some are better able to bear the loss than others. . . . Rich and poor crying out alike as they gaze appalled upon the tearful sweep of flame. Oh, what a shame! Our beautiful city! Was it not a great love when those who were cast out homeless and with no visible means of support, with their little families gathered about them, could still look beyond their own, even, and grieve first of all for their loved city?" The newspaper eagerly reprinted an article from the *New York World* which echoed the hyperbolic claim of unity across economic class and race lines. "The disaster," noted the local correspondent, "instead of crushing the people, seems to have had the effect of bracing their wills and stimulating their energies. Every one is hopeful, because all who live here firmly believe that the city has a great future." The public promotion of renewed vigor reflected in part the acknowledged need to attract outside investors.[63]

The newspaper accounts also reveal the often hazy line between claims to local status and assertions of outside interests. At least one local newspaper reiterated the Chicago connection, not only because, as Carl Smith has argued, of the cultural power of Chicago as a late nineteenth-century symbol of the struggle between urban disorder and control but also because of more direct economic and individual links. In the months after the fire, local politicians and businessmen determined to start a newspaper to rival the *Spokane Falls Review*, which they claimed represented external interests. Although originally established and owned by city residents, the *Review* had been in the financial control of the Portland-based *Oregonian* since 1888. The "local" status of this new paper, known as the *Spokesman,* rested predominantly in Horace T. Brown, a Spokane businessman and former investor in the *Review,* who spearheaded the effort and appeared on its list of publishers. Brown, however, depended on the financial backing and the journalists he had attracted to Spokane Falls from Chicago. Trained on the staffs of Chicago papers, the *Spokesman* editors followed the conventions of late nineteenth-century journalistic practice as they hyped the emerging city. The first issue of the *Spokesman* in March 1890 made the usual reference to the Chicago fire, included illustrations of the new business blocks, and headlined the "pluck and enterprise" of the "New Spokane Falls."[64]

As Spokane Falls residents, new and old, coped with the physical, social, and economic havoc wrought by the blaze, they too began to emphasize the positive, even in their private writings. The experience of Charles W. Clarke was typical. In his diary, the small businessman called the ruins "a ghastly and discouraging spectacle. 30 blocks gone—the entire commercial centre —nearly every brick block in town My Howard St store gone." Within two weeks, however, Clarke was less discouraged. Capitalizing on the inflated prices for downtown lots, he sold the ground lease for the Howard Street lot and received $300 insurance on the building. On August 23 he reported, "Spokane rising from the ashes in heroic temper. Tents up all over the burned district and all mechanics busy." Businessmen like Clarke and others who could reap economic benefits from the blaze quickly found a silver lining. On the morning after the blaze, for example, Albert Kelly recalled,

> We were up early,—daylight to a farmer; and out into the garden picking beans, cutting cabbage, digging potatoes, etc. We had an idea these vegetables would be in demand when so much was destroyed the night before. Wax beans were sold Saturday [before the fire] at around four cents per pound to the trade and Monday noon we had to advance to ten cents. Potatoes were a cent and a half Saturday and our small potatoes were sold at five dollars per sack. Nobody complained and if we had a conscience we didn't know it.

Regardless of Kelly's assertion, not everyone approved of this individual economic opportunism. In the first civic meeting held the morning after the fire, Mayor Frederick Furth, members of the city council, and a group of concerned businessmen passed a resolution that "all keepers of hotels, lodging houses, restaurants, and dealers in supplies who advance prices on this occasion shall forfeit their license."[65]

Resolutions and ordinances were passed immediately after the fire to reestablish civic control in the disordered space, to prevent the recurrence of fire, and to establish relief efforts. They also reflected the economic interests and civic concerns of a particular group of citizens. Prominent businessmen, who had suffered severe losses as a result of the fire, augmented the city government during the crisis. Bankers and real estate investors such as William H. Taylor and Cyrus Burns of Spokane National Bank, town site developers James Glover, president of the First National Bank, and Anthony Cannon, president of the Bank of Spokane Falls, dominated the city's relief committee. They attended the first morning meeting and called their own "citizens' meeting" to be held that afternoon. Members of a civic elite, most had previously served in city politics. At their afternoon meeting they passed additional resolutions, which were immediately approved by the mayor.

As the resolution against raising prices suggests, the town leaders rhetorically presumed that the duty of citizens during the crisis was to work for the common good rather than to seek individual profit. Another resolution, that "any person offered employment and refusing to work should be notified to leave the city," reflected their presumptions and self-interests even more directly. Because their own personal economic interests were closely aligned to civic interests, however, the line between individual and common good was somewhat blurry. The bankers competed with each other to acquire prominent corner locations on which to rebuild their establishments, raising the prices of downtown lots more than 25 percent. Yet when one hundred teamsters gave notice a few days after the fire that they would now require one dollar paid in advance for their services, the local business-oriented paper castigated their efforts "to take advantage of the present situation." Expanding upon the notion of general civic duty, an editorial asserted that "it is the duty of every citizen to enter a protest against so narrow a policy." Economic interests separated the experiences and the responses of the Spokane residents.[66]

Effects of the fire were hard on both the downtown working-class residents and the businessmen. Yet as the *Spokane Falls Review* pointed out, some residents were "better able to bear the loss than others." The evidence suggests that the businessmen may have even improved their positions, but the working-class residents faced more obstacles. Much of the transient population, burned out of their cheap lodgings, initially sought shelter on vacant lots, along the river, and on the outskirts of the city. Young Perry P. Kline explained his precarious circumstances in a letter to his friend Richard in Dillon, Montana, two days after the blaze: "Would pay any price for a Bottle of beer Will stay with the town all the same Slept on the bank of the River last night Catch as catch can tonight Will write you when the City is rebuilt which will be 10 years from now."[67] Those homeless who along with Kline decided to "stay with the town all the same," placed their hopes, like the businessmen, in the rebuilding of the city. In the optimistic language of the rebuilders, one city attorney claimed, "This fire

Looking East on Sprague from Lincoln

Looking East on Sprague from Lincoln Tents and scaffolding sprang up quickly in downtown Spokane Falls after the 1889 fire. The building in the foreground is also visible in the preceding photograph. By permission of Cheney Cowles Museum/Eastern Washington State Historical Society, Spokane, Washington.

has been a rich man's fire. It had destroyed property of those who could afford to lose it. The poor man has benefitted, it gave him work." When the *Spokane Falls Review* echoed the suggestion that the fire had provided "honest laboring men" with the opportunity for home ownership, however, "A Carpenter's Wife" complained about the blithe assumptions. Outlining her family's expenses and income she queried, "Will someone please show me where I can diminish expenses so that we may 'build a home and acquire a competence' as the REVIEW of January 20 states? I must be at fault for my husband is 'industrious, thrifty and sober.' " She continued with a bitter commentary on the "work" of real estate investors, "In regard to 'the men who are rebuilding our city' leaving the town, is there danger of this while they receive the rents now demanded?"[68]

The self-described town builders, the businessmen and town leaders, placed the blame for the fire not only on the waterworks employee who had neglected to turn on the water pressure after construction that previous Friday but also on the wooden buildings that housed the working-class residents. Following the example of Seattle leaders who had passed a similar law two months before, Spokane Falls leaders passed a city ordinance a few days after the fire prohibiting "frame, or wooden, or corrugated iron building of any kind or character" within fire limits.[69] A special permit was required to reopen a business within the fire district. Businesses whose applications for permits were accepted raised canvas tents with the allow-able wooden floors and three-boards-high wooden walls. Throughout the bitter winter of 1889–90, while the cattle industry received a death blow from freezing temperatures, businesses in Spokane Falls operated out of these canvas tents, which were heated by stoves. The metal stovepipes emerging from the cloth structures created an enormous fire hazard. But the Spokane Falls fathers were determined to allow only construction of brick, stone, and iron in their reenvisioned city.

In the months after the fire, the availability of work attracted skilled and unskilled laborers to the city. The bustle of Spokane Falls was undeniable, but so was the din, the clutter, and the dirt. Mounds of brick and stone clogged the city streets as crews of men labored to regrade them, lay new foundations, raise walls, and pave sidewalks. The new downtown Spokane Falls noisily proclaimed its future; it was not a stagnant place. The "process of becoming" was evident everywhere. The promise of the city, and hence of the region, was visible. Residents tolerated inconveniences and disap-pointments because of the power of this promise. J. Z. Moore, for example, welcomed brother lodge members to a Knights of Pythias convention and typically made a virtue out of the disruptions:

> As to our city, you'll find it somewhat disheveled, so to speak, building material often obstructing your way . . . and you may be disturbed by the busy ring of the hammer, the scraping sound of the trowel, the rushing of teams and men, the blasting of rock, and the loud roar of that great water-power which when harnessed up, and put to the uses of man, is destined to be so great a factor in the history of the Pacific Northwest, but these you will recognize as incidents to the thrift of a people and the upbuilding of a great commercial metropolis.

The constant activity bespoke the city's vitality and contributed to the emerging identity of the region.[70]

Change, excitement, and growth were evident in the short term. But so too was difference. A visible disparity emerged in the rebuilding city—the disparity between the tents and the five-story brick buildings. "Tents still dot the burnt district here and there in which thousands of dollars of business is transacted daily," reported the *Spokesman* in March 1890, "while at the sides of these dwarf-like temporary abodes rise high in the heavens monster blocks of artistic masonry." The disparity in architecture reflected class differences. Those on highly valued property who lacked capital to rebuild with the requisite stone and brick moved outside the fire limits. Those who did rebuild had or could get capital—the businessmen who spent the money for choice lots, built mortgaged commercial blocks, and passed ordinances. As John Fahey has pointed out, much of the money to rebuild Spokane came from outside investors, including a large percentage of Dutch bankers.[71]

Bankers and boosters approved the passage of the resolution regulating building materials to prevent a recurrence of a massive fire in a city of wood. It was passed out of fear of fire, of lack of control over one of the most unpredictable and destructive elements, and of uncontrollable nature. Less overtly expressed, though, other concerns motivated the ordinance, including a fear of the uncontrollable elements of certain social groups. The desire to harness perceived uncontrollable elements extended to aspects of social life. The fear of fire in a wooden city was also a fear of the uncontrollable.

In the confusion of that winter, tents made vice visible in the city. The noises from the canvas saloons and beer halls penetrated the tents of other businesses and entered public spaces. Although martial law closed down all liquor stores and saloons immediately following the fire, within a month they had reopened in the downtown area. Jacob Goetz and Harry Baer, two wealthy former miners from Idaho, well-known in Spokane for their saloon business, reestablished their enterprise on Riverside Avenue. They built a trestle to span a gulch and erected a gigantic tent to cover an entire city block between Riverside and Main, advertising the largest beer hall in the United States. As one white man noted, using the common racial and national terms of the dominant culture, "Here could be seen approximately four or five hundred men every evening courting the goddess Fortuna, lured on by the croupiers. White men, Negroes, Japs and Chinese stood as one great brotherhood, trying to beat the man at his own game."[72]

The streets seemed filled not only with building materials but also with scenes considerably less pleasing to a community striving to be a center city. As Joe wrote to his fiancée, Annie, in December 1889: "I saw a woman lying in the middle of the street in the mud bare headed and in her stocking feet apparently lifeless to a looker on but examination proved she was alive and a police was sent for." Later in the letter he told another story: "Then last saturday eve I found a drunken man abusing a woman who I thought was his wife and she appealed for help and I had a tussle with him to quiet her down I had him on the floor holding him down while the woman fled away. I learned afterwards that she was or had been living with him but she was not his lawful wife. Day before yesterday she looked me up and wanted me to keep quiet about the fracas."[73]

City residents responded in a variety of ways to this visible vice. While some took Joe's individual samaritan approach, others banded together to urge city authorities to regulate certain economic and social behaviors.

With the precedent of the post-fire regulations in mind, residents called upon the mayor, the chief of police, and the city council to purge the city "of the dangerous classes. . . . They are a clog in the wheel of progress and impart to the city an air of 'toughness' that repels many intending investors." In the ensuing public debate, Spokane Falls residents expressed their concerns about what constituted appropriate economic activity, social control, and civic responsibility. Who were these "dangerous classes"? What measures for control were appropriate? What were the moral boundaries of the community? What economic behaviors should be allowed?[74]

Gambling was a particularly thorny issue. Town merchants and businessmen distinguished between "tin-horn gamblers" who conducted "sure-thing games" and "legitimate gamblers" who ran "straight games." They considered saloon gambling "essential to the prosperity of a city." Other residents disagreed, arguing that "the gambler is living upon the labor of others. He is a simple operator upon the surplus. Nothing more. He does not produce sufficient for his own existence. Therefore we do not see how he can benefit a community." City ministers took the debate one step further when they conflated saloon gambling with real estate speculation and linked "the spirit of inflation and speculation" with prostitution and drinking. The Reverend Jonathan Edwards explained the ministerial response: "The spirit of inflation and speculation took possession of the people, and social and moral conditions were deplorable. . . . Good brother Bucholz, German Methodist pastor, and myself at the request of the Ministerial Association made an investigation of the redlight district, gambling halls and saloons. We spent two nights at it and witnessed scenes that made our hearts sick."[75]

The gambling fever existed not only inside Goetz and Baer's block-sized tent but also in real estate. Downtown lots exchanged hands rapidly in the days after the fire. The local newspaper quoted exorbitant prices, and the real estate boom spread throughout the city and its environs. Edmond Pendergast wrote to his family in an attempt to entice them to invest, "People here all seem to have more or less of a gambler disposition. They are willing to take great risks." To his father he reported, "I don't know when the 'boom' will collapse, if ever, it looks the bottom *might* drop out of prices in all outside property sometime and yet undoubtedly there will be fortunes made in the near future in just such land. It is a good deal like gambling anyway." Investors and real estate speculators became less inclined to equate gambling and speculation as the debate reached higher stakes.[76]

By January 1890, a self-appointed citizens' group, encouraged by city ministers, had established a Law and Order League to take the situation into their own hands. Conducting nighttime raids of suspected vice houses, the league soon became "a righteous power in the government of this city," according to its supporters. Other sympathetic antigambling advocates nonetheless complained vigorously that the league's activities deviated "from the proper pathway in interfering with the rights and liberties of others."[77]

One snowy evening, these familiar late nineteenth-century debates over economic activity and civic rights took on another twist when Harry Baer shot and killed "Big Mack" McCrossen outside Goetz and Baer's tent saloon. All sides seized upon the incident as evidence for their particular perspective on the gambling and vice issue. Some accounts condoned Baer's actions as self-defense, describing him as a businessman protecting his interests and even suggesting that he deserved praise for ridding the city of McCrossen, "a Gambler and a Bad Man Generally." Other accounts, caricaturing the German-born Baer's accented English, portrayed his quick acquittal as a grave miscarriage of justice and evidence of civic corruption. Such an equation of immigrant status, lawlessness, and immorality reflected a deep suspicion and dread of the foreign-born. For the prominent "citizens" of Spokane, the uncontrollable growth of the city, which was out of the hands of the "town founders," was matched by the "uncontrollable elements" of the city population, that is, the owners of saloons, wooden shacks, and lunchrooms as well as the frequenters of these establishments, who were mainly immigrants—German, Irish, Italian, Norwegian, and Chinese.[78]

City rebuilders linked the environmental chaos of that winter of 1889–90 to social disorder in a variety of ways. While the public debates over gambling and speculation, property rights and citizens' rights, difference and common interests continued, the rebuilt downtown stood as a tangible representation of their contested vision. Sanborn Fire Insurance maps reveal the changes effected in the city. In the downtown district before the fire, numerous saloons, gambling establishments, and female boardinghouses shared city blocks with banks, livery stables, merchandising establishments, and lodgings. After the fire, owners of such "unacceptable" businesses found permits difficult to obtain. City authorities, for example, effectively drove the Chinese out of the downtown and divided the Chinese presence in the city into two locations.[79] Before the fire, their lodgings and laundries dotted the entire downtown area. After the fire, they reopened their businesses on vacant lands south of the railroad tracks where the Chinese Mission and family dwellings remained.[80] Gambling houses, single men's dwellings, and employment offices moved to an upriver location, joining the exodus of saloons and houses of prostitution from the downtown blocks. In May 1890, when Goetz and Baer tore down "Dutch Jake's Tent," newspaper editorials claimed a victory for the antigambling efforts. The red light district, too, moved from its Front Street location under duress. City authorities and property owners worked together to prevent the return of prostitution to the downtown area. A few weeks after the fire, when "a French woman" put up a couple of tents in which to conduct "her nefarious vocation," she was arrested, fined, and ordered to leave the vicinity. The police tore down her tents. Initially these euphemistic "female boardinghouses" moved to a shantytown near the railroad tracks and later to an upriver location. Using a familiar, if oddly chosen, metaphor, a newspaper editorial noted the results of the public efforts to regulate vice, praising the "flame of public opinion . . . that may be relied upon to protect the homes of Spokane and shield the sons and daughters of this fair young city."[81]

While "undesirable elements" and "dangerous classes" were being forced out of the downtown, other changes in the social geography of the city were also taking place. In the long term the center of the business district shifted. The city effectively segregated the center of economic activity. The "invisible" business district—where businessmen engaged in real estate, law, banking, and other professions in which profits were often gained through abstract means such as the operation of invisible market forces—remained in the downtown area, but manufacturing moved out of the fire limits. Farm-related stores and livery stables also moved out of the business center. Joseph Boyd's hardware store, for example, moved from the Hyde block out of the business district. The most prominent residential areas rose above the city in the hills on the south side or in the addition platted by J. J. Browne around Coeur d'Alene Park on the bluff overlooking the river to the west. Nearly all the churches changed their locations as a result of the fire. The First Congregational Church moved to Fourth and Washington streets, where the members erected a stone building.[82]

The cityscape changed visually. Workers used the rubble from the fire to fill in a large ravine along the banks of the river and to close off one of the channels, joining Glover's Island to the downtown area. The downtown buildings rose five, six, and seven stories high. An organized grid of downtown brick blocks lined the street with construction right up against the sidewalk, crowding the downtown space. Paralleling the six- and seven-story structures were six-story-high poles that carried a network of electric wires along the city streets, stretched high above pedestrians. Replacing the ponderosa pines, these electric poles symbolized the emerging metropolis—a city of lights, of densely filled lots and street blocks. Gone was the world of sheds, stables, and Chinese laundries that was once visible behind the street-front stores. Other aspects of the city also receded from view. The falls were now visible only from the hill rising above the city where residential buildings congregated. Horse-drawn and electric streetcars obscured the roar of the falls.

Business blocks replaced the one-store or single-occupancy buildings.[83] The style of the buildings followed that of the noted metropolis Chicago. F. W. Lester, formerly of Chicago, was one of several architects working out of Herman Preusse's office, one of the busiest in the city. In the eight months after the fire Lester alone prepared fifty-six plans. "In almost every case," he reported, "I have followed the Chicago styles in designing the Spokane Falls buildings." By "Chicago styles" Lester was referring to the emerging Chicago school of architecture as it was being developed in that city during the last half of the nineteenth century. Characterized by tall buildings—five and six stories immediately after the 1871 fire and sky-scrapers two and three times that height by the end of the century—the style emphasized functional, utilitarian construction. Despite the anxiety about the recurrence of fire and the knowledge of steel technology, the need for rapid rebuilding, lack of ready sources of supplies, and high costs of steel structures meant that the buildings were fire-retardant, not fire-proof. Architects designed masonry shells with iron posts or columns hold-ing up heavy timber joists and followed Spokane city ordinances which banned the distinctive mansard roofs that had helped spread the fire from rooftop to rooftop. The rectangular blocks, tall and wide, included courses of different materials at the sill level to emphasize horizontality. Despite subtle variations on the facades, in the aggregate the buildings presented a remarkably uniform appearance.[84]

In Spokane Falls visitors came to marvel more at the human alterations of the environment than at the wonders of nature. It was not the falls but the dam and the hydroelectric plants that drew people's attention at the waterfront. Electricity from the plants provided streetlights at every corner as well as the power to run electric streetcars and elevators. The impressive downtown business blocks received more attention than the river. As a representation of the heroic rebirth of the city and physical articulation of a regional vision, the downtown came to define "the magic young city of the Inland Empire." "The Falls, (the city I mean) has grown to beat every thing," reported homesteader Alice Roberts six months after the fire. When her husband, Henry, journeyed to the city to "prove up" their Rosalia home-stead at the land office, he returned with news of the astonishing transfor-mation. "Henry says he never dreamed it had grown so fast. Street cars, electric lights water works, etc."[85] Streetcars brought residents and visitors into the center of the downtown world. Even rows of substantial brick blocks towered above their heads where electric wires crisscrossed the skies. But they reserved their greatest admiration for the evening hours. It was a dazzling vision. Spokane was luminescent. Arc lights brightened city streets, illuminating the darkness of the future. As William E. Jackson, who arrived in Spokane Falls after the fire, recalled, "I can never forget my feelings that first night as we looked out over the city and saw the bright arc lights in all directions. . . . We then realized that we were to make our home in a real city."[86]

What was the new Spokane like? One authority wrote in January 1892:

Look as you will, you cannot discover where were the thirty or more blocks burned that awful Sunday a little over two years ago, so rapid has been the march of progress. Here and there a vacant space, covered with crumbling foundations, tells where the fire was, but the outline has been wiped out. The only apparent result of the fire has been the reconstruction of the city on a more magnificent scale and the shifting of the lines of business. Her wholesale houses are now firmly established, mostly in one district; her banks have found permanent sites, and her great retail stores surround them and have established the main arteries of trade.[87]

Frances Fuller Victor, a more skeptical onlooker, noted on her 1890 visit to Spokane Falls that "much of the fine property in sight is covered with mortgages." Even so, she observed, "This fact does not seem to depress, much less dismay, the mortgators. They point to the wheat-fields of the Palouse country, the mines of Kootenai, Coeur d'Alene, Colville, and Okanogan, and enumerate with pride the several new railroads which will soon open up other districts, agricultural and mineral, and always mention the truly magnificent water-power which is destined to 'turn the wheels of progress.' "[88] Despite the fear that "dangerous classes" might clog those wheels, the businessmen and town leaders of Spokane thought of themselves within the context of an interlocking regional system.

Spokane and the Inland Empire

The emerging sense of region, as articulated by the businessmen of Spokane Falls—Victor's mortgators—reached its fullest expression in the fall of 1890 in the Northwestern Industrial Exposition. To introduce the newly rebuilt city, to assert its regional prominence, and to promote investment, the newly created Spokane Falls Board of Trade organized a commercial fair. Unlike the earlier agricultural fairs held in the city and other eastern Washington towns, this exposition, as its name implies, celebrated the urban industrialization process. Rather than rely on local talent, its promoters hired a professional specialist from Chicago, Charles W. Robinson, to manage the exposition. Following the pattern of the promotional fairs and expositions, along with their accompanying literature, that proliferated in late nineteenth-century urban development, Spokane Falls's version accentuated the importance of manufacturing, mining, and marketing in the city's economy. Its exhibits represented different aspects of the "active" market, "abundant" labor, and vast "natural" resources attached to "this inviting center." Fearful of the potential negative perceptions of Spokane Falls that outside investors might hold after the fire, the city promoters emphasized that "not a vestige of the ruins remains to be seen."[89]

The City Anticipates Its Future Accompanying the 1890 Northwestern Industrial Exposition oversized brochure, this bird's-eye view of "Spokane Falls and Her Natural Resources" presents the rebuilt city as envisioned by the Spokane Board of Trade. Disembodied hands point the ways from the city to agricultural, timber, ranching, and mining areas. The exposition buildings are located in the upper right. By permission of Cheney Cowles Museum/Eastern Washington State Historical Society, Spokane, Washington.

Despite some squabbling over the site for the extravaganza—various ex-position promoters, who were also real estate speculators, campaigned in the hopes that their own property would be selected—Spokane Falls's businessmen joined together to develop an area east of the city near the Northern Pacific Railroad yards. These "representative men," appropriately celebrated in the exposition's pamphlet, hired "an army of mechanics and laborers" to construct the three-story exhibition building.[90]

The businessmen's efforts to control the construction of this regionally oriented promotional space, both the exposition building and the percep-tual vision it represented, faced some opposition. In May 1890 the city's carpenters, mindful of the economic power they gained with the demand for their services after the fire and joining the national labor union move-ment in hopes of shortening their work hours, went on strike. Initiated by workers at the Spokane Milling Company, the strike for a nine-hour day spread throughout the city. Work stopped on all union projects—including the exposition building. In a shrewd promotional response, the exposition directors issued a call to "all good citizens . . . to report at the Exposition building tomorrow morning at 7 o'clock, with or without tools, to do what-ever is in their power to aid in the completion of the building." The next day 350 "good citizens" arrived, and the city's newspapers reported a "carnival" atmosphere. Significantly, after one day of manual labor, the businessmen and clerks returned to their desks and, using their more usual tools of persuasion, prodded private employers to release skilled nonunion workers from their jobs to work on the building.[91] Faced with the efforts of business-men-turned-workmen, the carpenters failed to prevent a complete work stoppage and to procure a shorter workday, but their resistance, con-sciously or not, had symbolic import. The architectural changes required by the post-fire city ordinances—especially the use of iron and steel—posed a potential threat to the skilled craftsmen who worked with wood. The industrial exposition itself, with its celebration of mass production, contributed to the deskilling process experienced by carpenters and other workers throughout the nation.[92]

Visitors to the exposition in October 1890 saw a wide variety of exhibits —products of the city's ironworks, foundries, lumber mills, and manufac-tories, displays by organizations and businesses, as well as the usual ag-ricultural produce. The exhibits and the fifty-six-page exposition brochure emphasized the economic relation between the city's manufacturing busi-nesses and the area's mineral, forest, soil, and water resources, all of which offered "the agriculturalist, the miner, the explorer, the capitalist and the investor . . . an extensive field of operation" and "unequalled advantages." Listing the city's businesses and industries, Major E. A. Routhe explained that "the presence of so many industries at a point where seven lines of railroad center is bound to invite other manufactures." The wish-fulfillment prose of the brochure echoed the perspective presented in the bird's-eye-view map created for the occasion. Entitled "Spokane Falls and Her Natural Resources, the Variety and Extent of which are not Equalled by any City in the World," the map defines in cartographic form the city's proposed relation to its surrounding area. The Spokane River, spanned by bridges and controlled by a dam, wends its way through the center of the map and the city. Attached to descriptive labels, disembodied hands with their index fingers pointing past the edges of the map encircle the city. The labels define the natural resources and districts lying beyond the boundary of the map but not outside the implied grasp of the city's economic control. Railroad lines, which snake through the regimented city blocks, provide a concrete manifestation of the economic connections of the city with its "hinterland." From the bird's-eye view, looking to the northeast, the city of Spokane Falls appears to blanket all the available land. The use of this standard lithographic form, as R. H. Schein points out, legitimated and promoted the new industrial order of late nineteenth-century America. Reliant on machine technology for its production, emphasizing order and control, the bird's-eye-view map participated in and promoted a particular ideology. As part of a new cartographic genre and a new vision of the city, the map defines the role the Inland Empire intended to play in the industrialized nation.[93]

In 1891 the Spokane Falls Chamber of Commerce, following a year-long campaign, voted to drop "Falls" from the name of the city. The message was clear: Spokane was a city of the future, a modern city created through human invention. Even its name no longer explicitly acknowledged the natural environment. The emphasis, as in other late nineteenth-century cities, was on signs of urban order to control the perceived instability of nature and culture. The horizontal lines of the Chicago-style business blocks and the electrical illumination of cardinally oriented streets defined an engineered city reliant on technology and industrial commerce. Linked stylistically and economically to the rest of the nation, Spokane as a modern city drew on familiar models to create its own identity. The reenvisioned and rebuilt city positioned itself as an imperial regional center. The Chamber of Commerce issued a new pamphlet to promote this identity. Although much of the work relied on the words and images of the exposition brochure, the new pamphlet reshaped its title, dropping the words "falls" and "natural" but adding others. "The City of Spokane Falls and her Natural Resources" became "The City of Spokane. Its Tributary Country and Its Resources."[94]

A new region, as well as a new city, emerged out of the ashes of the 1889 fire. In his 1889 annual report, W. H. Taylor, president of the Board of Trade, situated "our fair city, the capital of this Inland Empire." Describing the rebuilding process, he outlined one version of the regional vision. Specific ideas about change, speculation, difference, and control defined this regional consciousness. The Inland Empire, as seen through the prism of Spokane, was a place of promise and a region of the future. These visible signs of coming success allowed many settlers to create a place for themselves in an alien and uncertain environment. But clearly there were limits to the acceptance of change and uncertainty. The past, as the letters home reveal, continued to shape visions of the future. Social differences, defined along nineteenth-century understandings of race, class, and gender, for example, were perceived as elements to control, not to foster. Courting change as a speculator, as a "mortgator," was quite different from courting change as a gambler.[95]

The descriptions of Spokane after the fire erase parts of the city; people and places were left out of this selective vision of the Inland Empire. It does not include the shantytowns, for example, or the Spokane Indians who still camped alongside the falls. As this particular expression of the region and its future became encased and articulated in maps, buildings, electric lights, regraded streets, and social segregation, the rebuilt city came to have a larger influence on the regional consciousness as well. But it was not a vision that all residents of the Inland Empire shared. Many had reservations about empire.

INSET

Reservations about Empire

The signs on the edges of the Northwestern Industrial Exposition map of 1890—"To the rich gold and silver mines of the Coeur d'Alene," "To the Palouse farming & fruit districts, finest in the world," "To the Kootenai mining district and the great coal deposits," "The Big Bend stock country," "To Mica Peak and the timber tracts of St. Joseph and St. Mary's"—figuratively pointed the way to the "tributary" resources of the Spokane town builders' Inland Empire. In such representational constructions, the commercial empire depended upon the natural resources of the larger region and the manual labor of those who worked with the physical environment. The work of the business leaders and promoters centered on the built environment of the city, a few steps removed from the countryside. Deriving their profits from transportation, manufacturing, investments, and speculation, business leaders and their clerks handled paperwork, business transactions, letters, stock certificates, maps, orders, and other abstract language-based representations in their daily activities.

Although the distinction between city-based abstract work and country-based physical work resonated in the promotional literature emerging from Spokane, the economic realities of the late nineteenth-century interior Pacific Northwest often obscured such differences. Economic linkages between city and country helped to forge a regional consciousness. Spokane businessmen were not the only ones who invested their future in the varied economic opportunities found in the region. In ways large and small, other residents increasingly invested their time, money, and energy in ventures outside their immediate surroundings and economic niches. Ranchers bought city lots and mining shares; farmers tried their hands at prospecting, dabbled in irrigation company stocks, and found off-season work in towns. Town dwellers, including single women as well as men, registered for government lands in forested sections, often under the Timber Culture or Timber and Stone acts, then spent their summers living on the 160-acre plots to "prove up" their claims. Speculating in the region's natural resources and urban centers in these ways and others, many residents developed and conveyed an emerging regional consciousness closely akin to that of the town builders.[1]

Despite the increasingly pervasive rhetoric and economic linkages that drew diverse groups together into the Inland Empire vision, however, challenges to its proposed economic arrangements and alternatives to a single regional structure centered on Spokane persisted. Chapters 2 and 3 explore these reservations about empire, the debates over regional boundaries, from the perspective of those individuals and groups living outside the Spokane city borders. Whether considered by the town builders to be residents of "tributary" sections of the Inland Empire, such as the miners in the Coeur d'Alene and Kootenai districts, or viewed as obstacles to be set aside or displaced, such as the native peoples throughout the region—these groups operated according to their own visions of their place within the environment. While the Spokane businessmen celebrated their commercial enterprises with disembodied hands pointing to the city's tributary resources, from the reaches of northern Idaho territory other voices spoke of the dangers of losing such essential body parts.

"I would sooner cut off my right hand than give up my liberty to them [the mine owners]." These words of a Coeur d'Alene miner, Daniel Gillen, to the visiting Congressional Committee on Industrial Relations in 1899 express the vehemence behind the struggle over workers' rights in the industrial mines of late nineteenth-century northern Idaho. The labor-capital dispute, which erupted into violence in 1892 and 1899, is familiarly known as the Coeur d'Alene class wars.[2]

Gillen's words echo those of a participant in another late nineteenth-century northern Idaho rights struggle. Ten years before Gillen reported his indignation, a Coeur d'Alene leader, Andrew Seltice, negotiated with a different visiting federal government committee over the rights to land—the boundaries of his people's reservation. Relinquishing reservation land, Seltice explained during the 1889 negotiations, "was just the same as cutting my left arm off." The disputes over the Coeur d'Alene reservation lands, part of a longer struggle over native peoples' rights to land and self-determination, rested on assumptions regarding ideas about race and region.[3]

These two ongoing struggles over rights in northern Idaho in the late nineteenth century shared more than simply the language of amputation. The questions raised by these struggles over the rights to land, self-

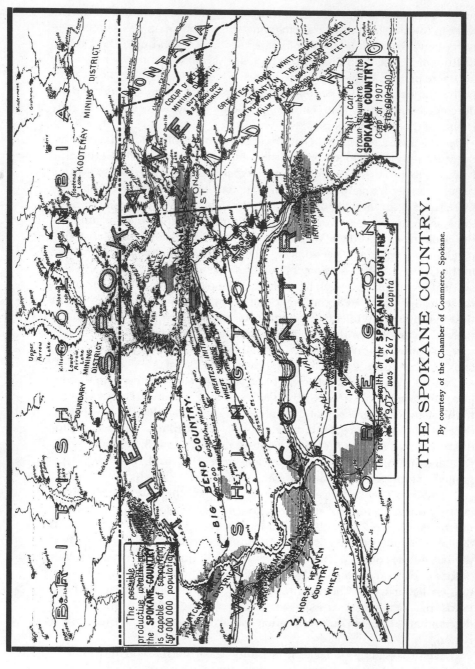

THE SPOKANE COUNTRY.

By courtesy of the Chamber of Commerce, Spokane.

Spokane Country This Spokane Chamber of Commerce map, reproduced in Ellis Davis's 1909 *Commercial Encyclopedia*, defines and quantifies the natural resources of the Inland Empire. County boundaries and reservation lands are not delineated. Courtesy, The Bancroft Library.

determination, economic control, identity, and the future engaged these and other inhabitants of the interior Pacific Northwest. Spokane businessmen and others who perceived the region as an Inland Empire, as a place of promise and a region of the future, offered particular answers to these questions. Those individuals and groups who had reservations about empire, such as the miners of northern Idaho and the Coeur d'Alene Indians, developed critiques of the emerging imperial vision.

Related in time and place, the Coeur d'Alene Indians and the Coeur d'Alene miners shared a similar set of circumstances as both independently responded to the pressures and power of capital and the state. The conflicts centered on the issue of rights over a particular environment— its appropriate use and ownership—and the rights of distinct social groups. They also shared, in the local public debates that surrounded these struggles, the nineteenth-century language of race and class.[4]

In the debates concerning the physical boundaries of the Coeur d'Alene Indian reservation, Coeur d'Alene Indians, miners, and government negotiators articulated competing visions of the region's social and economic boundaries. Historians of other regions have noted the ways in which an economically based regional identity developed in the face of oppositional voices. Andrew R. L. Cayton and Peter S. Onuf, for example, argue that "the formation of a middle class, midwestern identity depended on the denial of the legitimacy of alternative communities within the region." Situating its ascendancy in relation to the development of industrialization, they argue that "midwestern culture, in short, was born in a simultaneous celebration of the glories of capitalism and a rejection of divergent interpretations of the social and political implications of the market."[5] Similarly, in the Inland Empire, as Coeur d'Alene miners and mine owners, local residents and observers engaged in public discussions over the lines that contained striking miners in Coeur d'Alene bull pens, they spoke from different sides of social and economic boundaries.

The physical boundaries—of reservations and bull pens—carried symbolic meanings for those engaged in the conflicts. The reservation boundaries on the land reflected less tangible boundaries between races, cultures, and economies. As Coeur d'Alenes, Spokanes, missionaries, federal Indian agents, and Euro-American residents of northern Idaho and eastern Washington negotiated over the establishment, maintenance, and disbanding of the reservation, they contested critical social issues. Their discussions reveal distinct differences over questions of land and property, racial identity, and community membership.

In a similar way, despite shared racial and cultural assumptions, Euro-American miners and mine owners expressed divergent visions of their roles and rights through their own charged rhetoric. Boundaries, walls, and lines characterized the Coeur d'Alene mining conflict in a variety of ways. Workers decided whether to join the union or be escorted beyond the region's boundaries. Mine owners fought each other in litigation over subterranean mine boundaries. Soldiers corralled striking miners into bull pens and confined them behind fences. These physical boundaries, like those of the Coeur d'Alene reservation, carried both practical and symbolic meanings for those engaged in the conflicts.

The variant meanings attached to the terms of division, as shaped by race and class identifications, point to emerging discourses of difference and rights within the contexts of specific economic and social changes. Competing groups employed the same rhetoric of justice, freedom, equality, laws, authority, and rights. Where were the acceptable boundaries between property rights and human rights? How were competing claims to be resolved? What were the limits to social as well as economic freedom? Who defined those limits and those freedoms? In the larger cultural debate this language reveals competing ideologies of economic and social relations within the emerging region. The Coeur d'Alene boundaries, in both their physical and their rhetorical manifestations, mark differences; they reflect variant perceptions of appropriate rights. Chapters 2 and 3 explore these concurrent rights struggles, focusing on their discursive as well as their material components, as a way to examine the mental boundaries of the Inland Empire. A joint examination of these two Coeur d'Alene examples of late nineteenth-century debates over boundaries of race and class reveals the ways these boundaries were defined and maintained. As residents of the Inland Empire expressed their ideas about their place and their future in concrete and verbal terms, they contributed to the emerging regional vision.[6]

CHAPTER 2

COEUR D'ALENE
FENCES AND WALLS

In August 1889, as Spokane Falls faced the rubble of its devastating downtown fire, Andrew Seltice faced three U.S. Indian Department commissioners who had arrived at the northern Idaho lands of the Coeur d'Alenes "to
negotiate . . . for the purchase and release of such portions of its reservation not agricultural, and valuable chiefly for minerals and timber, as such
tribe shall consent to sell." At the opening council, Seltice reminded the
commissioners—Benjamin Simpson, John Shupe, and Napoleon Hum-
phrey—of a similar gathering held just two years earlier. In the 1887 council, the Northwest Indian Commission and the Coeur d'Alenes had
negotiated a written agreement stating that "no part of the reservation shall
ever be sold, occupied, opened to white settlement or otherwise disposed
of without the consent of the Indians residing on said reservation." That
agreement had yet to be ratified by Congress. In the 1887 negotiations,
Seltice pointed out, "We built a strong high fence with the Government; we
built it round so that the ends nearly met. We done our part, but the gap
that was left has never been finished by the Government at Washington.
Now, you three friends and headmen must close the gap. I am afraid, my
friends, of that treaty, I am doubtful. If I was not doubtful there would not
be hard work of this. That treaty is a wall we can no see through. When it
is down we can see through and talk."[1]

What did Seltice mean when he spoke of fences and walls? The "strong
high fence," the 1887 agreement establishing the Coeur d'Alene reservation
boundaries, was incomplete; it had not been ratified. Without ratification,
that same agreement became, in Seltice's words, "a wall we can no see
through." Rather than a marker of property, acknowledged by people on

Seltice, Chief of the Coeur d'Alenes Olin Levi Warner created this image of Andrew Seltice, one of six medallions he sculpted of Columbia River Indians in 1891. As the Portland writer and retired army officer Charles Erskine Scott Wood, Warner's patron and friend, explained in a *Century* magazine article two years later, Seltice sat for the portrait in a Union Pacific railway car. By permission of the Oregon Historical Society, OrHi 52378.

both sides of the line, it had become a barrier that prevented vision and communication. In Seltice's vision of the region in which he lived, fences served to demarcate the boundaries between his people and others. Walls, or insurmountable barriers between two spaces, threatened to disrupt their lives. The metaphorical fences and walls of which Seltice spoke at the 1889 council served as markers of property, as markers of racial rights to self-determination, and as markers of miscommunication between races.

Seltice was a seasoned veteran of negotiations. During the previous ten years he had been active in seeking compensation for Coeur d'Alene lands "taken possession of by whites." He had sent petitions to the government on the issue and, in 1887, traveled to Washington, D.C., with Pierre Wildshoe, Regis, Stephen Liberty, and others to lay their case before President Grover Cleveland, Secretary of the Interior L. Q. C. Lamar, and Commissioner of Indian Affairs J. D. C. Atkins. That 1887 group was as diverse as the population from which it was drawn, including natives—Coeur d'Alenes and Kalispels—and metis peoples, as well as Euro-Americans who had married into the tribes. They were all longtime residents, members of a multicultural community that had once typified the region. But now with the recent dramatic influx of settlers intent on creating a different world, they were in the minority.[2] They feared further reductions of the more than five hundred thousand-acre reservation guaranteed by that unratified 1887 agreement. Having seen the drastic reduction of the Coeur d'Alene lands since the 1850s, Seltice was "troubled . . . very much" about recent talk "by the whites of having their reserve thrown open to settlement."[3]

While Coeur d'Alene leaders and government negotiators may have shared words, the specific words contained variant meanings and often expressed distinct cultural views of land and boundaries. At the 1887 and 1889 councils, the commissioners and the Coeur d'Alenes spoke about the lands of northern Idaho and the need for lines and boundaries.[4] The discussions between natives and government negotiators concerning reservation boundaries frequently dealt with lines whose visibility depended on the observer. The lines that marked precise ruled boundaries on government maps were not visible in the northern Idaho landscape. There were no fences or walls that marked off the boundaries of a Coeur d'Alene reservation. Unmarked by physical objects on the landscape, created by words not wood, these lines were frequently ignored, moved, or erased. The experiences of the Coeur d'Alenes—their loss of four million acres "which the whites have taken away from us and they now occupy" and the constant intrusions onto the lands—influenced their desire for official recognition of the reservation. They sought firm control over their remaining land. "We do not care for money," Seltice and the other chiefs insisted, "it is land we want." Seltice spoke passionately at the councils about the Coeur d'Alenes' desire to maintain the core of their traditional lands: "We are on only a small part of our country—I mean this reservation. Here we have made our homes; here we have built our houses; here are our fences, our schoolhouses, our churches. Here are our wives and children; here are the graves of our ancestors; here are our hearts; here we have lived, and here we wish to die and be buried. We want these preserved forever." The connection Seltice made between heart and land is also evident in the native language in which he spoke. It is "impossible to detect any difference of form or function," notes Gladys Reichard, a Coeur d'Alene language analyst, in the use of the suffix "ilgwas." It refers to heart or stomach but also indicates property. "It is used to form a great many of the most figurative words," Reichard notes, "and the organ it describes is considered the seat of the mind or intelligence." For the Coeur d'Alenes, "centering" on traditional lands, placing their homes and hearts, fences and graves on specific lands, allowed them to maintain their cultural identity, their "sense of place on a disappearing land."[5]

Even as the Coeur d'Alene leaders and government negotiators were speaking across the boundaries, they misunderstood each other at basic levels. Government officials referred to the Coeur d'Alenes, for example, as a race, as "Indians." But the Coeur d'Alenes saw themselves not as Indians but as Coeur d'Alenes. In these negotiations the language of race became a pivotal marker. Referring to themselves primarily as Coeur d'Alenes, Seltice and other leaders continually made clear distinctions among the interior Salish peoples and used the reservation boundaries as a way of also marking the permeable boundaries—the fences—between themselves and others, whether those others were Spokanes, Colvilles, or "whites." Another measure of the different perspectives can be read in the complaint of an unsympathetic agency employee living among the Coeur d'Alenes in northern Idaho: "These Indians here according to the Priests are Christianized, which statement I am not in shape to deny, but I do know that they have never been civilized or humanized. They think they own the Earth and particularly that part known as the United States."[6]

An examination of the local debate among settlers, missionaries, Coeur d'Alenes, and other residents of the interior Pacific Northwest reveals that they bounded their often overlapping communities in distinct ways. In the creation of the Inland Empire, Seltice's conception of region was only one of many different perceptions of future and place. Some of these perceptions coalesced into the emerging vision; others did not. In the transformation of fences to walls between the Coeur d'Alenes and their neighbors can be seen other stories of walled-out groups. According to Seltice, the success of a multicultural regional community depended on building fences—permeable demarcations of difference—rather than walls—permanent fortifications—between these divisions. This chapter examines the local debates over the Coeur d'Alene reservation to reveal the problems of fence-building, of creating a regional community that recognized and incorporated, but was not pulled apart by, difference.

Missionary Fences

Seltice's words at the 1889 council reflected a long history of cultural connections among natives and Euro-Americans in the Columbia River Basin area. To understand the context of those words, we need to look at that history, particularly at the interactions of Coeur d'Alenes and missionaries. The Coeur d'Alenes of the 1880s employed rhetorical strategies to convey their cultural perspectives, strategies that grew out of their historical circumstances, particularly the physical, economic, and social alterations of the interior Pacific Northwest. The fences and walls of which Seltice spoke developed at least in part from experiences with missionary fences, both physical and mental.

By the time of the Northwest Indian Commission councils with the Coeur d'Alenes, the lives of natives and Euro-Americans in the interior Pacific Northwest had been interconnected for almost seventy years. Since the 1810s fur traders from the Hudson Bay Company, including French Canadians, Iroquois, and Scotsmen, had traveled and traded with the Salish peoples. The legacy of this intermixing was far-reaching. As Robert Burns points out, "The merchant or economic presence of the Hudson's Bay Company also interwove the white and Indian economies, creating a dependence and a modified human landscape."[7] These economic, cultural, and environmental changes accelerated as more and more Euro-Americans entered the region. The divisions among native populations, once characterized by flexible boundaries, became more rigid as a result of increasing limits.[8]

Natives and Euro-Americans had been in contact since the early years of the century, but native groups had a longer history of intermingling. The peoples who came to be identified as the Coeur d'Alene, Kootenai, Spokane,

Pend d'Oreille, Kalispel, Chewelah, Sanpoil, Nespelem, Okanogan, Columbia, Flathead, and Colville tribes shared linguistic, economic, social, and cultural bonds.[9] Speakers of the interior Salish languages, they understood each others' words. Seasonal gatherings at locations rich in subsistence resources, such as camas digging fields or salmon fishing falls, had fostered these bonds. These native peoples lived predominantly in bands, or loosely affiliated villages, often connected through family ties. The acquisition of horses had increased the contact among these various groups. Hunting and trading trips across the Bitterroot Mountains brought the Coeur d'Alenes into contact with the Flatheads and other Plains peoples.[10]

During the nineteenth century, as Euro-Americans established an increasing presence and exerted ever more influence in the interior Pacific Northwest, the resulting social and economic transformations, accompanied by related environmental changes, altered the Coeur d'Alenes' world. The physical environment of the plateaus and mountains from which the interior Salish drew their varied subsistence underwent dramatic changes. The eradication of beaver and substantial reduction of fur-bearing animals as a result of the aggressive fur trade, the intrusion of new plants crowding out existing species, and the prairie grazing of domesticated animals such as cattle, horses, and sheep all contributed to these changes. The ecological impact of new farming activities was noticeable by 1870. At one site in northeastern Washington, reported Special Indian Agent W. P. Winans to the territorial superintendent of Indian affairs, "The prairie . . . is covered with Timothy it contains about 1200 acres, but few acres were originally sown but is spreading from year to year and if not stopped will cover all the prairie on the north east side of the River." While new settlers of the Inland Empire celebrated these ecological changes as progress, natives faced the problems of responding to new ecological and cultural limits. Over a period of thirty years many Coeur d'Alenes chose to shift their subsistence patterns from a varied system of gathering, hunting, and fishing to one based primarily on farming. The shift to an agricultural-based economy implied a series of other significant cultural changes. Some of these changes, participation in a market economy, for example, had been underway since the early part of the century. Others, particularly the Euro-American sexual division of labor in which men engaged in work outside the home and women worked inside the home, represented significant transformations. The Coeur d'Alenes' choice to engage in agriculture was urged and supported by the predominant Euro-American group in contact with the Coeur d'Alenes during this period—Jesuit missionaries.[11]

Missionaries had interacted with the northern Idaho peoples since the 1830s, but it was not until 1842 that they came to live among the Coeur d'Alenes.[12] In response to the publicized visit of a Flathead delegation to St. Louis, Father Pierre-Jean de Smet led a group of Jesuits to the Pacific

Northwest. After the establishment of the St. Ignatius mission among the Flatheads on the eastern side of the Bitterroots, the Jesuits turned their attentions to the western slope. Bands of Coeur d'Alenes from that area had visited the St. Ignatius mission during their habitual hunting visits to the plains, and Father de Smet had returned their visits on one of his supply trips to the Hudson Bay Company's Fort Colville. In 1842 de Smet sent Father Nicolas Point and lay Brother Huet to establish a mission among the Coeur d'Alenes.[13] The missionaries brought their own cultural and individual perceptions along with them and measured the natives against Euro-American standards. In their progressive narratives about their interactions with the Coeur d'Alenes, they identified themselves as agents of change who moved the natives from "wretched misery" to "civilized life." Sharing the cultural perspectives of the Protestant missionaries who worked among the neighboring Columbia Plateau peoples, they linked Christianizing and "civilizing."[14] Father Nicolas Point's writings typically reflect these concerns. In his descriptions of a Coeur d'Alene village, for example, he connected physical cleanliness with spiritual cleanliness;

> What profound misery reigned among these poor people! What poor huts of straw and bark! Around them was the smell of animals, the remains of fish, and other filth of all kinds. Inside the huts bundles of roots were thrown in a corner, skins of animals hung from a pole, and fish were being smoked over a fire. What about the people? Dirty faces, hair in disorder, hands serving as comb, handkerchief, knife, fork, and spoon. While eating, fouls sounds came from the nose, the throat, from the mouth; in fact, from any part of the body capable of producing them. This gives some idea of the visible squalor, but it is a feeble image of the pitiful state of their souls.[15]

For the Jesuits, important elements in the civilizing process included transforming natives' personal habits, spiritual practices, gender roles, economic relations, and social organizations to conform to nineteenth-century Euro-American modes. Outward manifestations of "settled" or "civilized" Indians included "white man's" clothing, houses, fences, and farms along with participation in the market economy and adherence to Catholic or Protestant practice.

Father Alexander Diomedi, who lived and worked among Pacific Northwest tribes between 1875 and 1899, summarized his perception of the early Jesuit work among the Coeur d'Alenes: "We have made them first our friends, and then Christians; next, after inducing them to labor, we transferred them to good lands, where we made them practical farmers. We, then, with some help from the government, gave them schools, and so gradually trained them to the habits of civilized life."[16] The missionaries fostered the first stage of this process, that is, "making friends," with alms, dinners, and medical assistance. Living among the bands and learning their native tongue, the Jesuits established strong ties with the Coeur d'Alenes. Along with farming skills and Christian doctrine, the religious also taught their native tongue, whether English, Italian, or French. As the two groups learned each other's languages and customs, communication between whites and natives gradually came to be rooted in shared experiences and a shared discourse.[17]

The pervasive missionary cultural attitudes are visible not only in the writings but also in the experiences of the Jesuits among the Coeur d'Alenes. Father Point, for example, a sketcher and an artist, saw the land in fundamentally different ways than did the members of the band with which he traveled and lived. He translated these visions both onto his sketchpad and into the buildings and mission site he started constructing with Brother Huet in the spring of 1843. Selecting a location on the St. Joe River, Point followed the traditional Jesuit plans for mission buildings. Eventually a rude church, barn, and fenced-in field marked the land. The site Point had chosen was not ideal for such purposes. Each year spring floods washed over the fields. It was not until Father Anthony Ravalli came to take over the mission years later that the community moved to a new site more conducive to agriculture on a knoll two miles upstream.[18]

Convinced of their Christianizing mission, a succession of Jesuits continued the efforts of Father Point. In the fertile mountain valleys of northern Idaho, a successful farming mission emerged. In 1864, a visitor, Captain John Mullan, noted the cultivation of oats, barley, wheat, peas, and potatoes at the Old Mission. The missionaries seem to have regarded the Coeur d'Alenes' adaptation to horticulture as a sign of more fundamental changes in beliefs and cultural systems. Within the context of extensive cultural contact, however, the physical evidence suggests adaptation rather than transformation. Clearly the turn to agriculture enabled the Coeur d'Alenes to maintain self-sufficiency in rapidly changing circumstances.[19]

Not all of the estimated three to four hundred Coeur d'Alenes participated in the early mission life; many continued to depend on fishing, hunting, and trading.[20] And Coeur d'Alene women and men who engaged in agricultural practices usually combined Euro-American farming with such traditional economic activities. Women's work continued to include gathering camas, berries, and other plants along with tending vegetable gardens. Family groups continued to travel each fall to Kettle Falls on the Upper Columbia River in Washington Territory for the salmon runs.[21]

The Coeur d'Alenes increasingly adopted Catholic practices and established a settled agricultural economy. The written record emphasizes their ever greater involvement in agricultural pursuits, measured quantitatively by numbers of Coeur d'Alenes involved in agriculture, acres in cultivation, bushels of grain and vegetable varieties produced, buildings constructed, and fence miles erected. To provide "land enough for each to have his own farm and become, in time, self-supporting," the Jesuits moved the mission in 1877 to Nilgoalkoa, or Camas Prairie, a traditional site where the scattered bands of Coeur d'Alenes gathered in the summers to dig for camas. Ten years later, reported government officials, "The Indians have good productive farms, good houses, barns, gardens, horses, hogs, cattle, domestic fowls, wagons, agricultural implements of the latest pattern and indeed everything usually found on flourishing farms."[22] These farms included "large fields inclosed with post and board fences, or good substantial rails."[23]

Farms and fences, as physical structures, now marked the Coeur d'Alenes' environment. As representations of mental structures, as markers of an understanding of Euro-American beliefs and practices, they also influenced Coeur d'Alene rhetoric. Cultivated land contained with fences became part of a shared medium of communication. Most Euro-Americans, especially the government negotiators, spoke of land in terms of its commodities—timber, minerals, agricultural resources—as they pertained to its future. Increasingly the Coeur d'Alenes, long known as good traders, learned to negotiate with these terms as well. Requests for farming supplies joined demands for realistic reservation boundaries that included traditional lands.[24]

For nearby Euro-American settlers, shared economic practices distinguished the Coeur d'Alenes. When during the 1877–78 Nez Perce War, for example, bands of Nez Perce tore down the fences of the new settlers, Seltice and his band protected the settlers' lands and helped rebuild their fences. In return, at Seltice's request, the Pine Creek residents agreed to assist "in petitioning [the] Government to grant you a good title to your land."[25] The following year, when a reservation official, a "farmer-in-charge," first settled among the mission buildings and farms, he noted that the Coeur d'Alenes had integrated themselves into local social and economic networks, selling their products to military camps, railroad construction crews, and other regional markets. The farmer-in-charge, James O'Neil, remarked on "the extreme good feeling existing between the Indians and whites on the line of the reservation and in the adjoining towns of Farmington and Pelouse City, in business and social relations."[26]

As a result of these experiences and outward manifestations, Euro-Americans in the interior Pacific Northwest increasingly described the Coeur d'Alenes as the "most civilized" of the interior Salish peoples. By 1879, one Indian agent noted with approval that "their habits are completely changed; hunting and fishing are no longer looked upon as business but pleasure. . . . They no longer allow their stock to roam at large, but during the winter take care of it and feed it." He particularly pointed out what he perceived as changes in gender roles: "The women work, but not as slaves, they help their husbands in the field, and sometimes, during harvest, with machinery, but the heavier work, such as ploughing, chopping wood, etc., is done by men only." He added that "their government also has improved a good deal with their habits; they have unity and power."[27]

The "unity and power" of the Coeur d'Alenes derived in part from their ability to adapt to changing economic, political, and environmental circumstances. This flexibility, like the rhetoric of unity, did not mean that the Coeur d'Alenes constituted an undifferentiated bloc. Tensions and divisions, between those who closely followed Catholic practices and those who did not, and between those who adhered to Seltice's leadership and those who did not, are also visible in missionary letters, agent reports, and Coeur d'Alene actions. By the 1880s, Seltice and others had established an effective strategy dependent upon accomodations with Euro-Americans. Using the language drawn out of their experiences with missionary fences, the Coeur d'Alenes entered into negotiations for their place within the region.

Establishing Boundaries

While the Coeur d'Alenes continued to erect fences to mark their fields, the creation of the Coeur d'Alene reservation—their fence-building with the federal government—was a long, drawn-out process. During the 1850s Isaac Stevens, the Washington territorial governor, had negotiated a series of treaties with Pacific Northwest tribes at four great councils. But although the Coeur d'Alenes and other interior Pacific Northwest peoples, including the Spokanes and the Kalispels, met with members of the Treaty Commission in 1855, no treaty was signed. A reservation established by executive order in 1867 was never surveyed and never acknowledged or accepted by the Coeur d'Alenes. This imaginary reservation, with invisible lines that ran from the mouth of the St. Joe River to the headwaters of Latah Creek and from those two points west to the Washington territorial boundary, served as the basis for later negotiations. President U. S. Grant recreated the reservation by executive order in 1873. During the 1870s most Coeur d'Alenes moved within its boundaries even though "the necessary legislation confirming this negotiation" had not yet been entered and no compensation was granted for the forfeited lands. The Coeur d'Alenes had reason to expect that compensation; they had entered into an agreement with a special commission "sent to investigate the conditions of the Indians in Idaho and adjacent territories" that had met with the Coeur d'Alenes at the Old Mission in the summer of 1873. But by the time John P. C. Shanks, T. W. Bennet, and Henry W. Reed wrote up their report that fall, the commissioners had decided against a separate reservation and recommended "that the agreement entered into with the Coeur d'Alenes be not confirmed."[28]

As early as 1869 the Idaho surveyor general had urged the surveying of

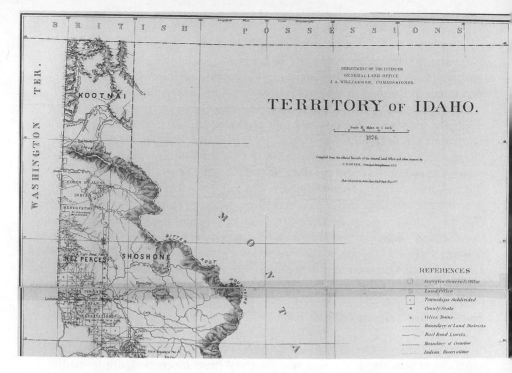

Idaho Territory On this part of the 1876 map, produced by the federal government, the Coeur d'Alene Indian reservation boundaries reflect the lines established by presidential orders but not yet ratified by the Coeur d'Alenes. The forty-mile limit lines refer to the extent of the Northern Pacific Railroad land grant. Courtesy of Map Collection, Yale University Library.

accurate lines: "If the *reservation lines* are not to be considered a myth by the settler, they should be surveyed and permanently marked as soon as possible." Not until 1883 was the survey accomplished. Even after its completion, local Euro-Americans treated the reservation lines as fictions. "For no sooner was the surveying done that some of the whites began to give us new cause of uneasiness," noted a letter written from the mission to the Indian agent John J. Simms in October 1883 and signed by a dozen Coeur d'Alene leaders. Their uneasiness derived from rumors of petitions circulating in local towns "to have the government open the very best portion of this reservation." The next year, another agent, Sidney Walsh, reiterated the "great need of placing monuments in reasonable proximity to each other defining the lines of survey of this reserve, so that settlers will not encroach thereon and cause trouble among the Indians."[29]

During the 1880s increased attention was being paid to the northern Idaho lands claimed by the Coeur d'Alenes. Mineral discoveries by prospectors in the mountainous area, agricultural settlement along the river valleys of nearby eastern Washington territory, and railroad expansion across the Bitterroot Mountains brought Euro-Americans into the region in

greater numbers than before. As the industrial development of mining discoveries increased, so too did the pressure to resolve the Coeur d'Alene
rights to those lands. Mining investors and local settlers exerted political
pressure to settle the question of legal rights and to gain access to lands
claimed by the Coeur d'Alenes. Native leaders, Catholic missionaries, and
government officials affiliated with the Colville Indian Agency, who held
responsibility for relations with the Coeur d'Alenes, also called for official
recognition from the federal government.[30]

The northern half of the reservation was particularly vulnerable to the
invasion. As Special Agent G. W. Gordon reported, "These mining prospectors are constantly on this portion of the reserve, and it seems next to
impossible to keep them off with the means at hand." Miners marked their
claims with notices posted on trees and stakes embedded in the ground.
The Coeur d'Alenes continually protested these incursions. Even their absentee agent noted their complaints and fears in his annual reports. "It was
feared in the early spring," he noted, quoting his resident farmer-in-charge
James O'Neil, in 1884, "that the great rush to the Coeur d'Alene gold mines
would cause considerable tresspassing upon their reserve." The following
year he wrote: "What they most dread is that their lands will be taken
from them some day by the whites, or they be forced to take up small
allotments."[31]

Not only the mining rush brought people across the lines. Encroachments on the reservation came from all sides as settlers cut timber, established mining claims, grazed cattle, or even took up farming on Indian
lands. The building of a Northern Pacific spur to the mines near Wallace is
a case in point. The Coeur d'Alenes objected to railroad lines intersecting
their reservation. The Indian agent Rickard Gwydir chronicled their objections in 1888: "It spoils their haylands along the Coeur d'Alene river, de-
stroys their trail to the old mission, has debauched the tribe, their Chiefs
having been bribed and bought by the R.R.Co. Whiskey has been brought
on the reserve, and the country flooded with unprincipled whites, either
connected with the R.R. or else taking advantage of that way of getting
in."[32] Nonetheless, Congress granted the Washington and Idaho Railway
Company a right-of-way through the reservation. The company then leased
the roadbed to the Northern Pacific, which built a line from Farmington,
through the reservation up the valley of the South Fork of the Coeur d'Alene
River, to reach the Wallace mines on December 9, 1889.[33] Subcontractors,
who operated illegal sawmills on Hangman and Trout creeks, stole the
timber used to construct the road's bridges and ties, an estimated three
and a half million feet, from the reservation.[34]

Some individuals legalized their usage or submitted petitions, such as
Z. J. Hatch's 1884 request "to land [the steamer *Coeur d'Alene*], receive
and discharge freight and passengers—and to cut and buy wood from the

Indians on the Coeur d'Alene Reservation."[35] Most did not. Often permits
were issued after the Coeur d'Alenes or their agent brought the trespass to
the attention of the authorities. The pervasive transgressions and the lack
of sufficient agency personnel made controlling the use of permits and even
the border itself a difficult and unrealistic task. Nelson Martin, for example,
used his permit for landing his steam launch on Coeur d'Alene Lake and
river as justification to build a warehouse.[36] In anticipation of allotment,
Indian agents often viewed the actions of trespassers with sympathy: "They
are doing no injury, however, further than simply locating mining claims
with a view to their possession when that part of the reserve is opened to
settlement, as it seems to be believed by them it will be at an early day."[37]
The trespassers, however, not only ignored the boundary lines but also
expected agents to uphold their rights to the lands. As an amazed Indian
agent reported: "There is hardly a week that someone is not complaining
to me by letter, that they have been treated badly by the Indians, or my
farmer on the Coeur d'Alene Reserve. Invariably I find upon investigation
that the complaining parties have been cutting timber on the Reserve,
which my farmer has seized."[38]

The boundaries of the Coeur d'Alene reservation were thus tenuous from
the beginning. Attempting to secure the northern Idaho lands, the Jesuit
missionaries also submitted petitions and requests, engaging Captain
John Mullan to act as their agent in Washington, D.C. Their intentions, as
outlined in an 1885 letter from Mullan to Father Joseph Cataldo, were
"First to save themselves [the Coeur d'Alenes] Second to save that Reservation to the Indian for all time." In consultation with Seltice and his people,
Father Cataldo pursued the interests of the mission, along with those of
the Coeur d'Alenes. At Mullan's request, for example, the mission land was
surveyed in advance of the general survey, expediting the Jesuits' patent.
Although Mullan, Cataldo, and Seltice acted together to gain official recognition of the reservation, their interests did not entirely coincide. Father
Cataldo did not follow Mullan's suggestion, for example, that the Jesuits
sell land to the miners. And Seltice ignored the proposition that the Indian
agent and missionary must approve all intermarriages between whites and
Coeur d'Alenes. Their joint efforts, however, included a 1885 petition
signed by Seltice and others and sent to Washington, D.C., asking the
president, secretary of the interior, and commissioner of Indian affairs "to
send them a proper commission of good and honest men . . . to make with
us a proper treaty of peace and friendship, and enter into such proper
business negotiations under and by which your petitioners may be prop-
erly and fully compensated for such portion of their lands not now reserved
to them; that their present reserve may be confirmed to them."[39] Recognizing the need to regularize the boundaries of the reservation that had been
established by executive order but never ratified or purchased, three ap-

pointed commissioners—John V. Wright, Jarred W. Daniels, and Henry W. Andrews—held a series of councils with the Coeur d'Alenes in 1887. These were the councils that Seltice mentioned when commissioners returned two years later to negotiate for additional Coeur d'Alene lands.

Defining Races and Places

During the 1887 and 1889 councils, when the commissioners and the Coeur d'Alenes negotiated over reservation boundaries, they delineated other boundaries as well. The process of defining distinctions among racial categories became intertwined with defining places. Negotiations over the boundaries of race became a crucial part of the debates over the boundaries of the Coeur d'Alene reservation in the 1880s. Depending on when, by whom, and for what purpose they were identified, the peoples who lived on the disputed lands were defined as half-breeds, metis, whites, squaw-men, Salish-speakers, Spokane, Coeur d'Alene, and civilized Indians. Along with these residents on the reservation lands, federal commissioners, native leaders, translators, missionaries, local settlers, and miners participated in the debates over identity, community, and region. In these debates, both the state and native leaders sought to impose control by employing sharpened racial distinctions within a region where blurred racial lines had been more common; these distinctions had new economic and political consequences. Individuals and groups, marked as "white" and "Indian," negotiated these imposed definitions, often with their own categories of "French" and "Coeur d'Alene," in discussing races and places in the Pacific Northwest.

Throughout the 1880s, as Seltice and native leaders protested the encroachments of Euro-American miners and settlers on their lands, they also registered complaints on other matters with local government officials. In June 1885, for example, J. P. Sweeney, who lived among the Coeur d'Alenes in Idaho Territory, wrote to his superior, the U.S. Indian agent in charge of the Colville Agency, located in Washington Territory, on their behalf: "Seltice the chief of this tribe wishes me to write to you that he has heard that a white man was killed by an indian near Spokane Falls, and that it is said by the Spokane indians and understood by the whites about there to have been done by a Coeur d'Alene indian. Seltice says that the man is not a Coeur d'Alene indian." In an effort to clarify the matter, Seltice explained that Whilcomte, the accused man, "has some Coeur d'Alene blood in his body, that his Grand Grand Father's mother was one half Coeur d'Alene which you can see is a very distant connection. All of the ancestors since that time have been either Colville or Calispel and this man . . . is more Calispel than anything else." Emphasizing that Whilcomte "is not a Coeur d'Alene and never lived here" and describing his behavior as "wild," Seltice asked the Indian agent to correct the misinformation.[40]

Seltice's attention to Whilcomte's tribal identity reflects his concern over the public perception of the Coeur d'Alenes and his resistance to a blanket racial identification as "indian." Speaking through an employee of the Colville Indian Agency, and translated by a Catholic missionary, Seltice referred to typical nineteenth-century European markers of racial identity—blood lineage, appearance, behavior—and asserted his own definition, as a tribal band leader, of who belonged and who did not belong on Coeur d'Alene lands.[41] In distinguishing among the various Salish-speaking peoples who inhabited the interior Pacific Northwest, Seltice marked out the boundaries between the Coeur d'Alenes and other native peoples. In particular, he disagreed with both the Spokane Indians and "whites" living in the growing town of Spokane Falls who sought to assign Coeur d'Alene identity to an accused murderer and "wild" man. Why did the Spokanes and "whites" claim Whilcomte was Coeur d'Alene? And why did Seltice protest their claims? To answer these questions we need to consider the relations among these groups during the 1880s.

For the town builders of Spokane Falls, the presence of Spokane Indians in the streets and camped alongside the falls presented an obstacle to their vision of the city's future. An 1881 editorial in the town's newspaper reported their perspective: "Indians are becoming unbearable in this vicinity. They will not work, and are continually prowling about in search of something to steal, something to drink or defenseless persons to molest. They have no shame. They let down fences, leave gates ajar, walk over gardens, and steal vegetables in their season."[42] The new urban settlers, who did not distinguish among different native peoples, encouraged Colville Indian agents, first John Simms and then Sydney Waters, to remove all Indians from the vicinity. Noting the adverse effect of the increase in Euro-American settlement, the Indian agents and the Catholic and Protestant missionaries—Father Joseph Cataldo, S.J., who lived among the Coeur d'Alenes, and the Reverend Henry J. Cowley, who had converts among the Lower Spokanes—had been attempting to move the Spokanes to reservations since the early 1870s. "The presence of towns and villages springing up all over Eastern Washington Territory," explained Waters, "places Whiskey (that damnable curse of the Indians) within easy reach of these tribes [Spokanes, Palouse, Kalispel, and Lower Pend Oreilles] resulting largely in making the males *vagabonds* and the females *prostitutes*."[43]

At least three bands of Spokane Indians lived in and around the new town. The leaders of these bands—Garry, Enoch, and Louis Weilsho—as their names imply, had long been familiar with Euro-American institutions and customs. Spokane Garry had been educated at the Hudson Bay Com-

pany's Red River school. Under the provisions of the 1875 Indian Homestead Act Enoch had laid claim to his farming lands along the river, now in
the midst of the town of Spokane Falls. They had all resisted attempts to
move them from the rich lands of the Spokane River Valley. Despite the
view of Spokane Falls citizens, reinforced by Waters, that all the Spokane
Indians were "hanging around the town of Spokane Falls, in idleness and
beggary," some members of the bands ran farms on the valley lands as part
of their economic livelihoods.[44] Like Enoch, various Spokanes took out
homestead papers but few completed all the necessary steps to secure their
lands. As a result, especially in the early 1880s, when the Northern Pacific
Railroad increased sales of their land grant sections, some lost their farms
when the property fell on lands allocated to the railroad. Others, who traveled seasonally to hunt in the mountains, gather camas, and fish at the
falls, found their choice lands claimed by Euro-American settlers in their
absence. Disputes over land increased cultural frictions between the Spokanes and Spokane Falls citizens; the murder discussed in 1885 was far
from the only violence between the native peoples and the new settlers.[45]

Unlike the new settlers, who generally lumped most Indians into one
racial category, government agents joined the missionaries in making distinctions based on a racialized understanding of "civilized" appearance
and behavior. According to these categorizations, the Coeur d'Alenes were
"settled" or "civilized" Indians, while the Spokanes were "wild" or "untamed" Indians. Sydney Waters, whose responsibilities as Indian agent
included the various peoples on the Colville, Coeur d'Alene, and Lower
Spokane reservations as well as all nontreaty Indians in the region (altogether numbering around four thousand), contrasted the Coeur d'Alenes
with the Spokanes and suggested that the Spokanes be removed to live on
the Coeur d'Alene reservation. "I feel that if they are so located," he explained in a letter to the commissioner of Indian affairs, "they will soon
imitate the example of their industrious and thrifty kinsmen the Coeur de
Alenes who are the peers of any farmers on the Pacific slope."[46] In 1884
and 1885 Waters met with Coeur d'Alene and Spokane leaders to try to
forge this arrangement.[47]

From the perspective of the Indian agent, Catholic missionaries, and
local citizens, it seemed an ideal solution; it removed the Spokanes from
the growing town of Spokane Falls, fostered "civilized" behavior, and united
them with other Salish-speaking people with whom they were related inas-
much as many Spokanes and Coeur d'Alenes were intermarried. According
to accepted Euro-American ideas about racial identity, in their shared ties
of kinship, language, and traditions, along with common biological factors,
the Spokanes and the Coeur d'Alenes, despite their differences in behavior,
could be categorized as members of a single race.

Yet the Spokanes and the Coeur d'Alenes protested the proposed arrangement. Viewing themselves as distinct peoples associated with specific lands, they preferred to remain apart. Although both the Coeur d'Alenes and the Spokanes sought to hold onto their traditional lands, they employed different strategies for dealing with Euro-Americans and faced different pressures from Euro-American settlers. Moving onto the unratified reservation lands, relying on the support of Catholic missionaries, and communicating with federal officials frequently through letters written in English, the Coeur d'Alenes managed to forestall drastic encroachments by Euro-Americans. The Spokanes, who often played the Protestant and Catholic missionaries off against each other, refused to acquiesce to requests that they leave the Spokane River valley, which now was inhabited by Euro-American settlers who greatly outnumbered the some three hundred Spokanes. "We would rather live among the whites," they explained, "than to be moved to a strange land." Thus, by the mid-1880s the Spokanes and the Coeur d'Alenes found themselves in different economic and social circumstances. These different strategies and circumstances affected their responses to Waters's overtures. The Coeur d'Alenes, writing with the aid of the Catholic priests, thanked Waters for taking "so much interest for the Spokanes," but also noted his faulty assumptions regarding the similarities between the Spokanes and the Coeur d'Alenes. They pointed out that the Spokanes "will not understand their own good and will not appreciate your troubles for them. We think that our presence will not do much, we know well their disposition." They warned him that he would face difficulty in getting the Spokanes to agree to the proposal. Indeed, the Upper Spokanes refused "to go upon any reservation, saying they first want the Government to settle with them for the land the whites took from them, and will, when such a settlement is made, go where the Government may see fit to place them, and then start to farming."[48]

Although Euro-Americans saw commonalities between the two groups, the Spokanes and the Coeur d'Alenes defined themselves by their differences. Contemporary white observers had early remarked on the distinctive relationship between these interior Salish-speakers in terms that reveal their own conceptions of, and priorities for, social and political organization. George Gibbs, for example, on an 1855 exploring survey for a railroad route to the Pacific, was puzzled by "a question of boundary between [the Spokanes] and the Coeur d'Alenes, which appears to be as complicated as some of those between more civilized nations. No resort to arms has, however, occurred, and the territory continues under joint occupation."[49]

The letter from Seltice to Waters regarding the tribal identity of the accused murderer Whilcomte needs to be read within the context of these complicated negotiations. The Spokanes and the Coeur d'Alenes both resisted association with the "wild" Indian. And Seltice, holding onto the "civilized" label accorded to the Coeur d'Alenes by the federal government readers of his letter, sought to turn back the attempts by "whites" to affiliate his people with those Indians defined as "gamblers and loafers" around Spokane Falls. The Spokanes, they explained, would be accepted on the Coeur d'Alene reservation only if they integrated themselves into the exisiting practices—especially adopting the outward appearance of "civilized Indians" and adhering to Seltice's leadership. Among the means used to regulate and enforce integration on the reservation were the actions of Seltice's police. "If the Spokan come," wrote Andrew Seltice to Waters, "we are all glad but one thing we will tell you we desire to have them but not all in one place separated from us, we want to make only one people."[50]

In 1885, as Seltice and the Coeur d'Alenes articulated the requirements for residence on the reservation—"civilized" behavior and traditional adherence to tribal band leadership—they welcomed other individuals onto their reservation lands under the same conditions accorded to the Spokanes. In that year four longtime residents of the region, Stephen Liberty, born Etienne Lalibertie, Julian Boutelier, Joseph Peavy, and Patrick Nixon, some of whom had married Coeur d'Alene women and others whose wives were the daughters of Hudson Bay Company fur trappers, moved onto the reservation with the approval of Seltice.[51] Although the new Euro-American settlers of nearby Farmington and Spokane Falls referred to these men derisively as "Squawmen, Irishmen, Frenchmen, Canadians, and Half Breeds," official federal Indian policy recognized these "whites" as Coeur d'Alenes and included them in all monetary disbursements.[52] By most measures, the Liberty, Boutelier, Peavy, and Nixon families integrated themselves as individuals into Coeur d'Alene society. Stephen Liberty also participated in the Coeur d'Alene reservation debates. He traveled with Seltice and other Coeur d'Alene and Kalispel leaders to Washington, D.C., in 1887 to meet with President Grover Cleveland, Secretary of the Interior L. Q. C. Lamar, and Commissioner of Indian Affairs J. D. C. Atkins about their land claims and the unratified 1887 agreement. And after 1889, he served as one of Seltice's main interpreters. Even after he divorced his Coeur d'Alene wife, Liberty maintained his Coeur d'Alene identity.[53]

So what did it mean to be Coeur d'Alene in the late nineteenth-century interior Pacific Northwest? Clearly the answer to this question depended on who was asking and who was answering. All the groups involved in the 1880s Coeur d'Alene reservation debates operated according to definitions of race that contributed to their understandings of place and region. For Andrew Seltice, racial identity relied as much or more on behavior, appearance, beliefs, and location as on blood lineages. Whilcomte, despite his Coeur d'Alene blood, was not a Coeur d'Alene, while Liberty, who lacked a single drop, was a member of the Coeur d'Alene people. As Seltice explained in words translated by his son Peter, "All the people that are on the reservation whether they are mixed blood or other wise if they are good people we want them protected for we feel that we are all one." Such an understanding of racial identity conflicted with the dominant nineteenth-century U.S. definitions of the Native American race. For federal government officials, missionaries, and Euro-American settlers, racial identity retained a biological determinant. Behavior, appearance, and location could make "whites" Coeur d'Alene, but such attributes never made the Coeur d'Alenes "white."[54]

Negotiating Reservations

Negotiations over establishing the boundaries for the Coeur d'Alene reservation were not simple. As temporary visitors to the interior Pacific Northwest, the 1887 and 1889 Indian commissioners had little understanding of the local distinctions concerning racial identity or attachment to specific lands. The official reports reflect their frequent mystification. They puzzled over the resistance of the Upper Spokanes to leaving their lands: "Their natural love of what was once their country, and their reluctance to leave it, was almost an insuperable impediment." The Coeur d'Alenes and the Upper Spokanes spoke of their emotional attachment to the land, whereas the commissioners defined the land in economic terms. They considered "idle and uncultivated" lands as "open" for use. "If your reservation was full of Indians," they argued with the Coeur d'Alenes, "the whites would not want it or ask for it." Seltice recognized the differences in perspectives; there were not only difficulties in reaching an agreement on the lines themselves but also in the ways the interested parties discussed those lines. For example, attempting to define the two positions, Seltice referred to the commissioners' reliance on maps: "That is your ideas about the boundary. You know we do not understand papers; in taking it that way we will not know the boundaries." Later he explained, "I do not quite like those boundaries; you are chief and have directed your boundaries; now, if you ask us where we want to sell, we could talk."[55]

And when the commissioners eventually reached an agreement with the Spokanes to move to the Coeur d'Alene reservation, where "they will be permitted to select their farms and homes on a tract of land to be laid off and surveyed" separate from "the Indians now on the . . . reservation," they were dismayed that the Coeur d'Alenes raised objections to this solution, which allowed the Spokanes to remain together. In the 1887 council and a second council held in 1889, the Coeur d'Alenes reiterated their insistance that the Spokanes would be welcomed, but only if they arrived as individuals, not as a tribal group.[56] Seltice prevailed, at least initially, in his efforts to maintain control of the reservation membership. As the 1887 and 1889 agreements made their slow way toward congressional ratification, some Spokanes moved to the Coeur d'Alene reservation, where, noted J. J. Walsh in 1893, "they are mostly working for the Coeur d'Alenes."[57] The Spokane agreement remained unratified by Congress until 1892, and two more years passed before ninety-one Spokanes finally settled—individually and not as a tribal bloc—on the Coeur d'Alene reservation. The rest of the Upper and Middle Spokanes, some 230 individuals, moved either to the Lower Spokane reservation or to the Flathead reservation in Montana; an even smaller number remained around Spokane Falls.

The Coeur d'Alenes were less successful in their efforts to maintain control of the reservation's physical boundaries. The 1887 agreements had included a guarantee against further reductions of their remaining acres, yet only two years later another Indian commission had been sent to renegotiate with the Coeur d'Alenes. The pressures of local and national government officials who continued to push for access to valuable resources within the reserve had held up ratification. The 1888–89 Idaho legislature sent a memorial to Congress requesting that the federal government reduce the size of the Coeur d'Alene and Lapwai reservations.[58] Commissioner Atkins concurred. He reported in 1888, "My own opinion is that the reservation might be materially diminished without detriment to the Indians, and that changes could be made in the boundaries for the release of some or all of the navigable waters therefrom, which would be of very great benefit to the public."[59] When the commissioners appeared on the reservation in the midst of the 1889 harvest, the wary Coeur d'Alenes asked that the previous agreement be ratified before new negotiations began. Taken aback by the Indians' tenacious insistence, the commissioners complained that the Coeur d'Alenes "displayed surprising business sagacity, coupled with an exalted idea of the fulfillment of promises. Much time was consumed in appeasing the grievances they fostered and in establishing confidence with them."[60] When they finally came to terms, the Coeur d'Alenes "insisted upon making the lines." They also received $500,000 for 2,389,924 acres of the northern half of the reserve. The government agreed to pay an additional $150,000 to compensate Indians whose improved farms with fenced lands were included in the ceded lands.[61]

The final irony of all these negotiations, however, is that congressional legislation had already doomed the reservation as a permanent Coeur d'Alene refuge. Finalized after the passage of the Dawes Act, the reservation was established only to be eradicated. The order of the day was dismantling, not establishing, Indian lands. The 1887 General Allotment or Dawes Severalty Act granted the president the power to divide Indian reservations into allotments, giving all tribal members varying amounts of land, then opening up the surplus to settlement by homesteaders. Expecting the reservation to be allotted in the near future, local settlers continued to ignore the reservation lines whenever it seemed convenient. Shortly after the passage of the act, Gwydir reported "daily receiving [letters] from whites who are eager to get on the reserve." Mr. Truax, a white resident of the nearby Pine Creek settlement, reported that "there has been forming for some time, near Farmington, a secret society whose object is to get on the Reserve, and will when their numbers are large enough to make the attempt."[62]

Coeur d'Alenes and Allotment

The pressures for allotment at the local and national levels coincided with the Coeur d'Alene reservation debates of the 1880s. For the next thirty years the Coeur d'Alenes, missionaries, local settlers, Indian agents, anthropologists, and ethnographers would struggle over their often divergent ideas about the appropriate use of the reservation lands, the boundaries between racial groups, and the future of the region. The Coeur d'Alenes, watching the gap in their fence close with the ratification of the reservation boundaries, faced new barriers as ethnographers, local settlers, and Indian agents took over the language of the debate and the land of the tribe. By the 1910s, the activities and discourse of local settlers, Indian agents, and ethnographers rendered the Coeur d'Alenes and their lands invisible or characterized the Indians as relics of the past.

In the midst of the 1880s negotiations about the reservation's simultaneous creation and reduction, non-natives pushed for its elimination. The national debate over the Dawes Act encouraged them to believe in their rights to the northern Idaho lands. Rare protests against allotment emerged in the region outside the reservation. The missionaries were particularly adamant in their objections. The Indian presses run at the St. Ignatius Catholic mission school on the nearby Flathead Reservation in Montana produced several pamphlets denouncing the petitions and the push for opening the Coeur d'Alene reservation. In an 1886 pamphlet entitled *The Coeur d'Alene Reservation,* Father Lawrence B. Palladino, writing under the pseudonym Indophile, queried, "Where then is the warrant for the white settlers in their neighborhood to assert that had the Indians their choice they would 'prefer to hold their lands in severalty?' Can these white settlers know the hearts of the Indians better than the Indians themselves?"[63] He did not, of course, ask such questions of himself. Many of the missionaries, while believing that assimilation was the desired goal, agreed with Myra Eells, a veteran Pacific Northwest missionary, who wrote to the Indian Rights Association and Congress *"that the time is not yet"* for even those landholding Indians "who have progressed the most."[64]

The argument for allotment found support from, and was influenced by, the work of anthropologists and ethnographers. Although most Euro-Americans continued to perceive American Indians as a subordinate race, late nineteenth-century anthropologists began to argue that there were no limits to any race's ability to "progress" to the state of civilization.[65] Franz Boas suggested that "the organization of the mind is practically identical among all races of men; that mental activity follows the same laws everywhere, but that its manifestations depend upon the character of individual experience."[66] Boas based much of his argument on his field experiences, particularly among the Pacific Northwest tribes. Although he did not conduct fieldwork directly among the Coeur d'Alenes, those who did perform early ethnographic studies on the northern Idaho peoples applied his methods and ideas.

In 1894, while in the Pacific Northwest to continue his work in British Columbia sponsored by the British Association for the Advancement of Science, Boas met a young "red-headed Scotsman . . . married to an Indian woman." This man, James Alexander Teit, was an ideal assistant, a "treasure," according to Boas. In the ten years since his arrival on the Thompson River to live with his uncle at Spences Bridge, Teit had learned the language, participated in the life of the Thompson River band, and, as Boas put it, "bummed around here a lot in all kinds of capacities." Boas hired the resourceful Teit on the spot. It was the first of several engagements between the two men. On field trips Teit assisted Boas and his team as they measured natives' bodies and made plaster casts of individual faces for anthropometric comparisons, collected melodies and myths, and studied vocabulary and language patterns. He guided them through the interior as they collected information on the Chilcotin. And Teit continued the work among other interior Salish tribes, including the Coeur d'Alenes, after Boas's departure.[67]

The ideas of men such as Teit and Boas gradually came to assert more influence than those of "Indophile" and other missionaries on outsiders' views of the Coeur d'Alene. While both groups agreed on the need for, and the ability of, natives to become "civilized," their religious and scientific perspectives guided them to different conclusions on the allotment issue.

Anticipating the dissolution of the reservation, settlers perceived that space as accessible, as open rather than closed, in their visions of empire. Official requests for access to Indian lands, as well as illegal entries, increased during the first decade of the century.[68] Although more of these requests were entertained, they were not always granted. As an Indian agent, Albert Anderson, explained in his 1903 report, "There is increasing pressure for leases of Indian lands, but I have steadily refused to lease lands belonging to individuals capable of working it themselves. The only hope of making decent citizens of the majority of Indians lies in tying them to their lands and making it necessary for them to work."[69]

Still, in the following year the federal government started to issue grazing permits for the use of reservation lands, at one dollar per head of livestock. Thirteen ranchers legally attained permits to graze a reported 1,872 head on the northern Idaho lands. Evidence of the anticipated opening can also be read in the right-of-way permit granted in 1904 for Rockford and Bellgrove Telephone Company lines and in the sale of lands for a railroad junction and depot at Plummer, Idaho, in the heart of the reserve. Squatters on Indian lands, such as the townspeople and farmers around Harrison, Idaho, concerned about their land titles, petitioned Congress for the right to purchase their lands. Special Agent John Lane, sent to answer the Harrison appeal, arranged for a $15,000 payment.[70]

In the accepted rhetoric of the Office of Indian Affairs, Indian agents advocated allotment. As Anderson, who had been urging allotment for several years, put it, "These Indians should have their lands allotted to them in severalty and be thrown on their own resources as promptly as possible."[71] The anticipated end result was their assimilation into the larger society. The walling out of the Coeur d'Alenes, their effective erasure from the debate, is also evident in the words of other contemporary commentators.

Ethnographers were anxious to capture native life before it disappeared into a "modern" mode. James Teit arrived among the Coeur d'Alenes in 1904 to gather data and details about customs, tales, crafts, and languages. Under Boas's influence, the amateur collector also noted comparisons that seemed to reveal larger truths about the process of cultural diffusion.[72] Teit's concerns were with the differences and similarities among and between various cultural groups. How were the 1904 Coeur d'Alenes different from their ancestors, that is, what cultural traits lingered in modern times? How did the Coeur d'Alene cultural practices compare with those of other interior Salish tribes, specifically those of the Thompsons? Teit's experiences with the Thompsons along with these interests and concerns did, of course, shape the ways he understood other interior Salish peoples.[73]

The sense of a lost culture pervades Teit's collections of information and tales. He regrets the loss of "traditional" activities and the infusion of what he characterizes as "modern" elements. In his perspective, the Coeur d'Alenes constituted a true community in the past, and his job was to uncover the shape of that past. During this nebulous earlier "traditional" time, Coeur d'Alene "land was communal or tribal, and the same applied to rivers and lakes. The whole country was considered the property and food preserve of the tribe." Through his writings, with their focus on a nostalgic past, Teit, along with the local settlers and Indian agents, contributed to the distortion of native voices. Yet echoes of the Coeur d'Alenes are still discernible. A picture of the Coeur d'Alenes at the turn of the century emerges from Teit's work. His concern was more with the past than the present, but his remarks reveal much of the Coeur d'Alenes' activities as part of the Inland Empire in 1904. After a description of traditional ball games in which both men and women once participated, for example, Teit noted that "nowadays the young men of the reservation have a good baseball team, and play against white teams from neighboring towns in Idaho and Washington."[74] But in addition to such specific references, these records reveal other information about the Coeur d'Alenes. Teit's ethnographical writings were composed in one sense not only by Teit but also by his anonymous informants. Although the outsider's recordings are, as James Clifford points out, "hierarchical arrangements of discourses," they nonetheless testify to the existence of some form of common language, of common ground, developed in the interaction of informant and enthnographer.[75]

The silences in Teit's account, for example, speak tellingly not only of the collector's preoccupations but also of his informants' perspectives. For example, Teit searched for "native" religious beliefs but found instead "modern" beliefs: "Nowadays the Christian idea of a reunion of the dead is held by some, but the Indians say that this has been learned from the priests. The form of the belief held seems to show that it is modern. I learned of no belief regarding animal underworlds or spirit worlds. There was no belief that infants, children, or other people were reborn."[76]

The most suggestive information comes from folktales collected by Teit on the eve of allotment. One tale in particular seems revealing. Collected in 1903 and presented in free form by Teit, it is a creation story that explains the moon's appearance. When Toad arrived at the Moon's crowded house for a feast and asked where to sit, she was told, "there is no place to sit." In retaliation Toad caused a heavy rain that penetrated all the houses; only in the Toad's house, situated on top of the Moon's face, did the people find a safe haven. When the rain stopped, "the people tried to pull Toad off his face, but did not succeed. The marks of Toad may still be seen on the moon."[77]

The story of Toad and the Moon speaks to the ongoing allotment process. The Coeur d'Alenes had long been "decidedly opposed to taking their lands in severalty under the general allotment act." When Atkins suggested that "this may be accounted for in part, I think, by the fact that some of them have individually much more land under cultivation than they would be entitled to under the act, and they naturally desire to keep all they have," he ignored any motives that were not materialist.[78] Toad-like, the Coeur d'Alenes sought a place to sit, a safe haven with secure fences, through the establishment of their reservation. They were not successful in maintaining control of their lands, but their marks on the land remain as evidence of their previous habitation.

Allotment Lands

On June 21, 1906, Congress passed the act authorizing allotment of the Coeur d'Alene reservation. By July 1909, when the procedure ended, less than one-fifth of the original reservation remained in native hands.[79] Over the next three years, the appointed agent distributed 160-acre parcels to 638 heads of households, breaking up, in the process, the largest and most established Indian farms. In 1908 Seltice's successor, Peter Moctelme, traveled to Washington, D.C., in one last unsuccessful attempt to forestall the process. The Dawes Act, which might have been expected to make few changes among the farming Coeur d'Alenes, worked against their economic self-sufficiency because self-preservation meant leasing and dependency. By 1913 most of the Coeur d'Alenes were no longer farming their own lands.[80]

Once the Coeur d'Alenes had received their allotted lands, the surplus two hundred thousand acres were opened to homesteaders. Using a lottery system, allotment agents distributed the lands to settlers in the spring of 1910.[81] John Eikum was one of the Coeur d'Alene reservation homesteaders. As he recalled the process, "In 1908 they opened three Reservations, they opened the Colville Reservation and the Flathead Reservation and the Coeur d'Alene Reservation. Then they had a drawing. And I happened to get one late number, 2438 was my number. So I got a piece of land. . . . Then after all the numbers were drawn, they waited so long and then they threw it open anybody could go in there and take a homestead."[82] Some lottery participants hired a locator familiar with the reservation lands to help them make their selection. In Spokane, Simms, the former Indian agent, charged a hundred dollars for the task.[83] Eikum scouted out the possibilities on his own.

The lottery participants came looking for different things; most valued the land for its timber resources or agricultural promise. Although John Eikum later regretted not picking the valuable timber land, he "was looking for farm land, I wasn't looking for timber land . . . it was mostly lodge pole pine. I didn't know anything about timber, but I could've had a good timber claim, you know. White pine timber. The best claim up there where I was on the Alder Creek country, you had over ten million of big white pine and 7 or 8 million of mixed timber." A friend of his settled on a timber claim: "He proved up and lived there about a year and then he sold out to the lumber company for sixteen thousand dollars." Eikum picked scrub brush land and cleared the lodgepole pines from it.[84]

Timber companies vied with settlers for the land. As later investigations by Senator Miles Poindexter's office revealed, a number of Weyerhaeuser Lumber Company representatives illegally entered the lottery for timber claims. A young forester who had recently joined the Indian Service, J. P.

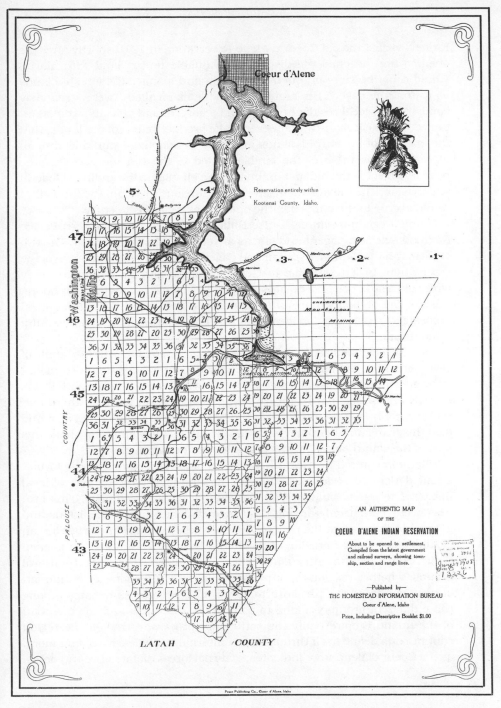

Coeur d'Alene Indian Reservation The Homestead Information Bureau, one of a number of local companies seeking to capitalize on the Coeur d'Alene land lottery, produced this 1909 map of the soon to be opened reservation lands. By permission of the Geography and Map Division, Library of Congress.

Kinney, visited the old Coeur d'Alene Reservation in 1910 shortly after the opening and watched the disposal of valuable timber land with alarm. Would it not be more productive to retain and manage the forested lands as a unit? he asked. His arguments, he later recalled, "were strenuously combatted by local residents and even by government officials, who maintained that the Indians would never make productive use of the lands, that the opening of the surplus lands and their development would lead to an increase in the value of the lands allotted to the Indians and that the primary object of the Indian administration should be the ending of federal supervision. The Indians themselves were anxious to obtain the funds that would accrue to them through the opening of the lands to entry."[85]

George Cecil and Minnie Louise Bailey worked for the Northern Pacific Railroad—he as an agent and she as a clerk—in Plummer, Idaho. The two of them ran the Plummer station and eagerly anticipated the opening of the reservation. In letters home to George Bailey's parents in Indiana they wrote of their hopes and dreams as they looked over potential purchases. Despite the preponderance of timber lands, they sought an agricultural homestead, a place for "an ideal fruit and chicken ranch," and a "beautiful building site."[86]

For a black stonemason named King living in Spokane with his family of seven children, the opening of the Coeur d'Alene reservation also meant the opportunity for a homestead of his own. Frank King described his father's choice as "just like a gambling deal, see, he went up there and there was a bunch of numbers on the board and he just pointed at it and said this is the number that I want . . . he didn't know anything about this part of the country at all, it was just a lucky number he drew."[87]

Whether acquired by luck, illegal entry, or careful planning, the former Coeur d'Alene reservation lands were now no longer the subject of local debate. The transformation from fences to walls was complete. This process occurred not only among the Coeur d'Alenes during the 1880s and 1890s but throughout the region. The Colvilles, Yakimas, and other Indian groups faced similar erosion of their land base as federal actions opened their reservations to entry and settlement. Other self-identified cultural groups, whether religious groups, such as the Dukhobors, or ethnic enclaves, also faced the pressure to conform. The complex debates among these different groups seeking to control the discourse and the direction of the Inland Empire typify the settlement process. Although the region continued to define itself through such internal struggles, more and more, as the Coeur d'Alene story indicates, external forces dictated the outcomes.

CHAPTER 3

COEUR D'ALENE
MINING DEBATES

In April 1892 the Coeur d'Alenes received the first payments for relinquishing the northern half of their reservation, which had been negotiated in the 1889 agreement. According to the *Spokane Weekly Review*, merchants rejoiced over the infusion of cash into the local economy as "quiet, orderly and dignifiedly polite" Indians purchased horses, hacks, wagons, saddles, and agricultural implements with their allocated funds.[1] Meanwhile, dispatches of another sort also filled the pages of the regional newspapers that spring. The recent battle over reservation boundaries mirrored other battles taking place in the mountains of Idaho. The mines centered around the towns of Wallace, Wardner, Burke, Kellogg, Gem, and Mullan remained closed for the fourth straight month in 1892 as miners and mine owners continued to dispute wages, working conditions, and rights. In the story of the confrontation between miners and mine owners, and in particular in the public debate between these two groups, the continuing contest over the meanings of the Inland Empire is evident.

The events of the Coeur d'Alene mining strife, particularly those of 1892, have been told in many ways. Historians have looked at these conflicts as the opening battle of the radical western labor union efforts, as the roots of the Western Federation of Miners (WFM) and the site of one of their early defeats, and as part of the "heritage of conflict" that characterized the nineteenth-century mining industry.[2] Participants in the conflicts have also told their versions. And it is those contemporary stories that are of interest here. How did those involved in the Coeur d'Alene struggles— miners and mine owners along with the entire community of which they were a part—speak of the issues at hand? What do their debates over

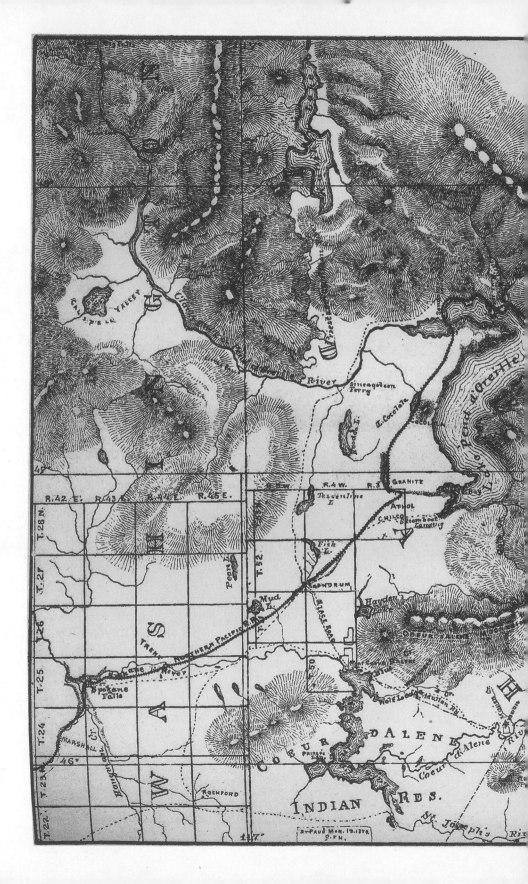

Map of the Coeur d'Alene Mining Region   Created for gold seekers, this map of the Coeur d'Alenes, published in 1879, shows the relation of the new mining region to the Coeur d'Alene Indian reservation and the town of Spokane Falls. By permission of The Huntington Library, San Marino, California.

the roles and rights of workers and owners reveal about the emerging region?

For Spokane town builders, the mining and farming lands of northern Idaho represented one part of their larger empire. Not all of the individuals and groups who lived in the "tributary" lands outside the city borders, however, agreed with Spokane's view of their relation to the region. Residents and promoters throughout eastern Washington and northern Idaho, in efforts to assert their own regional prominence, offered challenges to Spokane's version of the Inland Empire. From Wallace, Idaho, the *Coeur d'Alene Miner*, for example, responded defensively to the assertions of Coeur d'Alene's tributary status in relation to Spokane: "The MINER had no desire to cause any agitation that will be detrimental to the trade of Spokane merchants in the Coeur d'Alene country. . . . If they can lay down goods here as cheap or cheaper . . . they will probably get a good share of our trade. But it will not be because the Coeur d'Alene country is 'tributary to Spokane,' or that it owes Spokane any debt of gratitude."[3] Local promoters disputed the center of the Inland Empire but not its existence. The Republican *Coeur d'Alene Press* promoted its city, Coeur d'Alene, as an essential part of the Inland Empire. "The future will justify us," an editorial explained, "in joining with the people to build up one of the most prosperous sections of the Inland Empire, with Coeur d'Alene the hub, whose manufacturing industries will make it the largest city of northern Idaho."[4]

This multilayered struggle over the exertion of economic and perceptual control became entwined in the labor disputes of the 1890s, just as it had in the previous decade's debates over the Coeur d'Alene reservation. At local, regional, and extraregional levels, individuals, community members, unions, corporate groups, novelists, and others articulated competing visions over appropriate social relations in the emerging region.

Mining and Empire

In the area gradually becoming known as the Inland Empire, mining was part of the vision of a regional economic empire. During the 1860s, discoveries in the Colville area north of Spokane Falls and along the Clearwater River in the mountains of northern Idaho territory to the southeast had brought the first stampedes of miners to the area. Men from a wide variety of classes, backgrounds, and nationalities—French, Italian, Irish, and Chinese, for example—invaded the diggings, all seeking easy wealth. Many of the seasoned miners had pursued mining booms across the West, others were novices, drawn to the excitement of the mines from Oregon farms, for example, and some boomers arrived prepared to provide related services for the transient population. Regardless of their previous experiences, most of the 1860s immigrants left the region when the richest diggings played out. But camps of Chinese miners remained along the mountain streams, and prospectors continued to search for promising outcroppings. Ideas about the environment persisted as well; like other late nineteenth-century westerners, those who remained held onto the belief that mining offered economic rewards and judged mountains and streams by their mineral resources.[5]

When the Coeur d'Alene discoveries came a decade later, the boom coincided with and contributed to the development of Spokane. The town site promoters of Spokane Falls and other locales quickly boasted of any promising "showings" and included the latest rumors in their promotional literature. Publicized as well by the Northern Pacific Railroad, eager to draw business to its recently completed route through Spokane, the gold strikes made by Andrew J. Prichard and his associates after 1879 brought national attention, along with at least seven thousand placer miners, to the Coeur d'Alenes during the winter of 1883–84. As in the 1860s booms, the surface gold recoverable with placer mining techniques played out in a few short years, but the simultaneous discoveries of other metals such as silver and lead guaranteed continued interest in the area. The transportation networks, smelters, concentrators, flumes, and other materials that mine owners needed to process these minerals and to sustain industrial development required massive amounts of capital. Outside investors joined regional businessmen such as D. C. Corbin and James Wardner in providing the necessary financial support. Other individuals established stores, laundries, banks, saloons, and law offices to serve the needs of the new population. After its 1889 fire, Spokane's economic base was revitalized in part by the demands of these mining developments.[6]

As in other western mining areas, wage workers, both skilled miners and laborers, provided the necessary labor force. Although British, Italian, Scandinavian, and American-born men predominated, the ranks of miners included a range of foreign immigrants, except for the Chinese, who were barred from the district. Seasoned miners from Colorado or Butte, Montana, who sought jobs in the Coeur d'Alenes, shared ideas and experiences with their northern Idaho counterparts. The class conflicts between labor and capital that characterized the Coeur d'Alene region during the 1880s and 1890s were similar to those elsewhere during this period. Miners' concerns about working conditions, wages, and union recognition jostled with mine owners' concerns about profits, freight rates, and business control. Although the establishment of the first union in the Coeur d'Alene mines and the first strikes took place in 1887, in the subsequent three years the unions firmly established themselves in the district. On January 1, 1891, the various local unions organized into a single body led by the Central Executive Committee of the Miners' Union of the Coeur d'Alenes. Early on they achieved notable successes; they built a union hospital and engaged in a strike that won a $3.50 daily wage for all miners.[7]

The mine owners also organized into a single body in 1891; the Mine Owners' Protective Association (MOA) sought to protect their economic investments against increasing labor costs and freight rates in an era of fluctuating lead and silver prices. Bringing together local managers, regional owners, and absentee owners, the MOA identified and acted on their mutual interests. Active MOA members included John Hays Hammond, Victor Clement, of the Bunker Hill and Sullivan Mining Company, Spokane investor John A. Finch, and absentee owner Simeon Gannett Reed of Portland, Oregon. For the mine owners, it was "entirely a matter of business."[8]

The disputes over wages resulted in part from the introduction of new technology in the mines. The machine drill reduced the number of skilled miners needed and increased the demand for shovelers and laborers to move the additional ore materials. Many skilled miners found themselves relegated to unskilled positions. The union sought to keep the $3.50 wage for all workers, while mine owners argued that $3.00 was the standing wage for laborers. Essentially, they disagreed over the distinction between skilled and unskilled miners. The MOA argued for class stratification. "It is a recognized principle in business everywhere," explained the mine owners, "that men must be paid according to the skill necessary in the vocation they follow. Were it otherwise there would be no incentive for men to be anything but laborers." Union men, however, recognized that all underground workers faced the same risks, exerted similar efforts, and, aboveground, shared a dislike for company-run stores and boardinghouses. "It is the object of the union to hold up mining as a whole as skilled labor," asserted John W. Sweeney, president of the Wardner Miners' Union, "as it requires a certain amount of skill in any capacity in a mine."[9]

The union initially achieved its goals. Even the Bunker Hill and Sullivan Mine, the most adamant in its refusal to acknowledge the union, agreed to the uniform $3.50 wage in the fall of 1891. But on January 1, 1892, the MOA shut the mines down, ostensibly to force the Northern Pacific and the Union Pacific railroad companies to lower their freight rates. In late March, after reaching a settlement with the railroads, the MOA announced the reopening of the mines, but with a return to a graduated scale of wages; only certain of the underground workers would receive the $3.50 wage. The newspapers were filled with the ensuing debate.[10]

The immediate issue was the wage cut, but union workers also fought the continuing erosion of their control over the boundaries of their work and their region. As machinery took over workers' skills within the mines, issues of control over their lives outside the mines became increasingly important. The company-run stores, lodgings, and hospital facilities were important but not the only issues. When the MOA imported outside laborers into the district and used injunctions to restrain union activities, it directly challenged the workers' perception of their civic rights.

The mine owners also faced a loss of autonomy over their economic world. Their inability to control the workers paralleled their inability to control outside market forces. A part of late nineteenth-century industrial developments, the silver mines of Idaho were linked to complex economic networks within which the mine owners' actions and desires rarely made a significant impact. The battle over the railroad freight rates served as only the most recent manifestation of their loss of individual power, making it ever more difficult to sustain an imperial vision. The fluctuation in silver prices, triggered in part by the passage of the Sherman Silver Purchase Act in 1890, corresponding overproduction of silver, and resulting price decline, also contributed to the volatile nature of the silver economy. In the face of these mystifying invisible forces, the mine owners struggled to control the visible elements of their businesses. For the Spokane-based MOA members such struggles took on additional meanings.[11]

Though the union and the mine owners' association squared off along class lines in verbal debates, the boundaries between miners and mine owners were not always so easily distinguished. Many mine owners were former miners. Some union leaders became mine owners. Industrial spies infiltrated the union membership. The ranks of the miners themselves included skilled, self-identified miners and regional wage workers, as well as ranchers, farmers, and others seeking temporary wage work. Nonetheless, clear lines of difference infuse the contemporary discourse.[12]

Newspapers and Moral Suasion

The MOA and the union each sought to control the public debate. Adept at using the visible instruments of that debate—newspapers and other written documents—the MOA exerted strong pressure on public discourse. Daily newspapers published in Spokane, especially the *Spokane Review,* owned and operated by a couple of Coeur d'Alene mine owners, and its chief 1892 rival, the newly arrived *Spokesman,* which were circulated and read throughout the region, carried editorials, articles, and announcements on the labor conflict. In the Coeur d'Alenes, at least nine other weekly papers, situated in the towns of Wallace, Wardner, Mullan, Murray, and Osborn, vied for control over the ever-shifting story. Two of these papers had been founded precisely in an attempt to do so. In March 1892 the MOA established the *Coeur d'Alene Barbarian* to present its views. Local miners' unions controlled the *Idaho State Tribune* in nearby Wallace.[13]

Although the miners' perspective found voice through the press, that venue had limitations.[14] For immigrant workers without English language skills, communication rarely transpired directly through newsprint. The union miners' world depended primarily on the spoken word. As the later Industrial Workers of the World (IWW) free-speech fights illustrated, the unions relied on face-to-face communication with their transient and, in part, illiterate mining constituency. Spoken more than written words remained essential. Speaking in English and other languages, union advocates swayed fellow workers to their cause with persuasive oratory. Moral suasion, for example, became the byword of the union strategy in response to the importation of nonunion workers. As the president of the Central Miners' Union, Thomas O'Brien, explained their plans: "The union would use moral suasion. It would deal with the hearts of the men rather than resort to brute force; it would work on their sympathies and endeavor to induce them to keep away during this contest for bread."[15] An underlying threat of violence was always implied. As a sympathetic *Spokane Spokesman* correspondent explained, "moral suasion and honest labor eloquence will be the ammunition used" in attempts to persuade the intruders either to join the union or leave the district. Union men often employed a more vigorous interpretation of the term "eloquence"; "intimidation" and "coercion" of nonunion workers was the charge that mine owners leveled against the union.[16]

Most of the union members' words were not captured on paper. What is available, however, are the texts used to communicate with the mine owners' association and, more important, with the community at large. Pro-union local papers, especially the *Wallace Press* and the *Spokane Spokesman,* with its wider circulation, helped present their perspective. They printed extensive reports on union meetings, official statements, and letters from the membership. Although it is clear that words alone were not the only effective tool, union members needed to present themselves as "reasonable" and "intelligent" men in order to gain the sympathy and support of the larger community. In attempting to bridge the gap between the miners' world and that of the community at large, union leaders needed a flexible vocabulary.

Many local newspaper editors, guided by their political beliefs, personal interests, and economic constraints, chose up sides in the conflict. Adam Aulbach, editor of the *Wallace Press* and owner of the *Mullan Tribune,* along with young W. L. Taylor and F. K. Jerome, the *Tribune'*s editors, relied on the pages of their papers to advocate their passionate views in favor of the union. H. C. Piggott, editor of Osburn's *Coeur d'Alene Statesman,* mining engineer Robert Brown, editor of the *Coeur d'Alene Barbarian* (Wallace/Wardner) and later the *Coeur d'Alene American* (Wallace), and the brothers Alfred and John Dunn's *Coeur d'Alene Miner* (Wallace) most frequently articulated the mine owners' agenda. Brown asserted that his paper intended "to comment unreservedly and pointedly on topics of vital importance to the future of this section of the country, and to use the well worn motto, it proposes to 'Hew to the mark, let the chips fall where they may.' " And comment unreservedly and pointedly the editors did. In partisan purple prose they launched efforts to sway undecided participants, to evoke public sympathy, and, not incidentally, to attract readers to their pages. "The MOA came out with a great cock-and bull story in the Spokane papers last Sunday, telling of their grievances(?). Poor mine owners! The TRIBUNE pities them" ran a typically flamboyant *Mullan Tribune* editorial comment on the mine owners' statements.[17]

As the editors struggled for economic survival in a crowded press market, their words were colored the same vibrant shade in their rivalries with opposition papers. "Shame on you, Wallace Press! You, a supposed regulator of public affairs; a supposed fearless communicator on current happenings," thundered the *Coeur d'Alene Barbarian.* "You . . . have at last, cozened by politics or lured by the roar of the rabble, pitched your tent with the lawless, and have set in defiance every sense of justice and right." In their personal attacks, vivid prose, and partisan news articles as well as editorials, the northern Idaho editors engaged in prevalent if not always acceptable journalistic practice.[18] Underneath the attacks and excessive language, however, the newspapers articulated the points of contention not only in the labor-capital struggle but also in the ongoing debates about community identity and membership, civic rights and responsibilities, self-determination, and the appropriate relation of the district and the region.

In the Coeur d'Alenes of the 1880s and early 1890s, the unions had come to dominate local political and social life, largely because their perspective was shared by other members of the community. They agreed on the definition of terms. Like the Populists, to whose political party they flocked during this period, community members spoke more highly of the "honest" laborer, who worked directly in producing goods, than of the investor, who gained profits through the operation of the market. They advocated the rights of individual producers to all the profits realized on their products. In rhetoric, if not reality, the miners agreed.[19]

In 1892, the citizens of the mining towns of Gem, Wallace, Wardner, Burke, and Mullan became enmeshed in the dispute. At mass meetings the businessmen of each community passed resolutions in support of the striking miners. From the shopkeepers' perspective the labor of the miners, not the "skill and capital" of the mine owners, was entitled to more consideration. As one "prominent citizen" wrote to the *Wallace Press* under the pseudonym "Justice," "Who has made the mine owner what he is today? Labor. Labor creates capital, and the thing created according to the laws of Nature can never rise above its creator. We are citizens of a Republic, and good government demands that the citizens of a Republic shall be educated that they may understand and have the manhood to demand the rights

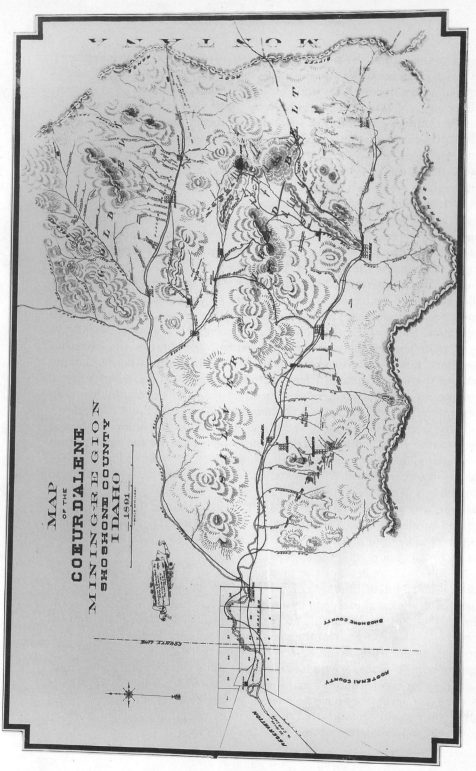

The Union Stronghold When Adam Aulbach, editor of the *Wallace Press*, published this 1891 map of the Coeur d'Alene mining region, he outlined the district in economic and geographic terms. Collections of squares mark the district's towns while rectangles identify some of the mining claims. By permission of the Barnard-Stockbridge Collection, University of Idaho Library, Moscow, Idaho, #8-A267.

and privileges of citizens." Although the businessmen's actions worked for their economic self-interest—their day-to-day success depended on miners' business and goodwill—they spoke of community interests as well. "While we recognize the right of capital to as large a share of the profits of its enterprise as it can legitimately obtain," one resolution read, "we believe more strongly in the principle of the greatest good for the greatest number."[20]

Clearly, however, the "greatest number" referred to a select group defined by locality and permanence as well as by manhood and citizenship. Allen Gill, a master mechanic for the Tiger-Poorman mines, identified 10 percent of the Coeur d'Alene population as "not desirable citizens," as a shifting population without permanent residences.[21] For many, these undesirable citizens were those without union cards. The issue "that has bound the citizens of Wallace, as well as those of the other towns in the Coeur d'Alene country, so closely to the mines," remarked one observer, and "the only question that threatens blood shed in the impending troubles is the simple one of importing cheap labor."[22] Local residents, whether miners, merchants, or settlers, who identified with the community and its future, vigorously denounced the importation of outsiders, "foreigners," and "scabs" into the region, across its boundaries. When the union miners refused to accept the lower graduated wages and the two sides failed to reach an agreement, the MOA announced its intention to reopen the mines on June 1 with nonunion labor. In April, imported laborers recruited by the MOA from Michigan, Colorado, California, and other mining camps began arriving by train. Union men, often armed, intercepted trains along the way, greeted the scabs at the station, picketed the mines, and, in each location, applied their techniques of "moral suasion" to convince the newcomers to join their ranks. By June, however, the district mines had reopened with some three hundred nonunion miners employed; the next month, according to MOA estimates, that number had risen to eight hundred.

The equation among unionism, manliness, and citizenship was frequently made. Using the language of race, Coeur d'Alene miners and their sympathizers accused the MOA of flooding the district with "the scums of foreign labor, who have nothing in common with us, and are more fitted for their condition of slavery than ever were the blacks of Africa. This scum is composed of men who have no ties to bind them to their fellows."[23] The MOA spokespiece, the *Coeur d'Alene Barbarian,* sought to inflame these sentiments with its calls for "Pure Americanism," calling the union leaders foreigners and "disturbing agitators" in opposition to "miners of actual experience" who needed to draw upon the liberty that "is the birth-right of every American" to denounce their "foolish leadership." "Our laws, habits, customs and system of government try to make men noble, strong and patriotic," responded the *Wallace Press,* "the Barbarian and the Mine Owners' Association would degrade manhood and make it disloyal, truculent and servile."[24]

Along with these efforts, the MOA recognized the need to appeal to the vision of a united community. The members emphasized the mutual interests of all citizens "to secure good order and to prevent outrages." Drawing attention away from the question of importing labor, which they considered their right, the mine owners pointed to the significant contributions they had made to the region's economic development. The region of which the MOA spoke, however, was not the "Coeur d'Alene country" but the Inland Empire centered on Spokane. Since most of the mine owners lived in Spokane, the Washington city was the location for most of the MOA meetings. And it was through the pages of the Spokane-based newspapers that the MOA issued its first March call to miners in the Coeur d'Alene district: "The Mine Owners' Association of Coeur d'Alene takes this public method of informing all former employees of various mines and mills as well as the public generally that . . . all mines will be ready to resume work on or about April 1st." A few days later the same notice appeared in the Idaho papers, which resentfully had to rely on copying the information from the columns of the *Spokane Review.* Subsequent public statements by the MOA and the Central Miners' Union of the Coeur d'Alenes also appeared first in the Spokane papers.[25]

The MOA particularly protested the union's control over the spoken word. Businessmen and miners "all fear to state their real opinions"; "the whole community is terrorized," argued the MOA, "nor dare any newspaper in this camp utter one word of comment upon the situation." They roundly condemned such intimidation, which forced "the majority of miners" to "keep their mouths shut." From the mine owners' perspective, a few agitators dominated the discourse, controlling the union and the community: "We hold that this is a free country, and that every man in this community is entitled to express his honest convictions, without being threatened for doing so. . . . We hold that it is not only the privilege, but it is the duty of every honest citizen to state his opinions, frankly and freely." The pro-owner *Coeur d'Alene Statesman* even suggested that the duration of the northern Idaho labor-capital struggle was a direct result of "meddlesome Coeur d'Alene papers."[26]

Meanwhile, the miners objected strenuously to the MOA's control over the written word, especially its use of legal papers. Injunctions, which included provisions against the union's oath of allegiance, challenged the union's base of power. They were unintelligible to the union both because of the language used and because of the intent behind the documents. When writs were served in Wardner, miners gathered on street corners where one of their number read the written documents aloud and attempted to translate the legalese. Not only did the miners question the legality of the writs, they also, noted one supporter, claimed they were "a usurpation of power by the association," power that did not "belong to" the MOA.[27]

The initial federal court injunction prohibited specific union activities, including conversing with strikebreakers or "in any manner interfering with the Coeur d'Alene Mining and Concentrating company." The temporary injunction named the most vocal pro-union newspaper editors, Adam Aulbach and F. K. Jerome, among the 118 district citizens enjoined from expressing their views. After being served with the writ, Aulbach released his next issue of the *Wallace Press* with blank columns adorned with the words "The injunction knocked this column out" and a torrid editorial entitled "The Press Gagged."[28] Drawing national attention to the censorship of the press, Aulbach, the local Associated Press correspondent, then promptly returned to his pro-union rhetoric. When the issue finally appeared in front of U.S. Circuit Court judge James H. Beatty in July, he upheld the injunctions but also clarified their limitations. Beatty upheld the liberty of the press, calling the "wild report that the public press has been muzzled" to be "untempered by truth," but he also cautioned the editors that if they interfered "by the use of force, threats or intimidation or by any other means" with the mine's employees, "they were rightfully enjoined." Although Beatty's ruling appeared to release Aulbach and Jerome from threats of imprisonment for their editorializing, it still meant that union members were unable to speak directly through the press.[29]

While the now constrained public debate continued, the MOA also gained private control over the union's written records. Charles Siringo, an undercover Pinkerton detective in the association's employ, infiltrated the union so successfully that he served as secretary of the Gem Miners' Union. Siringo's reports of union meetings made their way to the MOA membership. With access to these public and private venues for union expression, the MOA held onto the reins of the northern Idaho debate, drawing it into the Spokane-centered orbit.[30]

The final chapter in the contest over control of the organs of public discussion took place rather suddenly. On July 23, 1892, subscribers to the *Wallace Press* received in its stead a newly titled paper, the *Coeur d'Alene American;* "There are times in the history of newspapers, as in dynasties," noted the editorial page, "when sweeping and sudden changes are wrought." In a remarkable turn of events, staunch unionist Adam Aulbach had sold the *Wallace Press* to Robert Brown, editor of his rival, the *Coeur d'Alene Barbarian.* Although Brown explained in his first edition that "it is the aim of the new paper to maintain an independent attitude concerning all affairs," the columns clearly followed the antiunion perspective, style, and tone Brown had advocated through the *Barbarian.* Taking on the mantle of patriotism in opposition to the miners' union, Brown noted, "It is a fit

Phoenix of the dying embers of lawlessness that the paper should take the name AMERICAN. . . . It shall ever be the aim of the COEUR D'ALENE AMERICAN to see that no organization wearing the cloak of noble pretense and hiding its un-American face behind a mask of benevolence shall again, in this country, sit in judgment with thugs and agitators as its princes, to say whether this man or that man shall or shall not work as he himself sees fit."[31]

In early July the verbal struggle between the miners and the MOA was replaced by a physical one when violence erupted in the Coeur d'Alenes. Unable to combat the invasion of their boundaries—in the mines, in the region, or in the union—through words, unable even to control the words themselves, the workers turned to more aggressive means. News from Homestead, Pennsylvania, of the steelworkers' success against an army of Pinkerton detectives may have inflamed some, but the uncovering of Siringo's identity as a spy contributed another spark. After pitched battles at the Gem and Frisco mines in which three union and three nonunion workers were killed and the Frisco mill dynamited, the rest of the mines capitulated to union control. Bunker Hill and Sullivan Mine owners agreed to deport its nonunion miners beyond the boundaries of the district. The victory was short-lived. Governor Norman B. Wiley quickly declared martial law, and three days later federal troops and state militia took control of the district without incident. Mass arrests, including that of the county sheriff, were made, filling hastily constructed bull pens.

Outside the jails, the regional newspapers continued the dispute. While the pages of the *Spokane Review* denounced the riotous behavior of "mad" anarchists and the *Coeur d'Alene Miner* characterized the miners as "an armed and blood thirsty mob," the *Spokane Spokesman* wrote of the miners' "triumph" and included a full report of the local July 27 Haymarket Square labor rally in support of the Coeur d'Alene Union actions. Clearly the underlying issues relating to control of a particular vision of community were not resolved.[32]

The bull pens and county jails proved to be effective places for sharing information and perspectives.[33] Discussions among convicted miners in Boise's Ada County jail, for example, led to the formation of the WFM. Union miners soon regained their standing in the Coeur d'Alene community. Most prisoners did not remain incarcerated for long; within two months more than 550 of the 600 men who had been held in the bull pens without hearings had been released, and by March of the following year all miners were out of jail.[34]

"Our Rights as Free-Born Men"

Throughout the next seven years, the struggle between the miners' union and the MOA continued in the Coeur d'Alenes. The mines periodically opened and closed, not only in response to strikes but also as a result of the uncertain economy; repercussions from the Panic of 1893 and the repeal of the Sherman Silver Purchase Act resonated in northern Idaho.[35] The union, now affiliated with the newly established WFM, regained the $3.50 standard wage in most of the regional mines. The Bunker Hill and Sullivan Mine management remained the strongest opponent to the union demands. They rolled back wages, kept the union workers out, established their own militia, and thwarted two attempts to dynamite their concentrator. In April 1899, the union decided to focus its attention on the resistant company. Drawing on the strength of secretly enrolled union men in Bunker Hill's employ, they demanded the standard $3.50 wage and the right to organize. They achieved the wage raise, but management denied union recognition and required all union men to quit. The actions that followed became the center of the ensuing debate.

On April 29, a reported four hundred to one thousand union miners from Burke, Wallace, and Mullan gathered in Wardner to confront Bunker Hill en masse. Along the way, the Burke group hijacked a Northern Pacific train and picked up sixty cases of dynamite from the Frisco Mine. Upon receiving word of the gathering crowd, miners and managers deserted the Bunker Hill and Sullivan buildings. The union men, some masked, others adorned with white armbands, arrived amid gunfire and cheers and headed to the Bunker Hill mill. By the end of the day, the mill had been destroyed by dynamite, two men accused of being scabs had been shot, and the miners had returned to their homes. Martial law along with federal and state troops quickly returned to the Coeur d'Alenes.

The declaration of martial law allowed state officials to bypass local authorities. Governor Frank Steunenberg's representative, Bartlett Sinclair, arrested the sheriff and the Populist county commissioners and replaced them with state-appointed Republican men. The arrests were widespread. More than fifteen hundred miners were rounded up into bull pens— wooden barracks surrounded by fences—in Wallace and Wardner. Complaints about the abridgment of civil rights, as well as about the food and sanitary conditions, abounded. Unlike the 1892 debates, which ranged through a wide variety of local and regional newspapers, the 1899 discussion took place in fewer venues. The economic downturn in 1893 led to the failure of most of the district newspapers that had participated in the 1892 debates. In an effort to combat the power of the *Spokesman Review*, the Coeur d'Alene Miners' Union issued a boycott of the MOA-connected paper. The miners objected to the "false statements and misleading screeds" in its columns and its impact on the district's citizens, criticizing "the large daily papers whose improved machinery enables them to flood every district with their publications thereby turning the minds of the people into the wrong channels." The *Mullan Mirror* connected its complaints against the mine owners, the *Spokesman Review,* and Spokane, echoing the refrains of other districts that resented their "tributary" status. "The Coeur d'Alene country has made Spokane what it is," they editorialized in June 1899. "Yet the people and press of that hobo town are ungrateful enough to smite the hand that feeds them."[36]

Within the larger community, the public debate surrounding the events of 1899 decried the violence and focused on rights. It was a discussion infused with competing notions of political and social rights. While the union objected to the interference of the state on the side of "property privilege," mine owners spoke of "property rights." The MOA and the union both sought the freedom to exercise their rights, although they disagreed about the proper nature of civil rights. This disagreement was rooted in earlier debates. The MOA asserted its freedom to pursue economic gain: "We claim and will insist on the right to hire and discharge when we please without dictation from any man or organization." Miners sought an equal right with capital to organize for mutual benefit and protection:

> Tis for our rights as free-born men.
> On liberty's enlightened soil.
> We stand or fall beneath the stars and stripes
> Upholding noble toil.[37]

Again, union men presented the question as one of where to draw the line. As James Sovereign, editor of the WFM *Idaho State Tribune,* complained, "The line of criminality was not drawn on the raid on the 29th of April, or the destruction of the mill, or the killing of anybody, but the line of criminality was drawn at the membership in the miners' union . . . to be a member of the miners' union was sufficient evidence to warrant an arrest and incarceration." Mine owners, for their part, claimed no objection to unions per se, but, as John Finch explained, "unionism in the Coeur d'Alenes has been more or less socialism and anarchy, tyranny and lawlessness."[38]

To eradicate this force of social disorder and to regain power within the workplace, employers along with state officials instituted a permit system throughout the district. Owners required anyone seeking a job in the mines to sign a permit statement avowing no involvement in the April 29 events and renouncing union membership. "Believing that the crimes committed at Wardner on said date were actively incited, encouraged, and perpetrated through and by means of the influence and direction of the miners' union of the Coeur d'Alenes," the permit application read in part, "I hearby express my unqualified disapproval of such acts." "I would sooner cut off my right hand than give up my liberty to them [the mine owners]," responded the miner, Daniel Gillen. Speaking to visiting members of the federal Industrial Commission, Gillen went on to define the union position with a telling bull-pen story. Sailor Mike, one of the prisoners in the bull pen, "said for the boys not to sign permits: not to take out any permits, and not to sign their liberty away. The authorities took him and put him in the corner of the fence and made him stand there in the sun with his hat off for two hours." It was their liberty—defined by the miners, those "free-born men," in Lockean terms—that was under attack. The permit system was considered "an insult to a free American," explained T. N. Barnard, a Wallace photographer; the miners were "asked to practically sign away what they term their birthright." Confined within bull pens, controlled by written documents, union men lost the freedom to construct their own society, their own vision of the Inland Empire.[39]

While the miners spoke of "equal opportunity" and argued that "there is no line of society drawn in mining camps," it was clear from the 1899 debates that their vision of community was sharply bounded. Nonunion men were not welcome, nor were any outsiders. Their complaints about the bull pens, for example, were not only about sanitation problems. Their list of "horrors" included black soldiers in control of white miners.[40]

The federal troops maintaining order in the Coeur d'Alenes included eight companies of the Twenty-Fourth Infantry, a black unit, some drawn from Fort George Wright in Spokane.[41] Companies from the Twenty-Fourth had participated in upholding the 1892 martial law order, but they had made up less than one-fifth of the total complement of soldiers. This time the presence of black troops in the mining camps of the Coeur d'Alenes was larger, and it did not go unnoticed. May Hutton and other union sympathizers marshaled the role of "negroid" soldiers as further evidence of the intolerable actions of the state. Sovereign, the labor newspaper editor, described the soldiers as "quite domineering and overbearing." Even Job Harriman's socialist account used the soldiers as a potent symbol. Although, consistent with the Socialist Party's tendency to avoid the politically volatile race issue, the black troops were not mentioned directly, an emblem on the title page and cover of Harriman's pamphlet included them. The emblem, headed by the phrase "Remember the Bull Pen," depicts a striking worker being escorted through a fence by two U.S. soldiers. The only visible face is that of a black soldier with exaggerated features. In front of the Committee on Military Affairs, William Powers, a Mullan miner, described a community "terrorized" by the soldiers but was hard-pressed to describe any specific acts of terror the soldiers committed. As he tried to explain his objections, he noted: "The women were not used to nigger soldiers, or niggers of any kind, and they were afraid of them."[42]

Bull Pen These wooden barracks surrounded by wood and wire fences and flanked by military tents held the striking Coeur d'Alene miners. Federal troops guarded the bull pen in the town of Kellogg, Idaho, in 1899. By permission of the Barnard-Stockbridge Collection, University of Idaho Library, Moscow, Idaho, #8-X29b.

In the labor-capital discourse frequent references were made to women and children in appealing to community responsibility and respectability. Within the confines of the debate, affronts to women were described to illustrate the uncivil behavior of either side. A bull-pen complaint against restrictions on talking, for example, emphasized that wives were required to speak to their husbands through a wire fence. In typically excessive journalistic prose, the *Mullan Mirror* described "Scabtown" under martial law as "the only community in Idaho where bawds are the creme de l'creme of society, where young white girls under the eyes of their parents, walk arm in arm with colored soldiers, where the bawds and opium fiends find a place at the head of the Law and Order brigade, where young girls graduate for scarlet women, and where scabbery and all its attendant evils thrive and flourish at the shrine of mammon."[43]

Although the union men defined themselves in opposition to foreigners, from the perspective of Spokane they were the outsiders. Listing the names of the men in the bull pen on May 29, the *Spokesman-Review* commented on "the foreign character of the men who made up the mob. . . . Almost without exception the names prove either the Scandinavian, the Slavonian, or the Italian birth of the owners, good English names are few. The typical American names are almost entirely missing."[44] The union's use of the nineteenth-century language of race and gender as ways to define citizenship and community membership failed in its economic battles with the mine owners; nor did it succeed in enforcing its views about appropriate social relations and civic rights. Yet the union's reliance on this shared language reveals its ideological agreement with the Spokane-centered Inland Empire on the significant categories for regional definition in the late nineteenth-century United States.

Coeur d'Alene Miners and Indians

One of the women standing at the wire fence surrounding the bull pens in 1899 was May Arkwright Hutton. She was visiting her husband, Levi, the Northern Pacific railroad engineer whose train had been commandeered by the union men. May Hutton refused to be reduced to a symbolic entity. Although women were not usually accorded a voice, Hutton entered the public debate by claiming neutrality and relying on the appropriate nineteenth-century women's genre—romantic fiction. Her book, *The Coeur d'Alenes, or A Tale of the Modern Inquisition in Idaho,* was published in 1900. As Hutton explains, "Being in a neutral position—that is to say, being neither miner nor mine owner—the writer has been so placed as to be able to give a true and impartial account of the events which occurred. . . . Yet it has been deemed wise to exercise the usual licence of the novelist, and to mould the circumstances to fit the dramatic exigencies of the occasion." Her account, of course, is anything but neutral. Like the MOA and the union, with which her sympathies were allied, she projected a dichotomous vision of the rights and roles of competing Coeur d'Alene groups.[45]

Hutton was not the only woman who entered into the discourse in this fashion. From the other side of the debate, Mary Hallock Foote published her romantic novel set during the 1892 strike in *Century Magazine.* Foote, a magazine writer and wife of a western mining engineer, based her account mainly on discussions with friends who were members of, or sympathizers with, the Mine Owners Association and on published reports. Foote, too, asserted her neutrality, insisting that her narrative relied on the facts of history and the testimony of participants. In response to the *Century* editor's concern about the possible libelous aspects of her story, Foote explained how her "fiction" connected to the "facts" of the case: "The *story* is pure make up, except where it joins the story of the strike, which is history. I get my facts from the testimony given at the trial of the Union bosses, and from Mr. Heyburn who conducted the case for the State and the Government against the Union miners. . . . Any charges I may have occasion to bring in the course of the story against the 'Union' (in the Coeur d'Alene) you may rely will be *within* the proven facts."[46]

Both Hutton and Foote incorporated the events of the mining struggles into their fiction, aligning themselves on different sides. And both suggested the broader regional importance of the story.[47] Foote, who identified with an eastern literary elite and frequently expressed her dismay over her western environs, wrote her account from the perspective of an engaged onlooker. At the time of the Coeur d'Alene labor strife, Foote was living in southern Idaho near Boise. As a writer, she positioned herself as an outsider to the West, drawing upon its stories and landscape for the locations of her fiction.[48] Foote noted the western interest in the Coeur d'Alene struggles: "I find that nothing I have ever done in the West has 'taken' like this," she wrote to her *Century* editor. "Even the idea of it seems to excite unbounded sympathy, and I can get all the help I need, once they know I'm really going to do it and that it will be published. It is the burning question in every mining community of the West and in camp after camp it has to be fought out." From Foote's perspective, the "burning question" related to the "tyranny of mobs" and the responsibility of the government "to secure to all within its jurisdiction freedom to follow their lawful vocations in safety for their property and their persons while obeying the law."[49]

For Hutton, who wrote as an insider, a resident of the Coeur d'Alenes, the questions were different. She decried "the peculiar invasion of the constitutional rights of the individual in many ways." And though most participants in the Coeur d'Alene mining and reservation debates drew few connections between the boundaries of the reservation and those of the bull pens, for May Hutton, at least, there were direct parallels between the experiences of the Coeur d'Alene Indians and the Coeur d'Alene miners. As her hero, Jock Hazelton, loosely summarizes the history, the Coeur d'Alenes " 'viewed the encroachments of the whites with distrustful eyes. . . . They were accustomed to roam at will over a vast extent of territory, free as the birds of the air, and now were to be confined in narrow reserves.' " With more imagination than accuracy, Jock goes on to depict the Coeur d'Alenes as aggressive fighters engaged in battles to defend their rights. " 'In fact,' continued Jock, 'I think there must be some evil genii in the very atmosphere, for even the white race who inhabit the region at the present day continue to follow in the footsteps of the aborigines at the least provocation.' "[50]

The "very atmosphere" of the Inland Empire was changing by the turn of the century. Depending on one's perspective, either the threats posed by differences of race and class were subdued, or the potential of significantly incorporating such distinctions into the Inland Empire was diminished. In

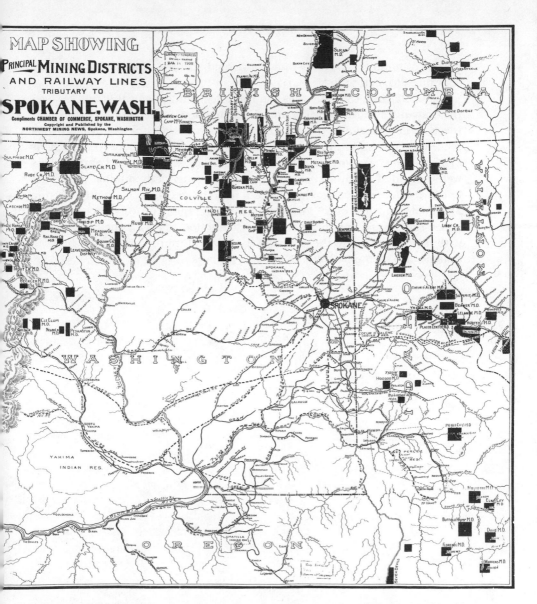

Tributary Mining Districts Large blocks throughout the mountains of Washington, British Columbia, Idaho, and Montana mark the mining districts claimed on this map to be tributary to Spokane as part of its Inland Empire in 1908. By permission of the Geography and Map Division, Library of Congress.

northern Idaho the WFM lost its stronghold and the mine owners' culture continued to dictate.[51]

The 1892 and 1899 debates, as rhetorical and physical struggles over the drawing of social and economic lines in a new settlement, helped shape the emerging regional definition. In these mining conflicts, which took place within a masculine public realm, women served more frequently as symbols than as participants. Even Hutton's and Foote's contributions were relegated to an arena temporally and generically outside of the debates. Yet, like the women homesteaders of the new Inland Empire, Hutton and Foote engaged in the discussions of the region's future. For our purposes they represent the increasing distinction between those who lived within and adhered to the notion of the Inland Empire and those who lived outside and reconstructed the region's borders.

INSET

Empire Building

Representations defined by race and gender served more than the Coeur d'Alene mining debates of the 1890s. During the 1910s, for example, the Spokane Chamber of Commerce developed a personification of the city's identity. Crafted to appeal to a touristic image of the western past, the "Miss Spokane" campaign centered on Marguerite Motie, a modern woman dressed as a Spokane Indian. In its promotional pitch to outside visitors, the Chamber called attention to "unmistakable signs of a new order of things" and celebrated signs of modernity. The advertising scheme received approval as a progressive concept. "The Miss Spokane plan," proudly reported the Chamber's Tourist Travel Committee chairman, R. E. Bigelow, "is declared by national advertising experts to be one of the most efficient publicity ideas in use today, as it gives unique personality to the city advertised." The selection of an Indian woman to promote the city revealed a particular interpretation geared to a national twentieth-century audience; it reflected stereotypical turn-of-the-century portrayals of Indians as representations of a once wild and now contained past, and it echoed other national personifications of women as icons of civilization and domestication.[1] In her Miss Spokane role, Motie presided at fairs and celebrations, clad in a headband and a fringed dress adorned by a sun. With her arms spread wide, she silently graced the city's promotional literature and advertisements. Through one ubiquitous photograph, her reign extended well into the 1920s. Her photograph superimposed over various updated graphs, scenery, and maps, Miss Spokane enveloped the region and its natural resources within her outstretched arms. Her open-handed gesture, in one 1927 brochure aimed at investors, even gathered railroad lines to her feet.[2]

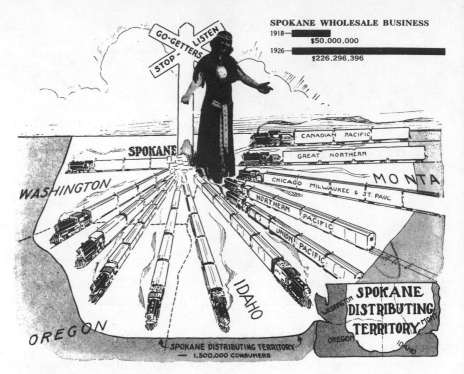

Miss Spokane and the Railroads From the Canadian Pacific to the Union Pacific, Miss Spokane controls the national railroad lines in this 1927 representation of the Spokane Distributing Territory. By permission of Cheney Cowles Museum/Eastern Washington State Historical Society, Spokane, Washington.

Railroads, according to conventional nineteenth-century wisdom about economic development, were the engines of change. They revolutionized industrial development, communication, and transportation. In the popular imagination, in investment circles, in communities and towns, railroads symbolized modernity, spectacular growth, technological magic, and future prosperity.[3] Throughout the late nineteenth and early twentieth centuries, representations of the Inland Empire highlighted its iron rails. On the promotional maps and on the landscape, railroad lines snaked through the region—over the mountain ranges and along the valleys, tracing the rolling hills of the Palouse, crossing rivers and streams, stretching across the Big Bend. And according to the city's Chamber of Commerce maps, they all hit the bull's-eye on Spokane. Marking completed, under construction, or simply proposed transportation routes, the lines depicted connections to markets as well as the dreams of the region's residents.

Four trunk lines—the Northern Pacific, Great Northern, Union Pacific, and Chicago, Milwaukee and St. Paul railroads—along with various subsidiary, branch, and local lines ran through the region. One of those latter lines, which plied the trade of the inland Northwest, was the aptly named

Spokane and Inland Empire Railway (S&IE). As an electric interurban rail
system, it connected Palouse farmers to Spokane and urban dwellers to
the Idaho mountains. Conceived by Jay Graves, a mining entrepreneur, in
the early twentieth century, the railway system relied on electric power,
not steam, and sought to capture the region's local traffic and tourists. Significantly, not unlike the region itself when viewed from the outside, the
S&IE was eventually, as were most such region-centered railroads,
subsumed into national networks, in this case, James J. Hill's Great
Northern.[4]

Railroads were not an uncomplicated blessing. They immediately involved their users in larger economic, political, and cultural networks.
Contests over rights-of-way, freight rates, terminals, and wages, among
railroad companies, steamboat lines, shippers, communities, workers,
and investors, also followed their tracks.[5] Like other material manifestations of change, the iron horses were caught up in the struggles both
within and outside the region, whether in tangible or symbolic forms. Unexpected as well as intentional interruptions brought attention to these en-
tanglements, when striking Coeur d'Alene miners stopped railroad cars
carrying scab labor into the region, for example, or when a special Spokane and Inland Empire train, filled with speculators and settlers seeking
Coeur d'Alene reservation lands, crashed into another on the same track.
The newspaper report of the 1909 disaster used the occasion to observe,
"In unusual degree the people had come to feel that the Inland Empire electric lines were peculiarly identified with their progress and
prosperity."[6]

From the outside, regional identity often seemed like a peculiar afflic-
tion. As competing railroad barons snapped up local lines or adjusted
freight rates and as tourists came to the inland West seeking an exotic
past, their interests increasingly diverged from local visions. While the inhabitants influenced, to some extent, outsiders' perceptions of their region, reaching beyond regional boundaries they competed with variations
of meanings. Farmers in the "Palouse Country," the agriculture-
dominated rolling hills of the Columbia Plateau in southeastern Washington and adjacent parts of northern Idaho, for example, by the early
twentieth century maintained a view of themselves as part of the region,
nation, and world. Producing wheat for expanded World War I markets, for
example, or participating in negotiations over freight rates, the Palouse
farmers considered themselves integrated into the economic and political
issues of the day. As part of the Inland Empire, they negotiated for economic benefits from their regional position. The freight rate struggles, however, which took place on a national stage, brought their views of
themselves and their region into a different arena.

In the reciprocal process of regional expansion and promotion, railroads were not the only markers and movers. The intertwined cultural and economic processes of Inland Empire expansion took place at a variety of levels. Visible in the personal accounts of those who settled across the international border in British Columbia, in the region-focused promotional literature, and in the actions of Palouse farmers, empire building was never simple. The following two chapters explore these processes as they participated in the creation of the mental territories of the Inland Empire. Examining, first, internal efforts to expand and promote the region, then the ways Inland Empire residents confronted often divergent external interests, the focus is on public rituals and presentations of regional identity.

CHAPTER 4

EXPANSION AND PROMOTION

In 1876, the U.S. centennial year, almost ten million people traveled to Philadelphia to attend the nation's Centennial Exhibition. Visitors marveled over the Corliss engine, technological displays, electrical wonders, and other signs of America's growth and mastery. Pavilions of exhibits included taxidermist specimens of western birds and animals, Albert Bierstadt's mammoth canvases depicting sublime western landscapes, and agricultural machinery and products. Across the continent in the nascent Inland Empire, a scattered population made the trek to a more local celebration. "The news was being spread all over the country and northern Idaho that a gigantic celebration, a sort of jubilee, was to be held at Spokane," recalled Ella Masterson, who was living on a Palouse ranch near Trent. "Everyone had heard about it, and everyone was determined not to miss this great 4th of July celebration." [1]

In 1876 homesteaders who knew of Spokane Falls's existence thought of the settlement as a way station, a crossroads stop on the east-west Mullan Road and the north-south Fort Colville trail. James Glover's store and post office offered services near the Spokane River ferry site. Few signs of an urban future marked the landscape. Indeed, for the Mastersons, notice of the impending jubilee was "the first news we had heard of this place." Attracted to the site by the reputed beauty of the falls, they also went to the celebration "to see . . . what kind of people lived there who could undertake to put over such a tremendous affair." Camping among the pines, the visitors marveled at the falls and the technological promise it represented. [2]

The 1876 Spokane Falls celebration, like its Philadelphia counterpart, extolled the virtues of mastery over the natural environment. Yet the Washington Territory organizers relied less on tangible exhibits and more on the power of words and imagination. Only one sawmill, which harnessed a fraction of the river's power, adorned the south bank. Compared to the Philadelphia exhibition, the Spokane Falls event was hardly a tremendous affair, but the presence of the mill, accompanied by promotional rhetoric, painted a suggestive portrait of a bustling industrial future aided by nature. As one contemporary description of the falls maintained, "Nature did not intend this mighty water-power for nought. But evidently it intended man should derive some benefit from them, as everything is arranged in such a systematical manner as to give him ample control of the entire body of water."[3] This Fourth of July celebration, like others in years to come, served as "a wonderful advertisement," and the Mastersons were part of a convinced audience who moved to the growing settlement.[4]

More than twenty years later, in a different small town, July celebrations also drew attention. In June 1898, the community of Moyie in southeastern British Columbia was in turmoil. The bustling town, settled as part of the Kootenay mining boom in the 1890s, was filled with rumors about the latest finds in the East Kootenays, about railroad plans to link isolated Moyie with Spokane, Washington, or Bonner's Ferry, Idaho; and about the establishment of a local union of the Western Federation of Miners.[5] But in the saloons and dusty streets where miners, merchants, and mule skinners congregated, in the hotels, boardinghouses, and homes where families and friends lived, these typical discussions were subsumed by a more important concern. Everywhere a pressing topic of conversation agitated the crowds until, finally, a public meeting was called to deal with the problem: Should Moyie celebrate Dominion Day on July 1 or celebrate Independence Day on July 4?

Why was this seemingly mundane issue such a dilemma for the Canadian town? For one thing, as the question suggests, the population was heavily American.[6] Prospectors from the United States had first uncovered the silver-lead outcroppings near Moyie by following mountain valleys and ridges north from Coeur d'Alene or Colville mining sites. The north-south mountain ranges—the Rockies, Selkirks, Kootenays, and Okanagans—cut off the area from the coastal cities of Victoria, Vancouver, and Seattle as well as from the prairie provinces. Miners, supplies, settlers, and information entered the area from the south, primarily through Spokane. From Spokane's perspective, the resources of southeastern British Columbia were "tributary" to the Inland Empire. They considered the Kootenay boom, like the earlier ones at Colville and Coeur d'Alene, as an extension of "Spokane Country" despite the fact that the discoveries were not within U.S. borders. "Between Spokane and the British Columbia mining communities of Nelson and Rossland," notes Carlos Schwantes, "the international boundary seemed to have lost all significance."[7]

To ignore an international, or any political, boundary for economic reasons is not uncommon. People are often drawn into a new area by the promise of financial gain. But in the Kootenays economics do not tell the entire story. Why did a simple question about a community celebration cause so much uneasiness? Residents eagerly accepted the proposal of a celebration. But asking them to choose a date demanded a declaration of national allegiance. At a time when Moyie residents were building connections among themselves, the question directly acknowledged the existence of difference. Most important, the celebration question caused a problem because it demanded that residents publicly identify themselves and their community in a way that contradicted their private images of self and place. That they were a community, that they had a group identity they did not doubt. But they did not primarily identify themselves as Americans or Canadians.

How did the community resolve its dilemma? Did they proclaim allegiance to the Stars and Stripes or to the Queen? Actually, they equivocated. The city's celebration was held on the Fourth of July that year but with two addresses, "one by J. W. Robinson, for the Canadians, and one by 'Judge' Fraser, for the Americans."[8]

Public celebrations do more than simply mark a holiday. They are, as these two Fourths of July suggest, self-consciously constructed rituals. Scholars in anthropology and sociology as well as history have examined holiday celebrations, festivals, carnivals, and other public rituals as events that speak tellingly about society and culture. As collective activities, they reveal community concerns and help define community identity. They can also, notes John Cawelti about world's fairs and exhibitions, "give us much insight into how men view the unity of their culture, how they understand the structure of its means, advertisements, and aspirations."[9]

Public celebrations are not, of course, pure reflections of "the people's mind." The organizers of the Spokane Falls jubilee, like those of the later 1890 Northwestern Industrial Exposition, exerted a strong influence on the ways visitors perceived the small settlement. Yet in some senses these events do echo a collective consciousness. The 1876 Washington celebration organizers presented a version of reality that attempted to bridge a gap between their own dreams and those of their audience. To entice others to participate in activities they needed to tap into shared assumptions.[10]

The Moyie Fourth of July dilemma reveals another aspect of the role of celebrations as expressions of cultural concerns. While public celebrations reflect a community's shared assumptions, they also reflect the multiplicity of perspectives which construct that consciousness. As Roy Rosenzweig has illustrated for the industrial Massachusetts city of Worcester, for example, differences in ethnic and class identification shape public celebratory activities. Not surprisingly, struggles within a society along ethnic, race, or other social lines are visible within these activities. The Moyie contest over the July date on which to mark a public holiday was also a contest over the cultural identity of the Moyie community.[11]

Taking these celebrations as a point of departure, this chapter explores regional expressions of identity and discord. In particular, it examines the actions and words that together worked to express the connections individuals or groups created and maintained as part of the Inland Empire. The citizens of Moyie resolved their differences by incorporating two traditions; more significant than their national identification was their regional identification. As part of the 1890s settlement of southeastern British Columbia, their actions and words—their "gestures"—expanded the limits of the Inland Empire across the international boundary.[12]

In Spokane Falls in 1876, words and actions combined to create a "wonderful advertisement" for a vision of a region dependent on a variety of natural resources controlled and tamed through human actions and technology, a region pointed toward the future. In the following decades, advertisements for the Inland Empire continued to outline a variety of imperial visions. In promotional literature designed to entice, at first, settlers and investors, and later, tourists and conventioneers, residents presented their competing understandings of their place within the empire and of the empire itself.

Contrasting the words and actions of residents, promoters, and visitors, examining their verbal and physical maps, this chapter explores the creation of the Inland Empire at the regional level. As the ceremonial public presentations reinforced and constructed regional identity, they also participated in ongoing struggles over that identity. Like community celebrations, promotional literature served as a public arena for debates about regional definition. These ritualized forms with their own exaggerated language contributed to the internal shaping of the region. The shape of the Inland Empire was also contested through the promotional literature created by outside investors and observers. As outsiders entered this discourse, using different frames of reference, the debate over regional identity broadened. The public presentations by Inland Empire residents, challenged by these externally created visions, increasingly revealed private doubts.[13]

Though individuals and groups within the region jockeyed for control over the terms of identification, they nonetheless agreed on the existence of the Inland Empire. Internal debates and conflicts, especially after the turn of the century, employed the language and framed their discussions within the physical and conceptual boundaries of the Inland Empire. For outsiders, regional boundaries were not as fixed. The Moyie dilemma suggests some important distinctions about the way regions are defined and bounded. When individuals come together and create their own boundaries, that is, when settlers collectively believe that what they share in common sets them apart, they act according to these beliefs. At times these mental boundaries, these self-created regions, diverge from the boundaries outsiders use to define the group. The conceptions that individuals or groups hold about the place to which they belong inform their behavior. The words and actions of the settlers in the Kootenays, for example, created explicit ties across the international border to maintain connections with the Inland Empire world.

Ties across the Border

The story of the settlement of southeastern British Columbia, of Moyie and other places, can be told in many ways. One way to tell the story is as an economic tale—the "discovery" of natural resources (land, timber, minerals) that could be turned to profit; the influx of people and capital into the area to exploit that resource; the acceleration of settlement as transportation lines, commercial networks, and institutional affiliations entangled the area into larger regional, national, and international networks. Another way to tell the story is revealed by the Moyie dilemma. The expressed anxiety over a public celebration suggests that a parallel cultural process joined these market forces in transforming the area. The actions and words of the mining rush settlers in the Kootenays reveal the personal and emotional lines, networks, and affiliations that contributed to the area's incorporation into the Inland Empire's regional identity.

The personal accounts of the settlement process—the diaries, letters, oral histories, and reminiscences of newcomers—hint at the attachments individuals felt to the region. But these private writings contain only fragmentary evidence. As elusive mental constructs, feelings, emotions, and perceptions often defy verbal and written expression. Movements, activities, and life decisions help to contextualize the words of the Kootenay settlers. How, for example, did these settlers describe the significance of the international border, and how did the international border influence their activities?

The boundary at the forty-ninth parallel clearly existed as a political line. As the creation of national treaty agreements, the international border demarcated the limits of national affiliation, responsibility, and claims. In personal accounts, however, individuals noted the environmental and economic lines that bisected the political line. Most important, they emphasized the kinship ties that deflated the border's significance in their lives within the region.[14]

Individual settlers carried more than mining expertise, capital, and labor across the border; they brought ideas, customs, and habits of thought; they extended personal attachments into the developing area. The words and actions of these new settlers help explain the importance of the community question for the residents of Moyie and reveal people's identification with place. Their voices, less well-known than those of the initial discoverers or the principal developers of the area's natural resources, tell of different "finds." The settlers, whether permanent or transient, speak of economic concerns and capital investments, but they also speak of familiar and unfamiliar scenes—of strangers who become neighbors, of alien environments that become familiar, of incomprehensible weather patterns that become predictable, of shacks and wooden houses that become homes. After the mining rush dissipated, these settlers remained attached to the place. Whether they physically remained or moved to a new location, they retained mental conceptions of the Kootenays that informed their future.[15]

For the individuals who settled in the border area, the international boundary was never a physical barrier. "You could walk back and forwards across the line just as often as you wanted to," recalled Stanley Jones about the turn-of-the-century period: "They did have an Immigration Officer there but he was just the kind of fellow that he never said anything to anybody when you went back and forwards just pretty much as you liked but the Immigration Officer knew who you was, where you was going and just about what you was going to do and if he wanted you, he knew just about where he could get you."[16] The environment, which allowed easy access across the British Columbia–Washington-Idaho borders, helped deflate the imaginary political boundaries in people's minds. The north-south mountain ranges frequently required that even travel within southeastern interior British Columbia include a detour into Washington. One young Bank of Montreal clerk who transferred from Rossland to Greenwood in 1896 found himself following a circuitous route: "In order to reach this Camp I travelled south on a railway newly built, connecting Rossland with Spokane. I left the train at Bossburg, in the State of Washington, and travelled by stage coach back over the border into the Kettle Valley Country."[17]

These transportation lines that connected Kootenay resources to United States markets represented and reinforced other economic linkages. The regional economic networks tended to deemphasize the international border, especially for individuals. Whether Spokane businessmen or northern Idaho miners, regional residents, especially those experienced with mineral resources, were receptive to overtures from British Columbia prospectors and pursued opportunities regardless of national location. Workers looking for employment in mining, lumbering, or railroading found jobs on both sides of the border. M. Allen was typical of those who followed the mining market; he moved from jobs in the British Columbia camps of Patterson and Rossland to work in Northport, Washington. In 1895 Robert Buchanan Graham went to stay in Trail, British Columbia, with his uncle, the skipper of a border-crossing steamer. Graham worked at the Trail smelter and later took a job on the railroad as an engine fireman. "Most of the engine men came across from the states," he reported, "across the line." In 1902 he returned to railroading in the states. Similarly, Jens Christian Hanson, a Danish miner and farmer, moved his family back and forth across the border from Coeur d'Alene to Spokane to Rossland to Lardo to Slocan between the 1880s and the 1910s.[18]

Kinship ties joined these economic incentives in linking the Kootenays to the Spokane-centered Inland Empire. Families seeking homes made no distinction between Canadian and American sites. Mormon families from Porthill, Idaho, settled in Creston, British Columbia, during the 1890s and worked in mining, logging, and canal-building jobs on both sides of the border. The Manley brothers, too, settled on both sides of the border; Sherry Manley practiced medicine in Colville, and Al Manley sold supplies in Grand Forks, British Columbia. Joe, John, Carse, and Lloyd Manley also made their homes in the area. Family letters reveal the extent of physical and mental movement across the border. Maria House's correspondence from the East Kootenays in the early twentieth century speaks of uncles Harry, James, Clark, and Robert, cousins Edith, Ida, and Candace, and reports on their lives in Walla Walla, Washington, Fort Steele, British Columbia, and Spokane. Correspondence and shared visits sustained their kinship ties. Cousin Ida, Maria reported to her niece in 1908, "came to see us all for a few weeks with Mary her daughter she stayed with Uncle Robert but has now returned to Spokane."[19]

Networks of kin and acquaintances encouraged and sustained people who moved to new communities in British Columbia from other parts of the Inland Empire. "Upon my arrival in Nelson in the fall of 1896," recalled Fred Smyth, a printer, "I was greeted by Seneca G. Ketchum, who was chief of police. . . . I had known Ketchum down at Pullman, Washington where I started to learn my trade." Newcomers were gradually drawn into these networks and into public celebrations. "Yesterday," reported English-born Harold Nation to his mother, "our violin neighbor came in and presented us with a layer cake and said 'I guess you folks ain't Americans but you can celebrate anyway.' It was Thanksgiving Day in the States."[20]

The kinship ties, job markets, and environmental conditions described in first-person accounts mark personal connections. These ties and connections extending over the international border were not in and of themselves unusual. But here the ties were invested with particular meaning; residents of the area perceived the invisible networks as signs of a larger regional identity. At key moments in these accounts—when the writers recall the past and dream of the future—they speak directly about their identity.

In their oral histories and reminiscences, Inland Empire residents took

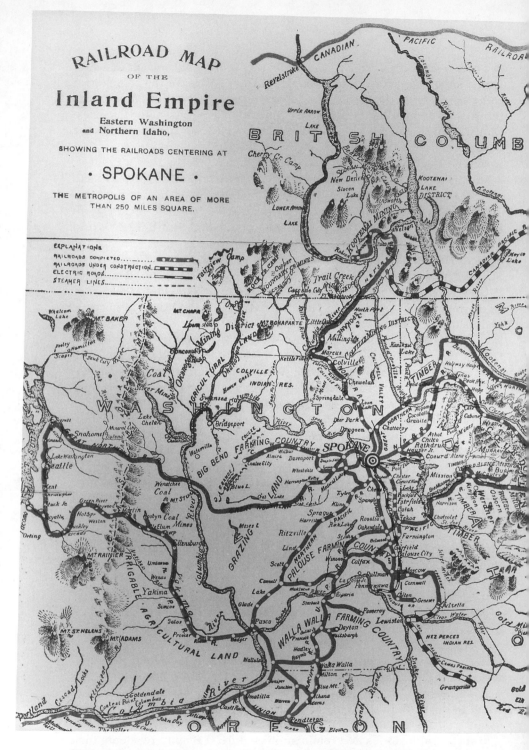

All Roads Lead to Spokane Hitting the bull's-eye, nine railroads lines converge on Spokane. The city's Chamber of Commerce republished different versions of this map throughout the 1890s. From its designation of "Irrigable Agricultural Lands" to its inclusion of Southeastern British Columbia to its erasure of the Coeur d'Alene Indian reservation, the map presents a particular version of the Inland Empire. By permission of Cheney Cowles Museum/Eastern Washington State Historical Society, Spokane, Washington.

pains to explain their former connections with the Kootenays. They repeated a litany of no longer existing ties that had been created by trails, mail, teamsters, steamers, and railroads. Mail was faster through the United States, whether addressed to a Canadian or American location, recalled E. Spraggett of Grand Forks, British Columbia: "At the same time that we were getting a mail once a month from our own government, we were getting it three times a week from Uncle Sam through Marcus, [Washington]." Carrie Allen, who grew up in Northport, Washington, spoke of frequent travel to Rossland, British Columbia, for shopping or visits. Trips by train south to Spokane or north to Nelson were equally treasured excursions.[21]

In their letters and diaries Inland Empire residents focused on the future. They wrote of their hopes and dreams by discussing individual plans, community actions, and regional events. The people of eastern Washington and northern Idaho considered southeastern British Columbia in their plans for the future. "We are seeking a new field and are impressed with the possibilities in British Columbia," wrote the Clarke Brothers, real estate promoters from Spokane, to W. D. Middaugh of Nelson.[22] When a group of twenty-five families from Lind, Washington, in the Palouse was looking for a new farming location in 1903, for another example, a representative of the potential immigrants requested information from the Canadian Pacific Railway on lands available in the Kootenays. The presence of the United States there was strongly felt. As one Kootenay settler wrote to his father, "Every where up here [in British Columbia] you can see the influence of the Americans that are coming into this country and although they do not hold the highest positions in the country yet they are getting there fast." But people in the Kootenays also looked south for opportunities. Eugene McGrath, the hired lad working for the Graham family near Trail, British Columbia, "left to seek his fortune in Ritzville, Washington." When Ed Tiegart wrote to his brother in 1890 that he planned to settle in British Columbia, he also indicated that his hopes were not tied only to Canada. "I bought some land out there last fall at the Columbia lakes where the Columbia river raises near Washington Territo[ry]," he explained: "it is a small valley between Mountains i think it is the best place I have seen yet to settle there is good land $1 per acre and plenty of timber and prairie land and the stock feeds out all winter I never have been in Washington I have heard a good deal about it I believe it is a good country."[23] Hearing and believing in the potential of specific locales, those who traveled across the international boundary created conceptual as well as physical links with both sides of the divide.

Perhaps the strongest indications of commitment to the Inland Empire are revealed in hopes for the next generation. Where, for example, did parents send their children for education? Dr. Edward C. Arthur of Nelson,

British Columbia, Canadian-born and educated in Ontario, sent his children to Washington State College in Pullman. So too did a Canadian judge, John Forin. Although Archie Coombs of Patterson stayed in British Columbia, eventually moving to Rossland, his sisters, he recalled, "went across the boundary into the State of Washington school (that was at Velvet Siding, about a mile below the boundary) every day for a few years. Two of my sisters eventually went to Spokane for business college and they are now living in the State of Washington." Local grammar school and high school classrooms, reported schoolteachers, included both American and Canadian students: "It was a good thing for both sides and helped to establish the 'Good Neighbor' policy," pointed out one teacher.[24]

The actions and words of individual settlers in the Kootenays suggest the importance of economic, environmental, and emotional ties across the border. Local public writings reinforced these private writings; regional public activities linked up with personal activities. Community, as well as individual, plans for the future emphasized Inland Empire ties. The Canadian settlement of Midway proclaimed itself "The Spokane of the Boundary Creek District." Rossland, British Columbia, was known as a "Spokane town." Kettle Falls, Washington, residents requested branch lines from the Canadian Pacific Railroad as well as from United States railways.[25] Larger regional events and celebrations also marked the extended boundaries of the Inland Empire. The annual Spokane Apple Fair and competition, for example, drew entries from throughout the region, from the British Columbia communities of Grand Forks, Creston, and Windermere, as well as from Wenatchee, Yakima, and Spokane, Washington. One-cent-per-mile special train fares to promote the Spokane Fruit Fair were available from points in British Columbia as well as Idaho and Washington. When Theodore Roosevelt stopped in Spokane to make a speech in 1903, the Washington city's mayor invited mayors from British Columbia cities to sit on the platform and be introduced.[26]

The arrangements for President Roosevelt's visit, like the Moyie Fourth of July compromise, mark the ties across the border that linked southeastern British Columbia with the Inland Empire. Yet they also reveal the persistence of the border, of individual beliefs, external forces, national affiliations, and international events that worked to weaken or cut these ties. In Nelson, British Columbia, the mix of Canadians and Americans in the schools went unnoted among the students, for example, until international events highlighted the differences and required them to take sides; during the Boer War, recalled Edgar Jamieson, a snowball fight took on a decidedly nationalistic fervor. "It happened that one captain was from the US and the other was a Canadian. In choosing their supporters, the choice definitely followed national lines . . . it was well past the noon hour before the teachers were able to restore peace and separate the contestants."

Vigorous efforts were also made by other Canadian nationalists to counter the pervasive over-the-border influences—one measure of the power of the regional construct. Jeremy Mouat traces the "Canadianization" of the Kootenays fostered by conscious efforts on the part of Canadian investors and the Canadian Pacific Railway to draw the mining region away from the Spokane orbit.[27]

The region's promotional materials, directed at external as well as internal audiences, most directly reveal both the required insistence and the habitual acceptance of the Kootenays within the Inland Empire. Pamphlets included the Canadian lands in their litanies of regional splendor. Drawing attention to "the vast Inland Empire of more than 200,000 square miles," one quantitative description listed "the east two-thirds of Washington, the northeast one-fourth of Oregon, all of north Idaho, part of western Montana and the best part of British Columbia." The photographs included in the *Souvenir of Spokane, Washington,* published in honor of Theodore Roosevelt's visit, depicted scenes from both sides of the border.[28]

During the 1890s, "the best part of British Columbia," at least according to some observers, was part of the Inland Empire. Through words and actions, individual settlers in southeastern British Columbia created and maintained personal connections across the border which, along with economic and environmental incentives, expanded regional boundaries across the international line. Their private writings reveal their participation in the larger public process of regional creation. In their stories of individual lives and in their matter-of-fact discussions of everyday activities, the settlers became actively engaged in the identification of the Inland Empire. Through the transition of their personal signs into regional signs, the distinction between public and private blurred.

Boomer Literature

The intermingling of public and private discourse concerning the identity of the Inland Empire, visible in the personal accounts of the settlement of southeastern British Columbia, can also be seen in the region's promotional literature. Anonymous authors created many of the pamphlets, brochures, and articles that described specific locations in wondrous detail for the potential settler, investor, or tourist. Indeed, once the words entered the public domain they were reprinted over and over again with little credit to the original source. A few authors, however, are known.

Charles Clarke was one promotional pamphlet writer. A former resident of Cincinnati, Ohio, where he and his two brothers ran a successful furniture concern, Clarke came to the region during the 1880s. The Clarke brothers had decided to expand their partnership to include joint speculation in western land, specifically the lands of the Inland Empire. They engaged in a wide range of businesses; among their early efforts, they provided supplies for Okanagon mines and ran a cattle ranch. Charles was not an enthusiastic partner in the latter venture. As one of his 1886 diary entries noted, "Worked all day doing chores at the barn. No farmers life for me! A round of primary drudgeries day after day Sundays and all! No wonder young men leave the farm." No wonder he was "trying to persuade Bob [his brother Robert Clarke] to abandon ranche next spring as something no longer practicable." Charles's interests lay predominantly in speculation and writing, two activities most of his contemporaries viewed as suspiciously impractical. In fact, much of his time at the ranch, if his diary is any indication, was spent writing.[29] Charles wrote more than promotional tracts—or, in his words, "boomer literature"—designed to attract investors in the Clarke Brothers' businesses. His short stories and series fiction graced the pages of such magazines and newspapers as the *Youth's Companion, McClure's Magazine, Christian Advocate,* and *New York Tribune.* In these fictional pieces Charles commented on the speculative activities in which he and his brothers were engaged as Inland Empire boosters.

The western boys featured in Clarke's articles for *Youth's Companion* faced adversity and adventure, learning behavioral and moral lessons along the way. In many ways his stories followed the typical patterns for this genre of late nineteenth-century children's literature. Armajo, for example, learned that "it was manly and improving to acknowledge errors frankly," especially those resulting from defects of temperament inherited from his Spanish ancestors. Varnum's lesson was that luck and good fortune come to those who work hard and persevere. These familiar Gilded Age prescriptions, similar to those proffered by Andrew Carnegie and Horatio Alger Jr., filled the pages of such magazine stories.[30]

There were other less familiar lessons as well. Clarke's first publication in *Youth's Companion,* winner of the First Prize Story for Boys, taught a lesson about speculation and control. Set in the Big Bend area of the Inland Empire, the story follows its young Audubon Club hero, Carlysle Calbeck, on a collecting trip for specimens to stuff and sell to the East. While spending the night at the cabin of a German immigrant and his Indian wife, Calbeck stumbles into a land dispute. His host, "Old Fels," complains of town site surveyors who are impinging on his "squatter's rights" to the land. In repayment for the man's hospitality, the rash Calbeck confronts the surveyors only to learn that the story is not so simple. Old Fels, the surveyors calmly explain, " 'is not a naturalized citizen. He exhausted his rights in Donation Lands in Oregon, and he has five other ranches in this neighborhood, all of which he claims. We have filed over him on this quarter at the land office, and have every legal right here.' " Calbeck is confused. Should his allegiance lie with "the crude 'squaw-man' " or the intelligent surveyors? As he conducts his internal debate, Old Fels and his "half-breed" sons, accompanied by armed reservation Indians, descend upon the surveying party. Wounded as a bystander in the ensuing battle, Calbeck escapes to safety, registering "an earnest vow never again to meddle in the affairs of other people, where he could not justly judge the rights involved and had no proper call to interfere."[31]

In the battle between Old Fels, a part of the "uncivilized" past, and the town site surveyors, who are platting the future, the latter are the obvious winners. The instinctual "savage" men of action are no match for the modern men who wield their technological advantages—guns and surveying equipment—as well as legal rights supported by written documents. The boy Calbeck and the *Youth's Companion* readers learn the moral of self-control. They also learn a few things about speculation and about the value of legal rights. At the start of the tale, the self-assured hero claims familiarity with "the wiles by which speculators 'boom' Western towns, and by which large values are created out of nothing." By the end, Calbeck and the readers are less convinced about the immorality of speculation. The wily Old Fels, who fooled the naive youth, has turned out to be the villain, not the surveyor-speculators. Calbeck's position is in the midst of the controversy. He is hardly an innocent interloper. His Audubonesque mission to kill and stuff animals for an eastern market makes similar use of the environment for economic gain. In telling the tale, Charles Clarke obfuscates the more traditional equation of hard work and financial success. For Clarke, a businessman engaged in Big Bend real estate speculation, creating values out of nothing was a legal, if not noble, enterprise.[32]

These fictional writings, along with his diaries and letters, reveal some of the ambiguities behind Charles Clarke's vision of the Inland Empire as presented in his promotional literature. The Clarke Brothers' pamphlets, circulars, and advertisements advocated just rewards for hard work and presented nature as a willing servant to human intervention. They raised no questions about the rights of investors to make profits or the morality of the use of technology to subvert natural processes.[33]

But Clarke's anxiety over the morality of speculation, "making something out of nothing," is clear in his fiction. His diary as well participates in the larger debate over the value and morality of different kinds of work. In its entries Charles distinguishes between labor and drudgery and between business and work. While he despises most ranch chores and housework as "drudgery," his worthwhile "labor" includes nonrepetitive jobs. The terms "work" and "business" apply to less physical moneymaking activities. Clarke speaks of "work" when he is engaged in producing a tangible product—writing stories and circulars, responding to his correspondence, or balancing the books. His "business" involves less visible results—discussing possible investments, selling lots, securing interests, or trading.

Clarke preferred manipulating words and clients to performing "drudgeries day after day" to acquire profits. Yet from the perspective of other regional residents—the Coeur d'Alene Populists, for example—who spoke of the virtues of "honest labor," Clarke and other individuals who proudly defined themselves as "capitalists" were the villains. In his moral-laden magazine fiction Clarke attempted to reconcile these discordances.[34]

As real estate speculators, the Clarke brothers invested in property throughout the region, including the city of Spokane and the mining areas in the Okanagons to the west and the Coeur d'Alenes to the east. Their activities were not always successful.[35] Their involvement in the promotion of Post Falls, Idaho, is a case in point. In 1871 a German immigrant, Frederick Post, had first established claims to the land around the Upper Falls of the Spokane River. Negotiations with the Coeur d'Alenes and later with the federal government gave him legal rights to the site. Although he laid out a town and started a sawmill, Post initially pursued more profitable ventures in Spokane Falls. It was not until 1879 that the area's increasing population, favorable economic conditions, and news of the opening of the northern half of the Coeur d'Alene reservation convinced him that the time for further development of the site had come.[36]

Post was not the only promoter who was drawn to Post Falls during the 1880s. In uneasy competition with Post, the Clarke Brothers joined other investors eager to be involved in the industrial development of the Upper Falls. They purchased some lands from Post and acquired legal rights to others.[37] A local branch railroad connected the northern Idaho town sites to Spokane. With waterpower, access to markets, and legal control over the land, the investors proceeded to "boom" the town.

The connection to Spokane extended beyond its railroad tracks. Even as Clarke and other investors sought to distinguish Post Falls from rival towns, they relied on its comparison and proximity to Spokane in their promotional activities. "The conditions which have made Spokane Falls a great success are repeated at POST FALLS, Idaho," read one advertisement. In fact, Charles Clarke used the same language and organization for his first Post Falls flyer that he had published as part of his Spokane Falls real estate endeavors. He simply plugged in the name Post Falls for any reference to Spokane Falls.[38]

In 1890 Charles Clarke moved his family to the new settlement, wrote and distributed advertising literature to attract investors, and worked at selling lots to prospective buyers. Capitalizing on, and in some cases fostering, rumors of the imminent opening of the adjacent Coeur d'Alene reservation, Charles sent news items to the Spokane papers and to the Northern Pacific's promotional magazine, the *Northwest*.[39] His pitch, which focused on technology rather than nature, was primarily to other investors. The Clarke Brothers' somewhat exaggerated advertisement in the *Spokane*

Falls Review, for example, listed nine mills and factories that "are already assured" at this "first class water power and townsite." At the time, the town limits contained only one operating mill. Not included as inducements were traditional signs of permanent settlements, such as schools, churches, or even restaurants. Although progress had been made in laying the cornerstone for a Methodist church, that fact was not noted in the newspaper copy. The emphasis remained on Post Falls as a "fine field for investment."[40]

Clarke's personal writings, however, paint a less rosy picture. Whereas his promotional works depict a place filled with tremendous excitement and growth, his diary entries describe "dull" and "very dull" days as he meets more prospective than actual clients. The entire venture rested on a precarious financial base. Dependent on the cooperation of the irascible Post, the Clarkes became increasingly discouraged with their prospects at Post Falls. As speculators, the Clarkes began to express reluctance at establishing permanent ties to the community. When asked to run for county commissioner, Charles refused; as he explained to his brother, "the future is too uncertain to penetrate," especially if the promised mills failed to materialize.[41]

In the early twentieth century the future of the Inland Empire became increasingly difficult to penetrate. Even in the ever-optimistic promotional literature, competing voices, both inside and outside the region, engaged in a public debate over its definition and future. As external voices intruded upon the region, other residents joined the Clarke brothers in questioning the underlying assumptions that constructed their vision of the Inland Empire.

Language of Promotion

"Probably no city in the Pacific Northwest is more widely known, by reputation at least," boasted one 1905 Spokane Chamber of Commerce pamphlet, "than Spokane, the Imperial City of the Inland Empire." If the claim was true, it was in part because of the outpouring of such pamphlets from Spokane and other regional cities, which contributed to the public's increasing awareness of the Inland Empire.[42] With titles such as *The Inland Empire and What It Comprehends* or *Catechism of the Inland Empire and the Pacific Northwest: Resources, Opportunities, Advantages*, the pamphlets published in Spokane captured a regional vision that was more than simple boosterism. In these "staged" writings, a variety of promoters presented their version of the Inland Empire. The region was "an ideal country for thrift, enterprise, money-making and comfort" with "the brightest prospects for a brilliant future."[43]

—OFFICE OF—

CHARLES W. CLARKE,

510 HOWARD STREET,

SPOKANE FALLS, WASHINGTON TERRITORY.

A SOUND INVESTMENT!

GOOD INTEREST EARNED WITHOUT RISKS.

You are invited to consider the peculiar and exceptional advantages of **SPOKANE FALLS, WASHING-TON TERRITORY,** as a field for safe and promising investment in town and suburban property.

This young city possesses conditions identical with those which have given Minneapolis such phenomenal success, and renews the opportunities for large profits in real estate which originally existed there.

THE SITUATION.

Spokane Falls lies at the edge of the Columbia plateau, a fertile prairie extending west and south for two hundred miles.

To the east is also an extensive prairie, while north and southeast are heavy timber regions in a mountainous country.

As a town-site this place challenges the continent for beauty combined with utility. It occupies an elevated plain lying between hills, everywhere commanding magnificent mountain and prairie views and bisected by a picturesque river. The charm of the locality alone stimulates quick settlement.

THE PRODIGIOUS WATER-POWER.

Spokane River, outlet of Lake Pend d'Oreille, trends westwardly in a sharp down-grade through Spokane prairie and pierces the heart of town in a series of cascades, falling 156 feet within corporation limits. It carries a swift, powerful and permanent current, which never freezes, and is never subject to great freshets. Islands in midstream divide it into numerous waterways, affording hundreds of admirable sites for mill purposes. Below the main fall—a distance of sixty-five feet—the river runs in a deep, wooded ravine. Expert engineers compute the available water power here during November, when at its lowest stage, at **114,000 horse-power!**

Lake Pend d'Oreille is in the heart of the Rocky Mountains, amid lofty ranges, snow-capped all the year. These vast deposits of snow yield a steadfast volume of water during the hot months, assuring a constant river supply.

AGRICULTURE AND MINING.

Stretching south and west of Spokane Falls is a broad semicircle of fertile prairie, comprising millions of acres, in all respects the peer of the Dakota and Minnesota grain fields. This country is being settled rapidly, and the output of grain and stock is already enormous.

North and east is an equally great semicircle of mines, consisting of seven successful districts—among them the famous Cœur d'Alene silver fields, only one hundred miles distant. These contribute liberally to the trade of the town, and when farther developed are expected to advance its importance still more rapidly.

This mountainous mining region is covered with a dense growth of superior timber, and large deposits of iron and coal are known. The lumber and flouring mill industries have already heavy plants here.

RAILROAD FACILITIES.

SPOKANE FALLS is on the main line of the Northern Pacific Railway. It is the terminus of the Spokane & Palouse R. R. and of the Spokane & Idaho R. R. The Union Pacific R. R. is building an extension toward us which is now within sixty miles. Another road has been projected northward to the Canadian Pacific R. R. Within twenty months it is expected there will be three trans-continental lines and six local roads centering at this point, giving additional advantages for wholesale and manufacturing interests.

PRESENT POPULATION.

Now 7,000. It has nearly doubled every year for three years past. The town has the Holley water-works system, sewers in the main business streets, gas, telephone exchange, and electric lights. It has in process a street railway. It has ten churches, two colleges, ample public schools, two daily newspapers and three weeklies, three banks with aggregate capital of $550,000, three fire companies, and 210 business and manufacturing firms. The streets are wide, regularly laid out, and perfectly drained. The latest hotels and commercial buildings are from three to five stories high, brick.

Best of all, it is settled by educated, energetic, wide-awake Americans, who have brought here modern methods, and have placed all public affairs on a systematic, economical and enterprising basis.

NO "BOOM," AS YET.

Values in property have steadily increased, but there has been no wild inflation or excitement, and city blocks and lots can still be had at very reasonable prices.

WHY INVESTMENTS HERE ARE SAFE.

SPOKANE FALLS is without an important rival for 300 miles. It commands an immense and fertile agricultural region. It is the natural distributing center for seven mining districts. It controls a vast area of timber, accessible both by rail and river. *Its water-power is the best on the continent, excelling that of Minneapolis in volume, frontage, and regularity.* Moreover, this region is in the direct path of immigration. From New York State westward the stream of progress has moved unceasingly for a century past. What Illinois was forty years ago Washington Territory is to-day, with this difference: that increasing railroad facilities, a narrowing area of virgin soil, and overcrowding of the eastern seaboard augment the rapidity of settlement. On the frontier, at present, one year's advance equals five or ten years' growth in those earlier days.

It is reasonable, it is conservative to believe that values here can never be *less* than they are at present.

WHY IT WILL PAY TO INVEST NOW

On the contrary, it is rational to believe that in a place having so many points of vantage, town property must logically increase in price, if selected with good judgment and bought at moderate cost. The influx of immigration is constant, and those stay who come, held by the wholesome attractions of our great natural resources.

The perfection of the climate (characterized by tonic days, cool nights, *mild winters* and dry air) is a factor of importance.

The tributary agricultural regions, the successful mining and grazing industries, the expanding market, all prophesy early increased utilization of the water-power and consequent town growth.

So far, investments have advanced in market value *from one to three per cent. a month* on unimproved property, while improved property has often paid *two per cent. per month in cash, besides rising constantly in price.* There is eager demand for brick business stands in good localities. For four years past the clamor for dwellings has been unceasing, arrivals outnumbering all possible accommodation, so that cheap houses have returned twenty per cent. per annum and doubled in market value biennially. All this without flurry or agitation, as the natural result of early investment judiciously placed in the line of immigration.

Those who buy in the primary stage of successful towns are the ones who reap the largest rewards, and this stage has not yet passed in Spokane Falls. We have as yet reached only that degree of development which discloses exceptional advantages and betokens a great manufacturing future.

PERSONAL.

Those who can come and see for themselves are urged to do so, and may rely upon finding unusual opportunities for wise purchases. All such are cordially invited to call upon Mr. CHARLES W. CLARKE, at the address below given, where every courtesy will be extended them.

To those who can not come in person, but who desire to invest little or much, the undersigned respectfully offers his services. Having made a special study of Spokane Falls, of its topography, its various tendencies, the qualities and prospects of its different neighborhoods, he is prepared to execute all commissions with care and promptness.

The profit following real estate investment depends upon the degree of judgment and vigilance used in selecting a location. *In this respect Mr. Clarke desires to give assurance of thoroughness and capacity, founded upon familiarity with the field and long and mature experience.* He cites by permission the following references as to his intelligence, record and integrity.

> SECOND NATIONAL BANK, CINCINNATI, O.
> GLAESCHER & CO., CINCINNATI, O.
> GEORGE S. BROWN, 32 Warren Street, NEW YORK CITY.
> FIRST NATIONAL BANK, SPOKANE FALLS.
> DR. J. E. GANDY, SPOKANE FALLS,
> REV. E. M. WHEELOCK, SPOKANE FALLS.

All titles here are by patent direct from the Government, or by deed from the N. P. R. R., and are indisputable. Money can easily be loaned at ten per cent. per annum (long time), and at one per cent. per month (short time) on gilt-edged security.

Parties desiring to buy town lots or business property, to loan money, to erect and rent houses, or otherwise invest here are invited to write me. Correspondence promptly answered. All trusts faithfully looked after.

Persons interested in any other respect and desiring information, etc., will also receive quick and courteous attention to letters of inquiry.

Very Truly,

CHARLES W. CLARKE,

REAL ESTATE AND FINANCIAL AGENT,

510 Howard Street.

Spokane Falls, Washington Territory.

Other regional cities and towns agreed with Spokane's depiction of the region as an Inland Empire. They disagreed, however, about exactly where the empire was centered. For the Washington cities of Walla Walla and Yakima, or the Idaho towns of Moscow and Sandpoint, the Inland Empire centered on themselves. The maps accompanying their promotional pamphlets depicted the region with somewhat distorted geographical boundaries and marked Sandpoint, Idaho, or Yakima, Washington, as the "center" or "gateway" to the Inland Empire. Well-established Walla Walla, the oldest of the urban locales, downplayed the role of other towns in its claims to regional prominence. In *Washington Territory! The Present and Prospective Future of the Upper Columbia Country,* the editor of the *Daily and Weekly Statesman* (Walla Walla) simply noted Spokane Falls along with other "comparatively new" towns of Spokane County.[44]

Claims to imperialism pervaded the booster literature of the nineteenth century. The term "empire" held a rich assortment of meanings for its readers, from classical allusions to commercial expansion, from ideas of dominion and control to those of unity and order, from extravagance to excess.[45] The malleability of the associations allowed its use in a variety of contexts. For the residents and promoters of the Inland Empire, the phrase took on specific local meanings. Introduced to the local concept of empire through promotional literature, railroad companies and other outside promoters gradually incorporated insiders' rhetoric into their own promotional campaigns after the turn of the century. In doing so, however, they molded the imperial vision into a different shape; it was the past, not the future, that these outsiders celebrated.

The Inland Empire pamphlet writers attempted to shape the ways others thought of their region. In their prose they addressed a skeptical outside audience, usually positioned in "The East." "These claims may sound grandiloquent to an Eastern reader," noted one Spokane author, "but they are facts."[46] Acknowledging the genre's overblown language, they claimed authority for themselves by virtue of their adherence to "facts." "I am not dealing in probabilities or fanciful conjectures, but in facts that tell their own story," protested the author of *An Ideal Country.* "We strive to avoid exaggerated statements and highly-colored accounts of interested parties who have town-sites to boom or real-estate to sell," explained another journal writer. "We aim to give the facts and let them speak for themselves." C. B. Carlisle of Spokane Falls claimed, "My position as a journalist has given me superior advantages for the collection and compilation of solid facts and results, and these, rather than eloquent language or beautiful embellishment, will be found in this work."[47]

Regardless of these protestations of exactitude and truth, "will" was the favorite verb of by the speculative writers. Projections, descriptions of the "obvious" future, gave the writers plenty of opportunities for superlative prose. Just one sentence in the *Handbook of Spokane Falls, W.T., the Queen*

City of the Pacific included the following parenthetical phrases: "which are now projected," "which is not many years ahead," "which are bound soon to come." Once these railroads, mills, manufactories, settlers, and capital arrived, of course, "all this vast country will be directly tributary to Spokane Falls." Other authors listed precise, although imaginary, numbers and data with the same literary license. "In five years Eastern Washington and Northern Idaho will be providing 50,000,000 bushels of wheat per annum and $25,000,000 in gold, silver, and lead," claimed one pamphlet.[48]

During the 1880s the Spokane Board of Trade, whose self-defined "object was to promote, by all proper and legitimate means, the prosperity of Spokane Falls, and to protect the varied interests of the town from the ruthless group of unscrupulous corporations," took a somewhat defensive position in its promotional rhetoric.[49] After the fire in 1889, and especially after the establishment of the Spokane Chamber of Commerce, the city presented itself as the center of the emerging region. Despite their rose-colored views, the pamphlets suggest a clear vision of the future, of the empire builders' hopes and dreams. As the chairman of the Spokane Chamber of Commerce put it, "Who wonders that the city of Spokane with a waterpower unsurpassed, in the center of a vast territory, has grown in a decade to be a city of 30,000 people and the greatest railroad center on the Pacific slope? Who doubts that it will maintain its position as the leading city of the 'Inland Empire?'"[50]

Reorganized during the 1890s, the Chamber of Commerce was one of many institutions seeking to promote a regional future. Newspapers and civic organizations in other towns and proto-cities contributed to the outpouring of exaggerated prose.[51] Advertising artists and cartographers portrayed the collective vision in pictorial representations. C. Winsor's "Birdseye View of the Falls and Factories," for example, was frequently published in the promotional literature. Copyrighted by a real estate businessman, L. C. Dillman, the painting depicted the Spokane River crisscrossed by a dozen bridges and lined with numerous factories, mills, and railroad tracks. A series of dams controlled the falls.

The natural beauty of the falls, and the beneficence of the region's natural resources contained the promise of Spokane and the Inland Empire. According to the literature, Spokane, as the "natural distributing center," "natural jobbing centre," and "natural railroad center," tied together the tributary mineral, timber, and agricultural resources of the Inland Empire. It was an empire based on the control of its natural resources through the machinery of mills, mines, smelters, harvesters—and advertising. As Charles Clarke preached from the pages of *Northwest Magazine*, "Under our modern system of competition, natural advantages alone, do not speed the growth of towns. There must be men behind; men of faith, pluck, enterprise, integrity, and advertising knack."[52]

For Robert V. M. Schawl, a Spokane writer, advertising compared directly

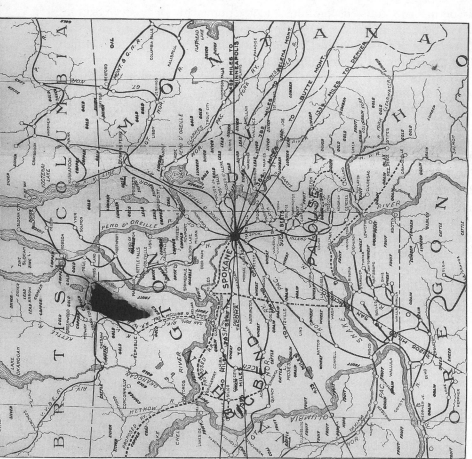

to machinery. Like the dams that harness the energy of Spokane Falls, he explained in *Nature's Energy. Who Pays for Advertising?*, advertising "utilizes and transmits the vital force of ideas." The merchant or manufacturer "merely utilizes the natural power"; buying advertising is "merely harnessing human psychology and making this natural power work for him." The purported ease with which words controlled the human mind lay behind the appeal of Schawl's argument. To gain power and profits one simply tapped into "nature's energy." This equation of control over nature, people, words, and ideas remained the ideal. The debates over the boundaries of the Inland Empire pointed to the difficulties of controlling public discourse. Still, as the promotional literature of the Inland Empire celebrated technology's control of nature, it aspired to similar control of human nature, thought, and psychology. In their attempt to control the way outsiders perceived the region, however, the Spokane promoters of the Inland Empire faced a difficult task.[53]

The Spokane Chamber of Commerce worked to draw outside attention, and money, to the area. The promotional campaigns included advertisements and articles in western and national magazines as well as its own separate publications. Spokane's 1890 Northwestern Industrial Exposition was not the only occasion for the creation of a brochure extolling the virtues of the region. Although Spokane made an effort to attract such groups to "The Convention City," when national events came to the West, they were held on the coast. Even regional expositions, conventions, and meetings were more likely to be in Seattle, Portland, or Tacoma. As a way to capture conventioneers, visitors, and tourists who would be passing through Spokane, "The Railroad City," the Chamber of Commerce petitioned the railroads to offer special "stop-over" rates. Visitors to the World's Columbian Exposition, the Lewis and Clark Exposition, and similar national or regional fairs also encountered Spokane-Inland Empire exhibits, maps, and brochures amid the cacophony of promotional efforts typical of such gatherings.[54]

Voices outside the area presented a different vision of empire. Oregon, for example, used the term "empire" to refer to its own grand ambitions. The state's immigration bureau and railroad lines published pamphlets describing a "New Empire" or "Columbia River Empire" that included the lands claimed by the Inland Empire. In direct competition with Spokane's claims, the Portland author of *The New Empire* relegated Spokane to second-class status: "Whilst it [the city of Spokane Falls] doubtless never will become the hub of 'The New Empire' which its ambition leads it to hope to be, it will always be one of the best of the interior points."[55]

Railroad companies—national concerns such as the Northern Pacific Railroad, Great Northern Railway, and Union Pacific, and local railways, all of which ran lines across the region—had a vested interest in attracting settlers and customers. While they joined the local efforts to promote the region, they presented a different version. Rarely, for example, did the outside promoters independently use the term "Inland Empire" in reference to the region.[56] When they did use the internal language, it usually reflected their reliance on local sources for descriptive prose. The Canadian Pacific Railroad's publicity department based in Calgary, for example, wrote to the towns along its Kootenay routes for self-descriptions and incorporated them with few changes into larger pamphlets. The editor, E. J. Smalley, also depended on local writers for the Northern Pacific promotional efforts. John Reavis of the Spokane Chamber of Commerce, like Charles Clarke of Post Falls, submitted articles and items to the St. Paul–based *Northwest Magazine*.[57]

When the national railroads created their own campaigns, the interests of the Inland Empire tended to be subsumed under those of the transportation companies. After the completion of the transcontinental route through Spokane, the Northern Pacific Railroad advertising campaigns presented the western region as "The Golden Northwest" or "The Pennsylvania of the West" rather than recognizing the designation used by residents. The Chicago and North Western Railway and the Great Northern Railway also incorporated the Inland Empire into larger regions.[58]

Gradually, however, the railroad campaigns came to accept certain aspects of the local version. The image they presented of the component parts of the region paralleled that of the Inland Empire promoters. They described "a country where the resources of Nature and the forces of civilization are coming together as nowhere else in America." This combination of nature and technology was praised as "a fascinating panorama of picturesque scenery and thriving industry."[59] The railroads also agreed with the extension of the region across the international border, especially the Great Northern Railway, whose lines followed the Kootenay River for sixty-two miles.[60]

Nowhere is the vision of empire better articulated than in the maps that accompanied the pamphlets' prose. The locally created maps were, as D. W. Meinig points out, expressions of regional identity: "For regions exist in the minds of men, and maps mirror their times, and such regional bounds and terms as appear today reflect the views that have quite a different image of order and arrangement in that part of the nation."[61] Real estate companies joined the chambers of commerce and railroad companies in producing and distributing maps of the region.[62] The maps labeled the various resources of the empire, highlighting the "soon to be opened" reservations and the potential locations of "irrigable agricultural lands," timber, and railroad lines, along with existing farms, mines, and towns.

The railroad companies generally published maps that included the portions of Idaho, Washington, and British Columbia claimed as part of the

Inland Empire. Although this sectionalism was perhaps pragmatic, it also reflected an acceptance of the regional perspective; their descriptive prose agreed with the Inland Empire designation. The Great Northern Railway's Northwest atlas, for example, which included mostly individual state maps, gave one page to northern Idaho and Washington. The accompanying text defined Spokane as "the center of a real empire, having in her mineral, agricultural, grazing and lumbering resources, four corners of wealth, as perfectly balanced as if specially designed."[63]

Outsiders found themselves trying to explain the regional conceit involved in claiming empire status. "The man of the East who has not been beyond the Mississippi and is accustomed to the congestion of humanity in the older States, may smile incredulously at the clause that here is an empire," noted Day Allen Willey in a 1908 *Moody's Magazine* article. He explained that westerners used a different frame of reference: "The West, however, is a country of big things. Its people are known not by numbers, but by achievements, and they make good . . . and this is a region which, as we have said, has been so lately penetrated by the white man that it is still almost a blank on the modern map."[64]

The Spokane Chamber of Commerce worked to fill in the blank on this modern map. Outsiders often preferred to keep the map vacant. Tourists, for example, were attracted to blank spaces that spoke of an uncharted romantic past rather than a known present. After the turn of the century, as railroad companies came to depend financially more on the business of travelers than of land purchasers, they aimed part of their promotional efforts at the tourist market. The version of the Inland Empire that they presented, as a place of the past where one could see traces of pioneer life, ran counter to the regional self-image. While the Spokane promotional literature celebrated the natural beauty of the region, its technological mastery, and its promise for the future, the railroad brochures emphasized virgin lands and sparse settlements.[65]

The Spokane Chamber of Commerce did recognize the need to appeal to a tourist audience. But even in the pamphlets geared for the new automobile tourist, it presented only a slightly revised regional definition. Still based on "the diversity of resources surrounding Spokane," the future of the region was part of "the new era in the west." Spokane was the "modern, substantially built, wide awake city." As in 1876, the vision was still more dependent on imagination than on reality and relied on future tenses. "You will see in the farming regions unmistakable signs of a new order of things, in which the great land barons are giving way before the onslaughts of intensive and diversified farming," one pamphlet noted in 1915, "and you cannot help but sense the coming of a great new era of manufacturing." Spokane now preferred to be known as "The Power City" of the Inland Empire.[66]

SEEING SPOKANE

A Tale of a Modern City Looking through their own lenses, railroad visitors to Spokane focus on the falls in another of the city's Chamber of Commerce efforts to attract Lewis and Clark Exposition tourists. This drawing graced the back cover of a promotional pamphlet titled *A Tale of a Modern City: Spokane.* By permission of Spokane Public Library

A preponderance of residents within this extensive area centered on Spokane believed in the concept of the Inland Empire and, although they sometimes differed in how they defined that concept, they acted according to beliefs in their united future. They shared a sense of self grounded in place, imbued by the environment of the Inland Empire as a physical place and a mental landscape. Yet as the changes in the regional promotional literature suggest, indigenous definitions lost credence outside and, to some extent, inside the region after the turn of the century. Tourists and outsiders presented a version of the Inland Empire that came to dominate the larger discourse.

The Law of Progress

One of these tourists was Elizabeth Bacon Custer. The widow of Colonel George Armstrong Custer came to the Inland Empire in 1890, staying as a guest at Fort Sherman. It was her first trip west in fourteen years, since the death of her husband at Little Big Horn. Now, having just finished her third book, which defended her husband's honor and recounted her experience of military life, she decided it was time to return. In July she arrived at the military fort near the city of Coeur d'Alene. From her north-ern Idaho base, she traveled about the region, gathering materials for her writings and visiting friends.[67]

For Elizabeth Custer the region was an "Out-of-the-Way" place, as she described it in an 1891 *Harper's Weekly* article, to be praised for its isola-tion and scenic beauty. The tourist Custer eagerly sought "wild places" and "wonderlands," and she saw both on an excursion to the northern reaches of the Inland Empire. She also looked for signs of the past—remnants that told her story of the triumph of white civilization over "wilderness" and "savages." Visiting the old mission near Kettle Falls, she noted, "My heart was full of the devotion and self-sacrifice of the early missionaries . . . and I walked reverently around through the old burying ground." But a disap-pointed Custer also found intrusive signs of the future. As she left the evocative cemetery and looked back at its entrance, she explained, "All that is belligerent in me rose to the surface, for across the front was the advertisement of a real estate firm. I had heard corner lots talked of so much in the 'booming' towns that I felt myself almost turning into one, but here, where the railroad had just penetrated, it seemed too much for one to endure calmly who loved these wild places."[68] Real estate speculation and advertising detracted from her tourist experience not only because they represented attempts to control land and ideas but also because their exaggerations pointed to the artificiality of "wonderlands" and unsettled her conception of "wild places."

Custer traveled northward on the recently built Spokane Falls and Northern Railroad line. The creation of the Spokane entrepreneur D. C. Corbin, the railroad promoted the region through which it ran in a different language than that of its famous passenger. Its promotional literature did include idyllic passages on scenery and romantic descriptions of the area's history. But it did not dwell on the imaginary past; the bulk of the commen-tary dealt with the imaginary future and the inevitable transformation of "a sort of semi-civilized state of society." "The law of progress is inexorable," explained the authors of *An Open Door*. For the farsighted promoters, even signs of the past were transformed into signs of the future; the old mission, which served as a romantic marker for Custer, "has lost its romantic qual-ity," they claimed, and now "remains as an educator of the young."[69]

In the journal Custer kept during her summer visit to the Inland Empire, she recorded other stories and traveling experiences that focused on the past. She celebrated moments when "the world" seemed "so far away." Her personal writings also told tales of colorful characters—the survivors of the Nez Perce War, an alcoholic Civil War veteran, or the soldiers stationed at Fort Sherman.[70] But the colorful character she decided to include in her *Harper's* article was Ranald MacDonald, the "half-breed" son of the Hud-son Bay Company's chief factor Archibald McDonald. Described as a jolly and eccentric host, Custer's MacDonald was a "quaint old man" who spoke in ludicrous language; his everyday talk included "the introduction, in the very midst of his most lofty flights of rhetoric, of slang phrases, which seemed all the more absurd, associated as they were with the stately language of by-gone days." For Custer, MacDonald was a curiosity, an exotic mixture, like his language, of the past and the contemporary West. She longed to acquire him as a souvenir of her trip, to take him east where she knew people who would "enjoy this witty, dramatic, and versatile man."[71]

Local residents, in particular Ranald MacDonald, objected to being rendered as a part of a nostalgic past. An editorial in the *Kettle Falls Pioneer* complained of inaccuracies, and, in a separate letter, MacDonald responded to Custer's article. He rejected her characterization of him as a "prince of paupers." Although, he admitted, he may have been "rather carelessly garbed, and had moccasins on my feet," MacDonald considered himself a man of substance firmly rooted in "my native homeland of the Columbia."[72]

Like Elizabeth Custer, Ranald MacDonald was engaged in the process of writing about his travels and life. Raised in the Pacific Northwest fur trade world and sent by his father to be educated in Ontario, MacDonald ran away to sea and traveled throughout Asia, his "Orient," as a young man. Enchanted by tales of Japan, he determined to find a way into the island nation that was closed to outsiders. In 1848 he deliberately capsized a small boat off the coast and spent most of the next year in Japan, mainly in prison, where he taught English to government interpreters. Following his release, MacDonald continued his adventures, mining in Australia, sailing around the Cape of Good Hope, and traveling through Europe. During the 1850s he returned to British Columbia and Washington, where he engaged in mining and ranching for the rest of his life.

He was writing about his adventures in Japan when Custer came to call. He knew something of the difficulties entailed in communicating with, and writing about, people quite different from himself. Although he viewed the Japanese from the perspective of an outsider, he considered them "fellow men" and endeavored to explain their customs and beliefs. Such consideration, he felt, had not been extended by his fellow writer, Elizabeth Custer. MacDonald collaborated with other writers; Judge Malcolm MacLeod reworked his manuscript for potential publication. As MacLeod explained his contribution: "I have improved on it; not by changing the style—for that is inseparable from the heart & mind in the expression of the truth within them—but in giving sharper point, and keener polish (with no less fervor however) to the story & its argument."[73]

MacDonald was never able to find a publisher for his memoirs before his death in 1894. Other authors continued to appropriate his story. Eva Emery Dye, author of a series of semifictionalized books about early Pacific

Northwest history, published *MacDonald of Oregon* in 1906. In Dye's account, MacDonald is "a hero of the vanguard" of "the migration of pioneer Americans to the Pacific coast." Although her portrayal was more sympathetic than Custer's, MacDonald remained a fictionalized figure.[74]

Clearly, not everyone's future was tied to the Inland Empire; not everyone perceived the boundaries of the region in the same way. Walter Van Arsdale, who lived in regional cities such as Spokane, Washington, and Fort Steele, British Columbia, tried in vain to induce his friend Charles Freeman to leave Tacoma for the Inland Empire. When Freeman finally did leave the coast in 1909, he headed for Denver: "I think British Columbia is alright and has a great future," he wrote to his friend, "but after all a man is getting a long ways from anywhere else when he gets there."[75]

By the first two decades of the twentieth century more and more people had come to share Freeman's beliefs. Even those individuals who remained within the Inland Empire faced a choice of lenses through which to view their regional identity. Outside forces shaped the region's destiny more powerfully than ever before. And outside observers, like Elizabeth Custer, presented an alternative way of perceiving this Pacific Northwest region. Today from the highway edging Moyie Lake you can see the weathered boards and slag heaps that mark abandoned turn-of-the-century mining shafts. There are ghost towns throughout the Kootenays, where old mining shacks and rusted railroad tracks mark the changing economic conditions. But more important than these ghost towns is the even more invisible ghost region to which they once belonged.

CHAPTER 5

OUTSIDERS IN THE PALOUSE

By the turn of the century, the Inland Empire, as a term and a concept, pervaded the region. The words adorned associations, railroads, maps, letterheads, and businesses; they appeared in private as well as public correspondence, newspapers, promotional pamphlets, and scientific studies. They marked a set of ideas, developed over time through negotiations among residents and others who invested their future in this particular place. The ongoing conflicts over the meaning of the term continued within the region and also extended beyond its boundaries. Residents engaged in constant negotiations with other sets of ideas, some of which altered their sense of the region, others which did not.

Regional identity did not develop in a vacuum. Despite the implied conceit, the Inland Empire, like other regions, was not an isolated unit. It existed within other perceptual categories, material realities, and time, whether as part of a nation, economic system, or geographical entity. Throughout this book, national and international trends, events, and actors have been kept at the periphery so as to examine indigenous perspectives and the subtleties of regional creation. To examine the ways national and international political and economic transformations affected mental constructs, this chapter pays close attention to the residents of one of the "tributary" areas within the region—the Palouse Country. It focuses on the farmers and ranchers who lived in this area, especially those who had succeeded in attaining a large economic, political, and personal stake and land base.[1] In particular, it looks at their encounters with influential outsiders who journeyed to the Inland Empire during the early twentieth century. James J. Hill, Harry Tracy, Brooks Adams, and Zane Grey each

THE INLAND EMPIRE

THE GREAT SEAL OF THE STATE OF WASHINGTON

of the North West

Where Fortune Beckons to the Farmer and Investor

Inland empire of the Northwest As the cover of this promotional pamphlet suggests, wheat farming was closely linked to the image of the Inland Empire. By permission of Cheney Cowles Museum/Eastern Washington State Historical Society, Spokane, Washington.

interacted with eastern Washington and northern Idaho farmers during their visits to the area. They also engaged in the perceptual formation of the Inland Empire as they brought their own ideas to these meetings and contributed to the larger public perceptions of the region. As representatives of particular economic, cultural, intellectual, and political national trends, these four individuals suggest the larger forces influencing regional perspectives. Their encounters with the farmers outline some of the emerging alternative visions that came to dominate public perceptions of this Pacific Northwest area. In some ways, their visions of the region were shared by the farmers they encountered during their visits. Yet in important ways these visitors defined the region differently. Hill, for example, saw the significance of external economic and cultural changes that those within the region failed to recognize. From an outsider's perspective, the Inland Empire farmers may have seemed like deluded rubes pursuing a hopeless dream, but the concept of a regional empire retained its power on a local level. The Inland Empire residents did not easily relinquish their claims to special status.

James J. Hill, Empire Builder

When the railroad capitalist James J. Hill spoke of "the imperial area of the American Northwest," he referred to a much larger area than that encompassing the Inland Empire. His Northwest Empire included all the states north of Missouri and west of Indiana—not coincidentally all the states through which his railroads ran. As "a great opportunity and a precious possession," this region constituted "one of the largest, most compact and most productive resources of the whole human race." In his story of the area's glorious recent history Hill was not shy in claiming credit. "The single influence that has contributed most" to the "astonishing" transformation of "a wilderness in half of a century into the home of plenty," he proudly asserted, "is, of course, the rise and scientific development of the modern transportation system."[2]

Canadian-born James Jerome Hill established his credentials as an independent entrepreneur in St. Paul, Minnesota. His vision of empire stretched from that city westward to "the Orient." Railroads and transportation lines were the essential linchpins of Hill's economic empire. From his development of the St. Paul and Pacific Railroad during the 1870s to the completion of the Great Northern Railway's transcontinental line in 1893 to the control of the Northern Pacific Railroad through the establishment of the Northern Securities Company in 1901, the self-proclaimed empire builder worked to create an interlocking system run on the principle of balanced expansion. Lacking the massive land grants that other transcontinental railroad companies received from the federal government to finance the construction of their lines, Hill relied on profits from the developing regions through which his lines passed. He promoted settlement and agricultural development to that end. In Washington and Idaho, for example, he worked to foster his vision of a productive and profitable territory by sponsoring agricultural demonstration trains and investing in irrigation projects. He succinctly outlined his business plan for the Great Northern in an 1891 letter: "I am more than ever convinced of the soundness of our policy of creating a good railroad with which to earn money, by developing in the best form, all the local interests along our lines. To do this successfully, we must be able to handle the natural products of the country at rates that will enable those handling or manufacturing those products, to do so with a profit. Our greatest profit will come in the enlargement of the business interests hereafter." In Hill's vision, the Inland Empire was only one piece in the jigsaw puzzle of territory and industries that he worked to control.[3]

For Hill, the Pacific Northwest was also the site of intense competition among railroads over territory. Four railway giants, the Canadian Pacific, Northern Pacific, Union Pacific, and Great Northern, battled within the region over routes and rates and outside the region in court, in Congress, and in the stock market. Key lines, such as those run by the Oregon Railway and Navigation Company, frequently changed hands in the high-stakes games of the robber barons. For example, the terms of business competition dictated Hill's acquisition of D. C. Corbin's Spokane Falls and Northern Railroad, the line Elizabeth Custer traveled in 1890. Purchased for a high price from the Northern Pacific in 1900, the Spokane–British Columbia line, Hill explained, "cost more than it is worth except for territorial reasons, and from that stand-point it is cheap enough."[4]

In some ways Hill's empire and the Inland Empire coincided. Both relied on their "mastery of natural conditions." But whereas the Inland Empire residents anticipated continued growth and prosperity, Hill cautioned against the "old order" in which everyone benefited from growth. In Hill's view of the future, the problem of the Northwest, indeed the problem of the nation, was to create new methods to deal with ever-increasing limits imposed by diminishing resources.[5]

The Inland Empire settlers embraced the railroads as signs of their participation in the economic mainstream and as an affirmation of their central role in the nation's future. During times of financial hardships, however, the railroads came to symbolize the various external economic forces that prevented the farmers and others from making profits on their products. Complaints about discriminatory freight rates, particularly those that benefited the coastal cities rather than the interior, were frequently heard.[6]

In the face of these complaints and potential threats to his profits, Hill strove to present himself as a friend and ally of the farmer. In some cases he succeeded in convincing the Northwest farmers in the Inland Empire's Palouse and Big Bend of his benevolence. One destitute Yakima farmer, John Walker, wrote to Hill directly requesting aid: "I am very anxious to hold a short conversation with you but that is not likely to be. With your kind approval and consideration we will have a short and special correspondence." The fifty-two-year-old father of six sought Hill's intercession in a land case involving Walker's farm that was currently under consideration by the secretary of the interior. "Your every act is one of extension and grandeur as a R.R. King," Walker wrote.[7] Whether Hill interceded on Walker's behalf is unclear, but Hill was given credit for responding to other requests by Inland Empire farmers. In July 1902, a group of Whitman County farmers sent telegrams to Hill; A. L. Mohler, president of the Oregon Railway and Navigation Company; and Charles Mellen, president of the Northern Pacific Railroad, inviting them to attend a summit conference in eastern Washington: "At a meeting of the farmers and producers of the Palouse country . . . it was unanimously agreed that you be invited to meet us at Colfax at a date most convenient to you to confer on matters of common interest to the railroads and the people and to see if our mutual interests could not be subserved by a reduction of freight rates." The three railroad kings accepted the invitation and came to the Inland Empire in August.[8]

The meeting of the railroad presidents, three "captains of industry," with the local farmers of eastern Washington was an "occasion unique in the history of American railroading," reported the *Spokesman-Review*. A crowd of more than six hundred met the visitors in Davenport on August 5. At "an old fashioned country dinner" Hill "rubbed elbows with a wheat grower from the Egypt country and a miner from the Cedar canyon camp." A thousand farmers gathered in Colfax the next day to attend the speeches and meetings. The impressive turnout, especially remarkable at the height of harvest season, included farmers and businessmen from throughout the region. The Colfax conference, though, was delayed in starting. All the principals were present, but, because of a change in plans, all the newspaper reporters had been left behind in Spokane. Hence "it was agreed to postpone the opening of the meeting until the arrival of the passenger train from Spokane at 11:05." Reporters were important, as we shall see.

The meeting's chairman, R. L. McCrosky of Garfield, opened the "frank and friendly conference" with the hope that the parties involved would "take the freight rate question out of politics." In his speech Hill also emphasized mutual interests: "Nothing can injure you without injuring us," he told the crowd in the suffocating heat of the courtroom, "nothing can benefit you without benefiting the railroads." As in his earlier speech at Davenport, Hill praised "the cornerstone of this country, the sheet anchor

of the nation . . . the farmer, the man who cultivates the soil." The an-
nouncement that made the next day's headlines, however, was the agreement that grain shipping rates would be reduced 10 percent from all points
in eastern Washington. In addition, a new crossroad would be built to
connect a branch of the Northern Pacific to the Great Northern. According
to the enthusiastic press accounts, "It doesn't need a philosopher to tell
the people of the State that such meetings between the railway presidents
and the farmers of Washington have borne more non-political fruit than all
the efforts which have been made in other directions could produce in an
hundred years!"[9]

Exclamation points aside, the 1902 "Hill-Mellen-Mohler-Farmers" summit can be interpreted in another way. Although contemporary newspapers
and public records presented the meetings as a response to the farmers'
petition, the conferences were actually instigated by the railroad companies. The meetings were not "conferences at which anybody" could "have
an opportunity to present his view" but staged events orchestrated for
public relations purposes. The impetus behind Hill's meeting with the Inland Empire farmers was a notice from the Interstate Commerce Commission (ICC) that the Great Northern's favorable lumber rates for timbered
regions discriminated against other Washington freight and localities. As
Hill noted in a private letter of May 1902, "At the present time there is
apparently a feeling of hostility to Railway Companies generally in Washington." In an attempt to stave off interference from the federal government, Hill decided to appease the wheat farmers directly.[10]

Despite the fanfare and hyperbole, the results of the meetings fell short
of local expectations. The 10 percent rate reduction was considerably less
than the Whitman County farmers sought, and the promised connecting
line benefited James J. Hill perhaps more than the local farmers. As a
result of the merger of the Northern Pacific and the Great Northern—companies represented at the summit as separate entities—Hill was looking
to consolidate and rationalize the maze of railroad tracks now under one
corporate control. Connecting the "orphan" Northern Pacific line, which
reached out and ended in the midst of the Big Bend, with the Great Northern line that ran all the way to the coast, enabled the newly merged railroads to save shipping costs from that area. The farmers who had
anticipated the further extension of the Northern Pacific line on through
the Big Bend faced the realization that they were part of a side loop, not on
the main track.[11]

Searching for Harry Tracy

The proposed meetings of the Inland Empire farmers and the empire
builder James J. Hill were widely covered by the regional newspapers in

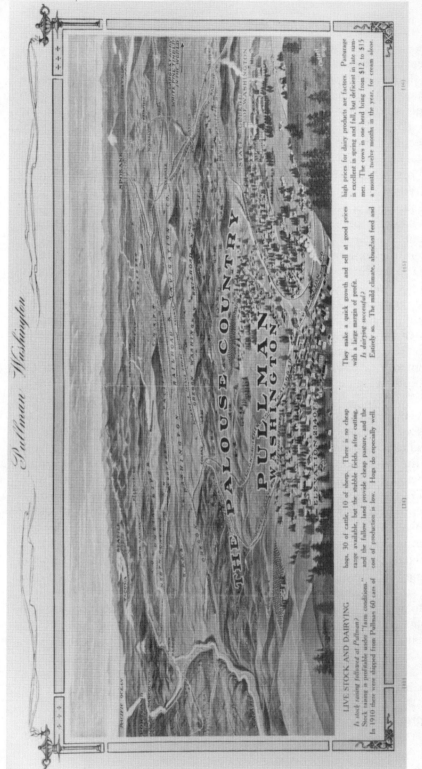

Palouse Country From the regional perspective of the promoters of Pullman, Washington, Spokane and Seattle are on the periphery. The Great Northern Railway stretches west of Spokane toward Wenatchee. Compare this "Palouse Country" map to the "Spokane Country" map that appears earlier in the book. From the F. M. Slagle Papers (Cage 4236), Washington State University Libraries, Pullman, Washington.

July and August 1902. But the summit shared headlines with another story. The ongoing saga of Harry Tracy, escaped convict, gripped local newspaper readers. In June, Tracy—convicted of murder and suspected of numerous bank robberies, holdups, and house break-ins—had escaped with his partner from the Salem, Oregon, penitentiary, killing three guards in the process. Rumors of their escapades and reports of sightings filled newspaper columns throughout the summer. On August 6, the day of the Colfax meeting, a posse in Lincoln County, Washington, cornered Tracy at the Eddys' ranch. Wounded in the ensuing shoot-out, Tracy, refusing to face recapture, shot himself in the head.

Regardless of Tracy's intentions for his escape into eastern Washington, the ways his actions were interpreted by regional newspapers are revealing. The newspapers continued to cover the Tracy case after his suicide, reporting on interviews with every conceivable "expert," including a courthouse janitor. Among those interviewed was the Northwest superintendent for the Pinkerton Detective Agency stationed in Portland. Captain James Nevins declared Tracy insane: "On no other theory can be explained the needless risks he took." "I am greatly interested," he said from his Spokane hotel room, "in hearing the report of the physicians who examined Tracy's brain." Proof of the escaped convict's insanity, Nevins explained, was his decision to leave the timbered country of western Washington and to venture into the empty, open spaces of the Inland Empire. Equally foolhardy was the young outlaw's insistence on "proclaiming his identity"; Tracy had the habit of announcing his name to his victims whenever he committed a crime.[12]

The Tracy story captured the national imagination. Throughout the nation, newspapers followed the trail of the western "desperado" into the barren lands of eastern Washington. Accounts of the Harry Tracy saga not only proliferated in national newspapers but also appeared as sensationalized popular fiction with elaborate titles such as *Harry Tracy, the Desperate Western Outlaw: A Fascinating Account of the Famous Bandit's Stupendous Adventures and Daring Deeds*. In these tellings, eastern Washington entered onto a national stage but not in a manner that entirely pleased the residents of the region.[13]

The juxtaposition of stories in the local press suggests that these two incidents—the escapades of the escaped convict and those of the farmers —shared a particular meaning for readers. Tracy and the farmers, both of whom found refuge in the arid lands of eastern Washington, worked for similar ends. The elusive Tracy was portrayed as an individualist who foiled the designs of powerful institutional machinery, a man who refused to surrender his freedom. Likewise, the farmers perceived themselves as individualists fighting to retain control over their region as they attempted to communicate on a personal basis with the railroad presidents. Both stories

fit easily into the larger discourse that celebrated western values of freedom, adventure, and personal control.

Outsiders, however, read these stories differently. By the standards that
Captain Nevins used to measure Tracy's mental competency, the Inland
Empire farmers were also a little insane, at least in the way they interpreted
the railroad meetings. Though the summit was clearly staged, the farmers
took the opportunity to air their views seriously. After the meetings were
over, they expressed their disappointment about the outcome, though
those complaints did not make the headlines. Their insistence on proclaiming their identity, in asserting their interests despite obvious disad-
vantages of power and influence, may seem absurd. Certainly outside
observers found it difficult to understand why the farmers insisted on perceiving themselves as equal partners. "A curious and unexpected result of
the farmers' meetings in Eastern Washington," wrote an amazed Thomas
Burke to Hill, "is that the thrifty and more prosperous among them are
talking seriously of putting their surplus in the stock of the Northern Securities Co. and thus becoming partners of yours in the railroad in real
earnest."[14]

Dissecting the brains, examining the ideas of Inland Empire residents to
gain insight into their dogged adherence to a mental territory reveals the
internal logic by which they ran their lives. In their perceptions of themselves as the center of a future-oriented region, the farmers, like others
who adhered to the regional vision, may have been myopic, but they were
not insane. What they did not see or recognize were the extraregional economic and cultural changes that placed them and their region off the main
track. In the coming years they became increasingly frustrated by their
inability to control their destiny.

The freight rates, for example, continued to be a bone of contention between the railroads and Inland Empire shippers and farmers. Beginning in
1887, Spokane and Inland Empire interests had sought redress for their
exorbitant railroad freight rates from the state legislature and railroad
commission, from the courts, from Congress, from the Interstate Commerce Commission, and, as the 1902 conferences suggest, from the railroads themselves.[15] The main complaint, as articulated in 1889 by
Spokane's Merchants' Protective Association in its case to the ICC, was
against the railroads' practice of charging higher rates for interior locations
than for the coastal region, whose cities paid lower "terminal rates." Farmers in Ritzville, Washington, for example, had to pay the "excessive, unjust
and unreasonable" rate of 32.5 cents per hundred pounds of wheat
shipped on Northern Pacific Railroad lines to Portland, instead of a 16.25-
cent rate.[16] The situation of Spokane and other interior western locales
came persistently in front of the Interstate Commerce Commission, but
even a favorable 1892 decision did not resolve the problem. Its implementa-

tion was stymied by the unsettled question of whether the commission had the power to set rates; during the 1890s the Supreme Court and Congress held that it did not. After the turn of the century, however, when the issue of railroad monopoly power was on the national agenda, the question resurfaced. As U.S. congressional attention focused on the matter, westerners sought to be heard. This time the Spokane Chamber of Commerce turned to a high-profile lawyer/historian to argue its case. In 1905, Brooks Adams, then a lecturer at the Boston University School of Law, testified on Spokane's behalf in front of the Senate Committee on Interstate Commerce.[17]

Grandson and great-grandson of two U.S. presidents and a friend of the incumbent president Theodore Roosevelt, Brooks Adams brought political connections and a national profile to the region's case. He also, one might assume, brought some understanding of the Inland Empire. Adams, who had visited Spokane periodically, held an economic interest in the region; the Adams family trust included Spokane real estate holdings, purchased by his older brothers. His brother Charles Francis Adams Jr. had long been involved in railroad development in the region, not only through his investments but also during his 1880s presidency of the Union Pacific.[18]

Brooks Adams took on the Inland Empire complaints, without fees, because they coincided with his own personal interests—political and intellectual, as well as economic. Like James J. Hill, he, too, saw the world through imperial glasses. For Adams, the United States was the "New Empire," which had achieved its supremacy through control of economic exchanges. But it was a success that followed the "law of civilization and decay," as he had outlined in his historical writings.[19] In his pessimistic view of America's future, the machinations of capitalists, such as Hill, when unregulated by the government and unresponsive to, or responsible for, the public, would lead to the collapse of social institutions. In the Spokane struggle, Adams saw his chance to combat the "greedy despot" who had "ignored public responsibilities." Traveling to Spokane for hearings and meetings with a local attorney, H. M. Stephens, and testifying in Portland and Washington, D.C., he connected the local complaints to his interpretation of the nation's ills.[20]

In many ways, Adams helped propel the region, albeit briefly, into the national political and economic discourse. In private correspondence and public addresses, he likened the Spokane case to the great antimonopoly campaigns of the day against United States Steel and Standard Oil. Along with other Progressives of his class, Adams argued against the "logic of capital" that had governed relations between railroads and western farmers and encouraged the president to expand the ICC's powers to control the industry.[21] When Congress finally passed the Hepburn Act in 1906, which allowed the Interstate Commerce Commission to fix rates, Adams assisted Spokane in filing the first complaint. Then, drawing on his political connections, he successfully lobbied President Roosevelt to aid his efforts with the ICC.[22]

As a national advocate for the Inland Empire, Adams echoed the concerns of the region's farmers and businessmen. In words similar to those of regional boosters, he described Spokane in his arguments as "the natural capital of the interior Northwest." One of the key issues, as Adams described it, was "sovereignty." Who held the rights to define the boundaries of the region? Was it the railroads or the "citizens of Spokane"? The railroads had "arbitrarily" divided the areas through which their lines passed into "zones" and determined their rates according to these zones. The existing zones did not recognize the Inland Empire, cutting through the region and thereby limiting Spokane's economic influence over its "natural" and "tributary" region. In its complaint to the ICC, Spokane asked for the "rights of American citizenship" to define itself and its region. The ICC drew on his language in its 1911 ruling in favor of the Inland Empire, agreeing with the region's imperial designs: "Spokane is a great distributing center and aims to be a greater one." This rhetoric trickled into contemporary writings on the railroad issue. As one writer explained, the city "although on the western slope, is not simply a town of the Pacific interior, as that designation ordinarily indicates. The surrounding country throughout a vast area is of such fertility that it is known as the Inland Empire." But this definition of the region was not the one that persisted.[23]

The residents' efforts to bring attention to the Inland Empire had succeeded; it became, however, an ironic success. Despite the series of state and national rulings against the railroads especially after 1909, Inland Empire shippers were never able to recover their losses.[24] Viewing the situation in that year, Charles E. Russell placed the blame for the region's failure to reach its potential on the "extortionist" railroad rates: "Because of these rates Spokane did not fulfill its obvious destiny, it did not become a great metropolis, the Spokane country did not become populous, the almost unexampled resources were not developed, the region capable of supporting many millions had a population of three hundred thousand."[25] This narrative of failed promise dominated outsiders' interpretations of the Inland Empire as other writers and observers defined the region as a railroad hinterland rather than an empire. Even those sympathetic to the farmers' and shippers' concerns contributed to the region's identification with loss. Frank Parsons, for example, who analyzed "the heart of the railroad problem," in his book of that name, singled out Spokane and the interior Northwest's case as "a specially aggravated one."[26] In his elaborate writings and vivid testimony, the often eccentric Adams too fostered the portrayal of a region of deluded farmers. In his words, "the good people of Spokane" had been "buncoed" by the railroad companies, particularly by "confidence man" James J. Hill.[27]

Wherever one placed the blame, the Spokane country once boosted as the Inland Empire, the region of the future, was now defined by its failure to achieve its early promise. From the perspective of the twentieth century, it became increasingly difficult to project a future empire solely based on natural resources, regardless of their diversity or quantity. As James J. Hill accurately observed, the recognition of environmental limits shaped the way Americans perceived places after the turn of the century. It was also increasingly difficult to define eastern Washington, northern Idaho, and southeastern British Columbia as a potential economic or cultural center. In the industrial transformation of the nation, as the powers of the state and of business expanded, local and regional centers became subservient to national and international centers of commerce and politics. The residents of the Inland Empire based their expectations on and assessed their region's value according to a worldview that was no longer shared by those outside its borders.

The Desert of Wheat

Fifteen years after the railroad summit and the Tracy suicide, the wheat farmers of the Inland Empire played host to another well-known visitor. Zane Grey, in search of material for his next best-selling western novel, spent part of the summer of 1918 living in the Palouse. He and his wife, Dolly, stayed for a few weeks at the Hooper Hotel, operated by the MacGregors, a successful and powerful Whitman County ranching family. The experience and information Grey gathered served as the basis for his 1919 novel, *The Desert of Wheat*.[28]

Grey's vision of the region, as the novel portrays it, was of "a lovely, hard, heroic country," the ideal setting for the mythic confrontations of his characters. Although the Columbia Plateau, his desert of wheat, is not officially a desert—it is classified as semiarid—Grey found a sublime beauty in the dry fields and scablands. In it he also found an avenue into the human psyche. He explained the lure of the desert a few years later: "Men love the forbidding and desolate desert because of the ineradicable and unconscious wildness of savage nature in them."[29]

Set in this epic landscape, Grey's novel tells the story of young Kurt Dorn, who must confront the ineradicable and unconscious wildness of his German heritage in World War I America. The outward manifestations of Dorn's inner turmoil include conflicts with his immigrant father, who refuses to reject their native land, and encounters with spies and saboteurs belonging to the Industrial Workers of the World. Grey portrays the "riffraff gang of tramp labor-agitators" as a recent threat to the Dorns and other wheat farmers: "In preceding years a crowd of I.W.W. men had been nothing to worry a rancher." Now IWW agitators corrupted the labor force and set fire to fields of wheat in order to aid the German war effort. Dorn's father dies fighting one blaze; the entire harvest is destroyed in another. Like James J. Hill's view, Grey's portrayal of the Inland Empire was part of his own personal vision. But as a novelist concerned with realism, Grey consciously attempted to reflect the ideas and attitudes of his time. His novel incorporates the perspectives and uses the words of the farmers with whom he spoke and the regional newspapers he read during his summer visit. He quoted local newspaper editorials directly in his novel, putting the words into the mouths of his characters. From a *Spokesman-Review* report on a board of county commissioners' meeting, Grey excerpted the extensive statement of a northern Idaho logging operator about the work of "an organization which calls itself the Industrial Workers of the World." An editorial titled "Suppressing the I.W.W." appears in *Desert of Wheat* as the comments of "Beardsley, a prominent and intelligent rancher of the southern wheat-belt."[30]

Grey incorporated other regionally produced words, ideas, and meanings into his anti-IWW novel. One of his central metaphors—identifying the IWW as a disease that needed to be eradicated—was familiar to a national audience; the World War I–era rhetoric against external and internal enemies frequently relied on such analogies. But Grey gave this metaphor a local twist by specifying the disease used in the comparison. Incorporating regional rhetoric into his novel, Grey presented the Wobblies as "smut."

The term referred to an agricultural disease—a parasitic fungus that grows in clusters on wheat plants. Inland Empire farmers had recently noted an unexplained increase in smut-infected crops; the Anti-Smut Club of the Inland Empire united regional farmers interested in combating the problem. In Pullman, Washington, local agricultural extension agents conducted experiments on ways to control the infections. The new farming technology, the agents discovered, had helped spread the disease because threshers broke up the clusters or balls, releasing "millions of minute bodies, the spores or 'seeds' of the smut fungus." The seemingly innocuous dust, emanating from the mechanical separators during threshing operations, contained the virulent spores, which were scattered and spread by the wind. Grey relied on a report by two agents of the Washington State Agricultural Experimental Station, F. D. Heald and H. M. Woolman, "Bunt or Stinking Smut of Wheat," for the language in his novel.[31]

The IWW, or Wobblies, as they were known, had been organizing the migrant laborers in the Pacific Northwest since the radical union's establishment in 1905. Much of the activity took place in Spokane, where the migrant laborers of the forest, fields, and mines gathered in their off-seasons. Seasonal farm workers, hired during harvest especially as the use of machinery expanded, joined the union seeking higher wages and better working conditions. Local strikes for a three-dollar daily wage proved un-

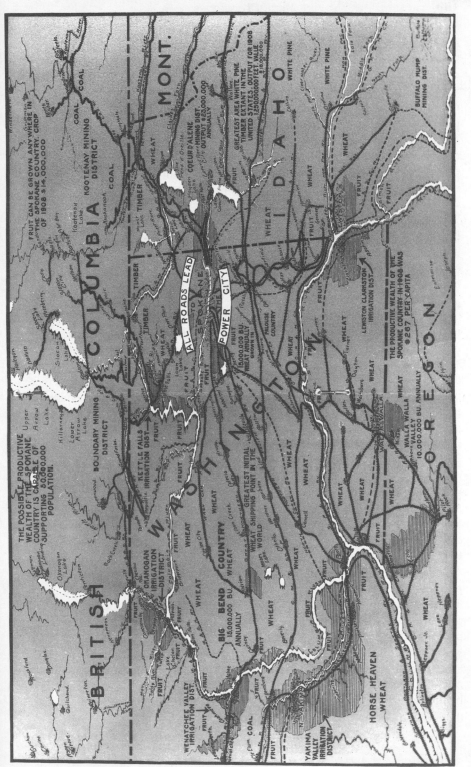

Map of Eastern Washington and Northern Idaho The farming and ranching country of the Palouse, Big Bend, and Yakima overshadow the mining districts in this 1904 Spokane Chamber of Commerce map of its region. Broken lines, indicating proposed railroad routes, crisscross the wheat lands. By permission of Cheney Cowles Museum/Eastern Washington State Historical Society, Spokane, Washington.

successful. Union activities were more successful in the region's lumber industry. In June 1917 workers in northern Idaho lumber mills and logging camps joined the general Northwest strike that tied up the industry throughout the summer. Distrust and antagonism characterized the relationship between the farmers and the union. Many farmers, for example, placed the blame for fires or unexplained machinery troubles on union agitators. Field fires, always a dreaded occurrence, had indeed become more common when farmers changed their harvesting procedures. At the time, few realized that sparks from machinery ignited grain dust and that static electricity led to what became known as smut explosions.

In *Desert of Wheat*, Grey employed the language and ideas of eastern Washington and northern Idaho farm operators. Like smut, he asserted, the IWW organizers spread throughout eastern Washington during the harvest, and their ideas infected other migrant workers. The only ways to eradicate the problem, according to Grey's analogy, were to prevent smut-infected seeds and crops from spreading any farther in the region and to poison existing smut and spores. Taking direct excerpts from the scientific study on wheat disease, Grey edited the scientific article in specific ways to highlight the implied parallels with the Wobbly menace; he removed, for example, references to the farmers' responsibility for the infections.[32]

The ongoing antagonism between farmers and union organizers received official sanction during World War I when the federal government, during a period of wartime hysteria, arrested IWW leaders on sedition charges. States passed criminal syndicalism laws aimed at the IWW, making it "illegal to advocate crime, sabotage, and violent methods of terrorism as a means of accomplishing industrial or political reform." Many Inland Empire farmers, including R. L. McCrosky, who had facilitated the 1902 railroad meetings, joined patriotic leagues and protective associations and used both vigilante and legal methods to eradicate the perceived menace. As McCrosky explained in 1918: "I tell you people the danger is grave. . . . More than $2,000,000,000 worth of property has been destroyed by these outlaws who sympathize with the Kaiser." The nine hundred members of Idaho's Latah County Protective Association agreed "to assist the sheriff . . . in protecting labor against the encroachments and interference of unpatriotic and alien influences" and supported his July 1917 roundup and incarceration in the Moscow fairgrounds of "all of the hotheads . . . and undesirables scattered over the agricultural section of the county" who belonged to the IWW.[33]

Throughout 1917, 1918, and 1919, similar officially sanctioned and vigilante roundups, reminiscent of the incarcerations of striking Coeur d'Alene miners, occurred throughout the Inland Empire. From Spokane's IWW headquarters, the district secretary, James Rowan, identified in local papers as the Wobblies' "leading spirit in the Inland Empire," called for a general strike in the harvest fields for August 20, 1917. On that day, a National Guard company from Fort George Wright raided the IWW headquarters, shut down the hall, "captured" Rowan and twenty-six others, and placed them as "military prisoners" in the county jail. The *Spokesman-Review* applauded the arrest of the "ring leaders of the conspiracy to paralyze agricultural and other production" as a patriotic duty. Other reform-minded organization members, such as Non-Partisan League organizers and unionists, faced similar suspicions, arrests, and abridgments of civil liberties. Spokane's Central Labor Council, which initially threw its support behind the IWW efforts, modified its stand in the face of the general hysteria. Even the state Grangers, newly led by William Bouck, found an inhospitable welcome when they gathered to meet in Walla Walla during the summer of 1918.[34]

Many eastern Washington and northern Idaho farmers believed Spokane was one of the sources of these troubles. This antagonism grew in part out of an older resentment against Spokane and its claims of regional dominance. "In our unbiased opinion," noted the Latah County Protective Association in a 1918 resolution, "the fair City of Spokane, by its sufferance of the I.W.W. to continue to preach its disloyal doctrines, is nursing a viper, which will ultimately strike, poison and paralyze even the industrial life of Spokane itself, as it has injured the farming, mining and lumbering industries of the Inland Empire, which are the life arteries through which Spokane receives such liberal sustenance." Despite their critique, the Idaho farmers, writing as a "tributary country to Spokane," identified with and accepted the parameters of their regional identity. Farmers and city residents alike perceived the threat as one against the Inland Empire. City officials, newspaper writers, and prominent businessmen who quickly responded to these accusations pointed to the city's own efforts to eradicate the IWW and aligned their interests with the farmers as members of the same threatened region. Edwin T. Coman, president of the Exchange National Bank, reported on the "embittered feeling that exists on the part of many of the very substantial citizens of this Inland Empire against Spokane by reason of this curse within our midst."[35]

During this period the requirements for membership in the Inland Empire clearly stiffened. The dramatic population increases, economic growth, and continual change that had once characterized the region eased off by the 1920s. As residents vainly sought to identify the causes of the region's stasis, they often blamed named or unnamed outside forces. Whether attributed to railroad rates, outlaws, or alien influences, the decline affected residents' self-perception, and narrower and narrower social boundaries came to define regional identity. At the same time, outsiders continued to define the region in terms of the past.

Like Zane Grey, Inland Empire residents were unable to control the way others perceived their place. Although acclaimed for his popular western fiction, Grey sought recognition as a serious American novelist. By setting *The Desert of Wheat* in the contemporary West, not the fictional western past, he attempted to engage subjects relevant to national concerns. More recent critics have recognized Grey's efforts at social criticism, but at the time of publication the novel was not well received. New York critics, for example, much preferred his earlier *Riders of the Purple Sage* and *The Heritage of the Desert,* both of which included the classic elements of the emerging western genre.[36] Inland Empire residents too sought recognition as part of the emerging West of machine-and-market-dominated natural resources, not the imagined, picturesque West of history. In the collective public mind, however, eastern Washington, northern Idaho, and south-eastern British Columbia, if they were identified at all, were considered part of a nostalgic vision of the nation's past, not a progressive picture of its future.

When outsiders such as James J. Hill, Harry Tracy, Brooks Adams, and Zane Grey visited the Inland Empire in the early twentieth century, they met residents imbued with a regional identity. Through their interactions, the meanings of that identity, especially beyond regional boundaries, un-derwent significant alterations. Residents of the region, like the Palouse farmers, as they strove for recognition, engaged in national political de-bates, participated in economic networks, and sought redress through fed-eral tribunals, contributed to the changing perceptions of the place. Seeking to understand the ways in which their visions and plans eluded full materialization, they negotiated with the world outside their mental territories. Yet their dreams of empire continued to lurk behind the specter of loss.

CONCLUSION

GHOST REGION

There was not one specific moment at which the Inland Empire came into existence, not one "turning point" at which the region appeared. Rather it was in the aggregation of people's actions and interactions that the place gained its identity. While the creation of a region, as an ongoing process, is influenced by economic, environmental, political, and social factors, it also relies on the ideas that lie behind these more visible forces. To identify the mental territory, the perceptual region known as the Inland Empire during the late nineteenth and early twentieth centuries, this book has focused on internal or indigenous texts—on the words, actions, and objects produced within self-defined regional boundaries. In this particular place and at this particular moment of time there existed a way of thinking endemic to the people who inhabited this space. Created out of internal conflicts and debates and responsive to external pressures and changes, the Inland Empire as a mental concept shaped experiences and lives.

The process of cultural change and the development of regional identity in Washington, Idaho, and British Columbia is not unique. As Marshall Sahlins notes about the South Sea world he studies, "The dynamic elements at work—including the confrontation with an external world that has its own imperious determinations and with other people who have their own parochial intentions—are present everywhere in human experience." The cultural confrontations generally studied focus on contacts between distinct national groups, for example, as part of colonial encounters. When Sahlins examines Captain James Cook's encounter with the Hawaiian islanders, he focuses on moments of contact between two distinct cultures. This dialectic approach reveals the dramatic discordances and

Market Facts about Spokane Country   The Heart of the Spokane Country, and the Pacific Northwest, in this 1927 version, blankets eastern Washington and northern Idaho. While centered on Spokane, this regional vision defines itself in relation to cities and markets outside its boundaries. By permission of Cheney Cowles Museum/Eastern Washington State Historical Society, Spokane, Washington.

misunderstandings that ensue from such meetings of peoples with opposing worldviews, with their own "cultural signatures." Similarly, studies of the American frontier as "a territory or zone of interpenetration between two previously distinct societies" analyze sharp differences between natives and "intrusive" cultures during opening encounters.[1]

The dynamic elements at work within the Inland Empire were neither so sharply drawn nor so clearly contained. The internal struggle for definition, which took place after the period of initial contact, was often a muddle of contradictory impulses. Yet in ongoing encounters among new settlers and old, reservation Indians and government agents, miners and mine owners, real estate speculators and tourists, different voices constructed a regional identity. In their uneasy transitional state as a settled frontier, the peoples of the Inland Empire developed their own subtle codes of meaning. As they engaged in the development of a particular way of thinking, they forged a mental territory.

Mental territories reveal much about regions and regionalism. Regions are about definition, setting out boundaries, and intentional markings, but they are also about often unexpected intersections, controversies, and interminglings. They are as much about the future as the past. Like the Inland Empire, the West as a whole maintains a protean regional identity while its history retains a powerful ghostly presence in the national consciousness. For those who live within its boundaries, and those who do not, the West is a landscape that holds ruins and memories with contested significances. Depending on the angle of vision, and faith, the West can be defined by its losses and ruins or by its hopes and portents. And perhaps that is the magic and the promise of place. Invisible to all but believers, the ghosts of the past flicker into view in the continuing debates and conflicts that define region and nation. One can scoff at those who speak of visions, but if we take these claims seriously we gain a better understanding of the ways in which history and memory participate in the present.[2]

Focusing attention on what transpires at a regional level, at the emergence of an "interior regionalism," suggests links to forces involved in the emergence of nationalism. Scholars who pay close attention to the power of the nation-state often define nationalism as an ideological movement and examine the practices involved in bringing competing groups into a shared consciousness of belonging. Regions, in this formulation, maintain "separate interests" that need to be reconciled with the national project. Frequently influenced by concerns drawn out of western European historical circumstances, this model of nation-region dynamics applies only partially to the United States West.[3]

The mapping of the Inland Empire took place within a more distinctive American set of historical and ideological contexts. In the "Janus-faced boundary" between insiders and outsiders, between region and nation, where conflicts defined groups and places apart from each other, new systems of meaning emerged. As late nineteenth- and early twentieth-century westerners articulated a local sense of belonging using the language of rights and citizenship, for example, they drew on a cultural narrative of nationalism. And in their struggles against certain aspects of that national narrative, especially ones that relegated their material and rhetorical position to a colonial periphery, to a touristic locale, or to a wild past, they employed a cultural narrative of regionalism. The reciprocal process in which they engaged—creating meanings at the intersection of regionalism and nationalism—mutually reinforced the construction of overlapping identities in the turn-of-the-century United States.[4]

If there was not one moment at which the Inland Empire was created, there was also not one moment at which the region-specific way of thinking ceased. In one sense, the Inland Empire has not disappeared—it persists as a region-based construct—altered and reshaped over the years. Yet in another sense, the Inland Empire never materialized; the desired control over time and place remained frustratingly elusive. Perhaps the best way to mark the gradual erosion of this particular regional identity, as understood by nineteenth-century residents, is to step outside the region, to look at the dialectic between outsiders and insiders. As Elizabeth Custer's encounter with Ranald MacDonald illustrates, visitors to the region came with different expectations and saw the area through different eyes. Never static, never totally controlled, regionalism changes through confrontations with alternative perspectives.

The insular turn-of-the-century inhabitants who created a region based on their own conceptions of the future left their marks on the land. Some of them, including Oscar Amos, Luvina Buchanan, Andrew Seltice, Charles W. Clarke, and Ranald MacDonald, left a written record. Their lingering words and ideas about this place constitute a ghost region—a region with layers of memory, history, and meaning which continue to haunt the present. Part of the legacy that they wished to leave, that is, their specific vision of the Inland Empire, has not survived intact. Their ideas remain only as ghostly images. The creation of the Inland Empire offers a vivid example of the power of perceptions. As individuals, as groups, as regions, as nations, our perceptions of place are haunted by ghost regions. The challenge for us is to materialize these ghost regions, to look into the minds of their inhabitants and to see what those minds reveal about our own.

NOTES

Abbreviations Used in Notes

Annals, AAG   *Annals of the Association of American Geographers*
EWSHS   Eastern Washington State Historical Society, Spokane
FtS   Fort Steele Provincial Heritage Park, Fort Steele, British Columbia
GAI   Glenbow-Alberta Institute, Calgary, Alberta
GPO   Government Printing Office
JJH   James J. Hill Reference Library, St. Paul, Minnesota
LCHS   Latah County Historical Society, Moscow, Idaho
PABC   B.C. Archives, Victoria British Columbia
RHM   Rossland Historical Museum, Rossland, British Columbia
UW   Special Collections, Manuscripts, and Archives, University of Washington Libraries, Seattle
WSU   Manuscripts, Archives, and Special Collections, Holland Library, Washington State University, Pullman

Introduction

1. Oscar Amos Papers, WSU. The quotes that follow are from the Amos Papers.

2. "Has Dug His Way with Pick and Shovel from Pullman to Spokane," *Pullman Herald*, August 17, 1928, p. 11. Between 1904 and 1918 Whitman County directories occasionally listed Amos as a laborer or clerk for a baker, Murray D. Henry. See *Directory of Whitman County, Washington, 1904* (Spokane: R. L. Polk, 1904) and the directories for 1910–11, 1912–13, 1915–16, and 1917–18.

3. Donald W. Meinig, "Spokane and the Inland Empire: Historical Geographic Systems and a Sense of Place," in *Spokane and the Inland Empire: An Interior Pacific Northwest Anthology*, ed. David H. Stratton (Pullman: Washington State University Press, 1991), p. 1; Ruth Feser Hale, "A Map of Vernacular Regions in America" (Ph.D. diss., University of Minnesota, 1971).

4. *Report of Committee on New State, Submitted to the Spokane Chamber of Commerce* (Spokane, [1909]), quoted in D. W. Meinig, *The Great Columbia Plain: A Historical Geography, 1805–1910* (Seattle: University of Washington Press, 1968), p. 465.

5. Northwest Homeseeker and Investor, *The Inland Empire and What it Comprehends: Together with a Sketch of the Principal Cities and Surrounding Country That Should Be Seen by Every Visitor to the Lewis and Clark Exposition at Portland* (Spokane: Hutchinson and Bronson, 1905), p. 9.

6. Ibid., pp. 9–10.

7. Ibid.; Northwest Homeseeker and Investor, *Inland Empire,* "Introduction." See Yi-Fu Tuan, *Topophilia: A Study of Environmental Perception, Attitudes, and Values* (Englewood Cliffs, N.J.: Prentice-Hall, 1974), pp. 153–60.

8. Fanny Kemble Wister, ed., *Owen Wister Out West: His Journals and Letters* (Chicago: University of Chicago Press, 1958), p. 136.

9. The information in this description is derived from John A. Alwin, *Between the Mountains: A Portrait of Eastern Washington,* Northwest Geographer Series No. 1 (Bozeman, Mont.: Northwest Panorama Publishing, 1984); Nevin M. Fenneman, *Physiography of the Western United States* (New York: McGraw-Hill, 1931), pp. 183–273; Charles B. Hunt, *Natural Regions of the United States and Canada* (San Francisco: W. H. Freeman, 1974), pp. 373–77, 409–23, 537–44, 553–71; and Meinig, *Great Columbia Plain.*

10. *Northwest Monthly Magazine* 5 (June 1892): 45. See, e.g., R. T. Stritmatter to Mamie Aldridge, September 13, 1902, R. T. Stritmatter Papers, MSS 4185, WSU; Josephine H. Dunning to Mr. & Mrs. Kenyon, May 22, 1881, C. B. Dunning Papers, MsSc 186, EWSHS; J. Z. Moore notebook, June 1907, Archives, EWSHS; James Wardner, *James Wardner of Wardner, Idaho* (New York: Anglo-American Publishing, 1910).

11. U.S. Bureau of the Census, *Ninth Census of the United States, Statistics of Population 1870* (Washington, D.C.: GPO, 1872); U.S. Bureau of the Census, *Tenth Census of the United States, 1880, Population* (Washington, D.C.: GPO, 1883); U.S. Bureau of the Census, *Twelfth Census of the United States Taken in the Year 1900* (Washington, D.C.: GPO, 1901); U.S. Bureau of the Census, *Thirteenth Census of the United States Taken in the Year 1910* (Washington, D.C.: GPO, 1911); U.S. Bureau of the Census, *Fourteenth Census of the United States Taken in the Year 1920* (Washington, D.C.: GPO, 1921); Canada, Department of Agriculture, *Census of Canada, 1880–81,* 4 vols. (Ottawa: Maclean, Roger, 1882–83); Canada, Department of Agriculture, *Census of Canada, 1890–91,* 4 vols. (Ottawa: S. E. Dawson, 1893–97); Canada, Census Office, *Fourth Census of Canada, 1901,* 4 vols. (Ottawa: S. E. Dawson, 1902–6); Canada, Census and Statistics Office, *Fifth Census of Canada, 1911,* 6 vols. (Ottawa: C. H. Parmelee, 1912–15); Canada, Bureau of Statistics, *Sixth Census of Canada, 1921,* 5 vols. (Ottawa: F. A. Acland, 1924–29).

12. Otis A. Pease, "Comment on Raymond D. Gastil, 'The Pacific Northwest as a Cultural Region,'" *Pacific Northwest Quarterly* 64 (October 1973): 160. See also Dorothy O. Johansen, "A Working Hypothesis for the Study of Migration," *Pacific Historical Review* 36 (February 1967): 1–12.

13. Anthony P. Cohen, "Belonging: The Experience of Culture," in *Belonging: Identity and Social Organisation in British Rural Cultures,* ed. Cohen (St. John's: Institute of Social and Economic Research, Memorial University of Newfoundland, 1982), p. 2.

14. The term "region" and the boundaries of American regions have been variously defined. See Merrill Jensen, ed., *Regionalism in America* (Madison: University of Wisconsin Press, 1951); Howard W. Odum and Harry Estil Moore, *American Regionalism: A Cultural-Historical Approach to National Integration* (New York: H. Holt, 1938); Raymond D. Gastil, *Cultural Regions of the United States* (Seattle: University of Washington Press, 1975); Joel Garreau, *The Nine Nations of North America* (Boston: Houghton Mifflin, 1981); Edward L. Ayers, Patricia Nelson Limerick, Stephen Nissenbaum, and Peter S. Onuf, *All Over the Map: Rethinking American Regions* (Baltimore: Johns Hopkins University Press, 1996).

15. In thinking about the role of words, language, and structures of meaning I have found useful Roland Barthes, *Mythologies*, trans. Annette Lavers (New York: Hill & Wang, 1972); Joan Wallach Scott, "On Language, Gender, and Working-Class History," in *Gender and the Politics of History* (New York: Columbia University Press, 1988), pp. 53–67.

16. Frederick Jackson Turner, *The Frontier in American History* (New York: H. Holt, 1920), p. 41. See also John T. Juricek, "American Usage of the Word 'Frontier' from Colonial Times to Frederick Jackson Turner," *Proceedings, American Philosophical Society* 110 (February 1966): 10–34; Frederick Jackson Turner, "The Significance of the Frontier in American History," *Annual Report of the American Historical Association for the Year 1893* (Washington, D.C.: GPO, 1894), pp. 199–227, and "The Significance of the Section in American History," *Wisconsin Magazine of History* 8 (March 1925): 255–80.

17. The settlement of the Inland Empire occurred largely in the late nineteenth and early twentieth centuries after the 1890 "ending" of the frontier, according to the frontier thesis. Yet American scholars tend to apply the frontier thesis to these later settlements without question. Comparative frontier scholars have noted differences between the Turnerian frontier settlements and those of the late nineteenth century in other parts of the world. For insight into the debate over these "settler societies," see Donald Denoon, "Understanding Settler Societies," *Historical Studies* 17 (July 1979): 511–27; John P. Fogarty, "The Comparative Method and the Nineteenth Century Regions of Recent Settlement," *Historical Studies* 19 (April 1981): 412–29; Graeme Wynn, "Settler Societies in Geographical Focus," *Historical Studies* 20 (April 1983): 353–66.

18. Benjamin Burgunder Papers, MsSc 110, EWSHS.

19. William G. Robbins, "Landscape and Environmental Change in the Intermontane West," *Pacific Northwest Quarterly* 84 (October 1993): 140–49.

20. David M. Potter, *People of Plenty: Economic Abundance and the American Character* (Chicago: University of Chicago Press, 1954); Thompson R. Smith, "The Ecology of a Massacre: Indian-White Relations on the Columbia Plateau, 1805–1847" (Senior essay, Yale University, 1983); Christopher L. Miller, *Prophetic Worlds: Indians and Whites on the Columbia Plateau* (New Brunswick, N.J.: Rutgers University Press, 1985); William Cronon, *Changes in the Land: Indians, Colonists and the Ecology of New England* (New York: Hill & Wang, 1983).

21. Carlos Schwantes, "Farmer-Labor Insurgency in Washington State: William Bouck, the Grange and the Western Progressive Farmers," *Pacific Northwest Quarterly* 76 (January 1985): 2–11; Harriet Ann Crawford, *The Washington State Grange, 1889–1924: A Romance of Democracy* (Portland: Binfords & Mort, 1940); Joseph Smith Papers, UW.

22. John Brinkerhoff Jackson, "Concluding with Landscapes," in *Discovering the Vernacular Landscape* (New Haven: Yale University Press, 1984); George W. Pierson, *The Moving American* (New York: Knopf, 1973).

23. See, for example, Catharine Burgess Carr to William H. Carr, June 6, 17, 25, 1914, Hamptonetta Burgess Carr Papers, WSU.

24. While my focus here has been on the notions of frontier, settlements, and the West, other nineteenth-century ideas and language, of course, also shaped the rhetoric and experience of Inland Empire residents. Changing views of society, particularly American society, for example, influenced their vision of a multidimensional region centered on an urban place. The impact of industrialization on theories of human interaction, that is, the intrusion of the machine into personal lives and therefore into personal concepts and ideas, also resonated in the creation of the Inland Empire. In the late nineteenth and early twentieth centuries United States society was often conceived as a thermodynamic machine, one that thrived on disequilibrium, replacing an earlier view of society as a mechanical machine, one that needed cooperative meshing of parts or unanimity. This distinction had a particular resonance for the people of the Inland Empire. It contributed to a sense of social cohesiveness—recognizing differences among individuals and within individuals as an integral part of their notion of a region. See Henry Adams, "The Dynamo and the Virgin" (1900), in *The Education of Henry Adams* (Cambridge, Mass.: Riverside Press for Massachusetts Historical Society, 1951); G. Charbonnier, *Conversations with*

Claude Lévi-Strauss (London: Cape, 1969), pp. 32–39; Emile Durkheim, *The Division of Labour in Society* (1893; rpt. New York: Macmillan, 1984); Ilya Prigogine and Isabelle Stengers, *Order Out of Chaos: Man's New Dialogue with Nature* (New York: Bantam Books, 1984). See Victor Turner on "communitas" and "liminality" in *The Ritual Process: Structure and Anti-Structure* (Chicago: Aldine, 1969), esp. pp. 94–97, 125–40, and "Liminal to Liminoid, in Play, Flow, and Ritual: An Essay in Comparative Symbology," *Rice University Studies* 60 (Summer 1974): 54–92.

25. Recent interdisciplinary collections within cultural studies that participate in the definition of this field include Angelika Bammer, ed., *Displacements: Cultural Identities in Question* (Bloomington: Indiana University Press, 1994); Nicholas B. Dirks, Geoff Eley, and Sherry B. Ortner, eds., *Culture/Power/History: A Reader in Contemporary Social Theory* (Princeton: Princeton University Press, 1994); Lawrence Grossberg, Cary Nelson, and Paula A. Treichler, eds., *Cultural Studies* (New York: Routledge, 1992); Tony Bennett, Graham Martin, Colin Mercer, and Janet Woollacott, eds., *Culture, Ideology and Social Process* (London: B. T. Batsford, in association with Open University Press, 1981).

26. For discussions of the "new regional studies" that use interdisciplinary approaches, see Glen E. Lich, ed., *Regional Studies: The Interplay of Land and Peoples* (College Station: Texas A&M University Press, 1992), and David Jordan, "Introduction," in *Regionalism Reconsidered: New Approaches to the Field,* ed. Jordan (New York: Garland, 1994). On historical approaches see Howard W. Odum and Harry Estill Moore, *American Regionalism: A Cultural-Historical Approach to National Integration* (New York: Henry Holt, 1938); Richard Maxwell Brown, "The New Regionalism in America, 1970–1981," in *Regionalism and the Pacific Northwest,* ed. William G. Robbins, Robert J. Frank, and Richard E. Ross (Corvallis: Oregon State University Press, 1983); Andrew R. L. Cayton and Peter S. Onuf, *The Midwest and the Nation: Rethinking the History of an American Region* (Bloomington: Indiana University Press, 1990); Ayers et al., *All Over the Map.* Works in geography that tackle the regionalism issue include Michael Harloe, C. G. Pickvance, and John Urry, eds., *Place, Policy and Politics: Do Localities Matter?* (London: Unwin Hyman, 1990); A. Jonas, "A New Regional Geography of Localities?" *Area* 20 (1988): 101–10; Allan Pred, "Place as Historically Contingent Process: Structuration and the Time-Geography of Becoming Places," *Annals of the Association of American Geographers* 74 (1984): 279–97; Michael Bradshaw, *Regions and Regionalism in the United States* (London: Macmillan Education, 1988); Ann Markusen, *Regions: The Economics and Politics of Territory* (Totowa, N.J.: Rowman and Littlefield, 1987). See also Marilyn Strathern, ed., *Shifting Contexts: Transformations in Anthropological Knowledge* (New York: Routledge, 1995). The most comprehensive survey of this literature is Michael Steiner and Clarence Mondale, *Regions and Regionalism in the United States: A Source Book for the Humanities and Social Sciences* (New York: Garland, 1988).

27. Benedict Anderson, *Imagined Communities: Reflections on the Origins and Spread of Nationalism,* rev. ed. (London: Verso, 1991); Jonathan Rittenhouse and Courtice G. Rose, "Introductory Remark," *Journal of History and Politics* 9 (1991): 1–4; Roberto Maria Dainotto, " 'All the Regions Do Smilingly Revolt': The Literature of Place and Region," *Critical Inquiry* 22 (Spring 1996): 486–505; Peter Jackson and Jan Penrose, eds., *Constructions of Race, Place and Nation* (Minneapolis: University of Minnesota Press, 1994); Homi K. Bhabha, ed., *Nation and Narration* (London: Routledge, 1990).

28. Robin W. Winks, "Regionalism in Comparative Perspective," in *Regionalism and the Pacific Northwest,* ed. Robbins, Frank, and Ross, pp. 16–17; William G. Robbins, "Introduction," ibid., p. 1. See also Carl Abbott, "Frontier and Section: Cities and Regions in American Growth," *American Quarterly* 37 (1985): 395–410.

29. Edwin R. Bingham and Glen A. Love, "Introduction," in *Northwest Perspectives: Essays on the Culture of the Pacific Northwest,* ed. and comp. Edwin R. Bingham and Glen A. Love (Seattle: University of Washington Press, 1979), p. xv.

30. See, e.g., Joseph Schafer, *A History of the Pacific Northwest* (New York: Macmillan, 1905). For overviews of Pacific Northwest histories see Kent D. Richards, "In Search of the Pacific

Northwest: The Historiography of Oregon and Washington," *Pacific Northwest Quarterly* 72 (1981): 415–43; and George A. Frykman, "Regionalism, Nationalism, Localism: The Pacific Northwest in American History," *Pacific Northwest Quarterly* 43 (October 1952): 251–61.

31. N. W. Durham, *History of the City of Spokane and Spokane Country, Washington, from Its Earliest Settlement to the Present Time,* 3 vols. (Spokane: S. J. Clarke, 1912); Julian Hawthorne, ed., *History of Washington, the Evergreen State: From Early Dawn to Daylight,* 2 vols. (New York: American Historical Publishing Co., 1893), p. 425. Nelson Durham's history was commonly referred to as *Spokane and the Inland Empire,* the short title embossed on the covers of each volume.

32. George W. Fuller, *The Inland Empire of the Pacific Northwest, A History* (Spokane: H. G. Linderman, 1928), pp. 1–2; George W. Fuller, *A History of the Pacific Northwest* (New York: Knopf, 1931).

33. Carlos A. Schwantes, *The Pacific Northwest: An Interpretive History* (Lincoln: University of Nebraska Press, 1989), p. 2.

34. See, e.g., Dorothy O. Johansen and Charles M. Gates, *Empire of the Columbia: A History of the Pacific Northwest* (New York: Harper & Brothers, 1957); Oscar Osburn Winther, *The Great Northwest: A History,* 2d ed. (1947; New York: Knopf, 1950).

35. John Fahey, *Inland Empire: D. C. Corbin and Spokane* (Seattle: University of Washington Press, 1965), and *The Inland Empire: The Unfolding Years, 1879–1929* (Seattle: University of Washington Press, 1986); D. W. Meinig, *The Great Columbia Plain: A Historical Geography, 1805–1910* (Seattle: University of Washington Press, 1968). See also the series of articles by Herman J. Deutsch, "Geographic Setting for the Recent History of the Inland Empire," *Pacific Northwest Quarterly* 49 (October 1958): 150–61, 50 (January 1959): 14–25, "The Evolution of the International Boundary in the Inland Empire of the Pacific Northwest," *Pacific Northwest Quarterly* 51 (April 1960): 63–79, and "The Evolution of Territorial and State Boundaries in the Inland Empire of the Pacific Northwest," *Pacific Northwest Quarterly* 51 (July 1960): 115–31.

36. Other, more prosaic, external factors often define the boundaries of regions. Earl Pomeroy, for example, includes six western states in his 1965 regional study, *The Pacific Slope.* The inclusion of these particular states was, as Pomeroy explains, a function of publishing needs. His book was designed to complement the works written by Robert Athearn and W. Eugene Hollon. See Pomeroy, *The Pacific Slope: A History of California, Oregon, Washington, Idaho, Utah, and Nevada* (New York: Knopf, 1965); W. Eugene Hollon, *The Southwest: Old and New* (New York: Knopf, 1961); Robert G. Athearn, *High Country Empire: The High Plains and the Rockies* (New York: McGraw-Hill, 1960).

37. Accounts of the intellectual development of the "semiotics of culture" include Irene Portis-Winner, *Semiotics of Culture: "The Strange Intruder"* (Bochum, Germany: Universitatsverlag Dr. N. Brockmeyer, 1994); Milton Singer, *Semiotics of Cities, Selves, and Cultures: Explorations in Semiotic Anthropology* (Berlin: Moutonde Gruyler, 1991), pp. 291–96; and Irene Portis Winner and Thomas G. Winner, "The Semiotics of Cultural Texts," *Semiotica* 18, no. 2 (1976): 101–56. For examples of the ways scholars in different disciplines have worked in this vein, see Giles Gunn, "The Semiotics of Culture and the Interpretation of Literature: Clifford Geertz and the Moral Imagination," *Studies in Literary Imagination* 12, no. 1 (1979): 109–28; Yoshihiko Ikegami, ed., *The Empire of Signs: Semiotics Essays on Japanese Culture* (Amsterdam: J. Bejamins, 1991); Alec McHoul, *Semiotic Investigations: Towards an Effective Semiotics* (Lincoln: University of Nebraska Press, 1996). The term is closely associated with Russian theorist Yuri Lotman; see his *Universe of the Mind: A Semiotic Theory of Culture,* trans. Ann Shukman (Bloomington: Indiana University Press, 1990); Ju M. Lotman and B. A. Uspenskij, *Semiotics of Russian Culture,* ed. Ann Shukman (Ann Arbor: Michigan Slavic Publications, 1984); A. D. and A. S. Nakhimovsky, eds., *The Semiotics of Russian Cultural History: Essays* (Ithaca: Cornell University Press, 1985).

38. See, e.g., Peter Benes, *The Masks of Orthodoxy: Folk Gravestone Carvings in Plymouth County, Massachusetts, 1689–1850* (Amherst: University of Massachusetts Press, 1977); James Stevens Curl, *The Victorian Celebration of Death* (Detroit: Partridge Press, 1972); Catherine Ho-

wett, "Living Landscapes for the Dead," *Landscape* 21 (Spring–Summer 1977): 9–17; Ronald A. Dixon and Jack W. Thomas, "Cemetery Ecology," *Natural History* 82 (March 1973): 60–67; John R. Stilgoe, "Folklore and Graveyard Design," *Landscape* 22 (Summer 1978): 22–28; Stanley French, "The Cemetery as Cultural Institution: The Establishment of Mount Auburn and the 'Rural Cemetery' Movement," *American Quarterly* 26 (March 1974): 37–59; John Brinkerhoff Jackson, "The Vanishing Epitaph: From Monument to Place," *Landscape* 17 (Winter 1967–68): 22–26; Carl Edison, "Motorcycles, Guitars and Bucking Broncos: Twentieth-Century Gravestones in Southeastern Idaho," in *Idaho Folklife: Homesteads to Headstones*, ed. Louie W. Attebery (Salt Lake City: University of Utah Press, 1985), pp. 184–89.

39. Fred Kniffen, "Necrogeography in the United States," *Geographical Review* 57 (1967): 426–27; Richard V. Francaviglia, "The Cemetery as an Evolving Cultural Landscape," *Annals, AAG* 61 (September 1971): 501; Michel Ragan, *The Space of Death: A Study in Funerary Architecture, Decoration, and Urbanism,* trans. Alan Sheridan (Charlottesville: University Press of Virginia, 1983), p. 182.

40. John R. Stilgoe, *Common Landscape of America, 1640–1850* (New Haven: Yale University Press, 1983), p. 231.

41. Yi-Fu Tuan, *Space and Place: The Perspective of Experience* (Minneapolis: University of Minnesota Press, 1977), pp. 173, 179. See also E. Relph, *Place and Placelessness* (London: Pion, 1976).

42. Edward W. Soja, *Postmodern Geographies: The Reassertion of Space in Critical Social Theory* (London: Verso, 1989); David Harvey, *The Condition of Postmodernity: An Enquiry into the Origins of Cultural Change* (Oxford: Basil Blackwell, 1989); Michel Foucault, "Space, Knowledge, and Power," in *The Foucault Reader,* ed. Paul Rabinow (New York: Pantheon, 1984), pp. 239–56.

43. Richard C. Poulsen, *The Pure Experience of Order: Essays on the Symbolic in the Folk Material Culture of Western America* (Albuquerque: University of New Mexico Press, 1982), p. 5, see also esp. pp. 1–25; Henry Glassie, *Folk Housing in Middle Virginia* (Knoxville: University of Tennessee Press, 1975). Poulsen's use of the term "symbol" is closer to the term "sign" in a semiotic context than to the use of the term in an American Studies context. For a clearer distinction between the two terms see Victor Turner, "Symbolic Studies," *Annual Review of Anthropology* 4 (1975): 145–61. See also A. P. Cohen, *The Symbolic Construction of Community* (London: E. Horwood; New York: Tavistock, 1985); Henry Nash Smith, *Virgin Land: The American West in Symbol and Myth* (Cambridge, Mass.: Harvard University Press, 1950).

44. In cognitive psychology, studies in spatial problem solving, "mental mapping," and cognitive mapping examine internal representations. On cognitive mapping see Roger M. Downs and David Stea, *Maps in Mind: Reflections on Cognitive Mapping* (New York: Harper & Row, 1977); Roger M. Downs and David Stea, eds., *Image and Environment* (Chicago: Aldine, 1973); Kevin Lynch, *The Image of the City* (Cambridge, Mass.: Technology Press and Harvard University Press, 1960); Peter Gould and Rodney White, *Mental Maps* (Harmondsworth, Eng.: Penguin, 1974); Benjamin Kuipers, "Modeling Spatial Knowledge," *Cognitive Science* 2 (1978): 129–53. They are concerned with discovering the conceptual abstractions that mediate between stimuli received by sense organs and behavioral responses, that is, abstractions that serve as the basis for perception and comprehension. As Charles Frake observes, "Culture is not simply a cognitive map that people acquire, in whole or in part, more or less accurately, and then learn to read. People are cast out into the imperfectly charted, continually shifting seas of everyday life. Mapping them out is a constant process resulting not in an individual cognitive map, but in a whole chart case of rough, improvised, continually revised sketch maps. Culture does not provide a cognitive map, but rather a set of principles for mapmaking and navigation. Different cultures are like different schools of navigation designed to cope with different terrains and seas" ("Plying Frames Can Be Dangerous: Some Reflections on Methodology in Cognitive Anthropology," in *Language and Cultural Description: Essays by Charles O. Frake,* selected and intro. by Anwar S. Dil [Stanford: Stanford University Press, 1980] p. 58). See also Gaston Bachelard, *The Poetics of Space,* trans. Marie Jolas (1958; rpt. Boston: Beacon Press, 1969), on the interwoven relationship between place and self-identity.

45. See Charles O. Frake, "Cultural Ecology and Ethnography," *American Anthropologist* 64 (1962): 53–59; Thomas J. Schlereth, "The Above-Ground Archaeology of Trees," *Orion Nature Quarterly* 3 (Autumn 1984): 36–45.

46. More recently cultural geographers have looked to less traditional sources. "The nature of human experience," points out Christopher L. Salter, "whether that between fellow humans or in their relationship with place, cannot be captured in a rigidly objective framework," ("John Steinbeck's *The Grapes of Wrath* as a Primer for Cultural Geography," in *Humanistic Geography and Literature: Essays on the Experience of Place,* ed. Douglas C. D. Pocock [London: Croom Helm, 1981], pp. 142–58, quote on p. 142). Trying to uncover "underlying systems" (p. 156) and "attitudes that shape environmental manipulation" (p. 143), Salter looks to works of literature. Yi-Fu Tuan similarly finds "perceptive writers" a source for expressions of "intimate experiences of place" (*Space and Place,* pp. 136–48), and, more generally, the evocative power of art, architecture, ceremonials, rites (pp. 166–78). See also Salter, "Signature and Settings: One Approach to Landscape in Literature," in *Dimensions in Human Geography,* ed. Karl W. Butzer (Chicago: University of Chicago Press, 1978), pp. 69–83.

47. Tuan, *Space and Place,* pp. 173, 179, 178.

48. Anthropologists and folklorists speak of "performance." A written transcription of an oral myth, for example, takes the myth out of context. All the elements involved in the transmission of the myth, including the tone of voice, the time of day, the individuals involved, the physical surroundings, and other aspects of the performance are essential in understanding the myth's cultural components. See Alan Dundes, "Texture, Text and Context," *Southern Folklore Quarterly* 25 (1964): 251–65; Dan Ben-Amos, "Toward a Definition of Folklore in Context," *Journal of American Folklore* 84 (1971): 3–15; Dell Hymes, "Folklore's Nature and the Sun's Myth," *Journal of American Folklore* 88 (1975): 345–69; Dan Ben-Amos, ed., *Folklore Genres* (Austin: University of Texas Press, for the American Folklore Society, 1976); Elizabeth C. Fine, *The Folklore Text: From Performance to Print* (Bloomington: Indiana University Press, 1984). See also Clifford Geertz, "Thick Description: Toward an Interpretive Theory of Culture," in *Interpretation of Culture* (New York: Basic Books, 1973), pp. 3–30; Victor Turner, *From Ritual to Theatre* (New York: PAJ Publications, 1982). The idea of "performance" has taken on additional meanings when appropriated by other cultural scholars; see Jean-Christophe Agnew, *Worlds Apart: The Market and Theatre in Anglo-American Thought, 1550–1750* (Cambridge: Cambridge University Press, 1986); Joseph Roach, *Cities of the Dead: Circum-Atlantic Performance* (New York: Columbia University Press, 1006).

49. Cohen, "Belonging," p. 12.

50. See Jonathan Culler, *Ferdinand de Saussure,* rev. ed. (Ithaca: Cornell University Press, 1986); Michael Silverstein, "Shifters, Linguistic Categories and Cultural Description," in *Meaning in Anthropology,* ed. Keith H. Basso and Henry A. Selby (Albuquerque: University of New Mexico Press, 1976), pp. 11–54; Gunn, "Semiotics of Culture."

51. John W. Berry, *Human Ecology and Cognitive Style: Comparative Studies in Cultural and Psychological Adaptation* (New York: Halsted Press, 1976), concludes that ecological demands placed on a group of people plus their cultural adaptation to this ecology ("cultural aids") led to the development of certain perceptual skills. Specifically, nomadic hunting groups with loose social organization and socialization for autonomy developed field-independent cognitive style while sedentary agricultural groups with tight social organizations and socialization for conformity developed field-dependent cognitive style.

52. See Nicholas Pastore, *Selective History of Theories of Visual Perception, 1650–1950* (New York: Oxford University Press, 1971); George A. Miller, *Language and Perception* (Cambridge, Mass.: Belknap Press of Harvard University Press, 1976); Umberto Eco, *A Theory of Semiotics* (Bloomington: Indiana University Press, 1976); David E. Sopher, "Place and Location: Notes on the Spatial Patterning of Culture," *Social Science Quarterly* 53 (September 1972): 321–37.

53. In the American West, the "Mormon Culture Region" has received most attention. Geographers have primarily been interested in the visible symbols on the landscape that reflect this distinctive Mormon worldview. Hay derricks, irrigation ditches, central hall houses, Mormon

chapels along with Mormon town sites and the cardinal orientation of streets, for example, are all seen as components of the Mormon landscape. The most prominent works on this topic include D. W. Meinig, "The Mormon Culture Region: Strategies and Patterns in the Geography of the American West, 1847–1964," *Annals, AAG* 58 (1965): 191–220; Richard V. Francaviglia, *The Mormon Landscape: Creation and Perception of a Unique Image in the American West* (New York: AMS Press, 1979); Seth Budge, "Perceptions of the Boundaries of the Mormon Culture Region," *Great Plains: Rocky Mountain Geographical Journal* 3 (1974): 1–9; Lowry Nelson, *The Mormon Village: A Pattern and Technique of Land Settlement* (Salt Lake City: University of Utah Press, 1952); Richard H. Jackson, ed., *The Mormon Role in the Settlement of the American West* (Provo, Utah: Brigham Young University Press, 1978); Richard H. Jackson and Roger Henrio, "Perception of Sacred Space," *Journal of Cultural Geography* 3 (1983): 94–107. See also David Lowenthal and Marguita Riel, *Environmental Structures: Semantics and Experiential Components*, David Lowenthal, *Publications in Environmental Perception*, No. 8 (New York: American Geographical Society, 1972).

54. My focus is on "interruptions," moments when individuals and groups act more consciously than reflexively, when they create verbal, literary, or structural responses to their environments. See L. S. Vygotsky, for example, on the distinction between "tool" and "sign" in *Mind in Society: The Development of Higher Psychological Processes*, ed. Michael Cole, Vera John-Steiner, Sylvia Scribner, and Ellen Souberman (Cambridge, Mass.: Harvard University Press, 1978), esp. pp. 52–57.

Chapter 1. Mapping the Inland Empire

1. "Letter from the Secretary of War, transmitting in response to Senate Resolution of April 5, 1882, a letter from the Chief of Engineers of yesterday's date, and the accompanying copy of a report from Lieut. T. W. Symons, Corps of Engineers, embracing all the information in this Department respecting the navigable water of the Upper Columbia River and its tributaries, and of the country adjacent thereto," 47th Cong., 1st sess., Sen. Exec. Doc. 186 (1882), pp. 96–97. On the influence of fur trade information on early western United States maps, see William H. Goetzmann, *Exploration and Empire: The Explorer and the Scientist in the Winning of the American West* (New York: Vintage, 1966); John L. Allen, "The Cartography of the Rocky Mountain Fur Trade," paper presented at the Western History Association Conference, October 1992.

2. *Spokane Falls Review*, May 19, 1883; Ralph E. Dyar, *News for an Empire: The Story of the Spokesman-Review* (Caldwell, Ida.: Caxton Printers, 1952), p. 5, and D. W. Meinig, *The Great Columbia Plain: A Historical Geography, 1805–1910* (Seattle: University of Washington Press, 1968), p. 323, also note the designation.

This discussion is based on a survey of nineteenth-century maps, which were produced in the United States and included or focused on this section of the country. While the maps are located in a variety of repositories, the largest collections are in the Geography and Map Division, Library of Congress, Washington, D.C., and University of Washington Library, Seattle. Meinig, *Great Columbia Plain*, pp. 177–82, discusses some of these early maps.

3. Recent studies of the settlement process and the roles of homesteaders and town builders, although focused on different times and western locales, include Michael J. O'Brien et al., *Grassland, Forest, and Historical Settlement: An Analysis of Dynamics in Northeast Missouri* (Lincoln: University of Nebraska Press, 1984); Paula M. Nelson, *After the West Was Won: Homesteaders and Town-Builders in Western South Dakota, 1900–1917* (Iowa City: University of Iowa Press, 1986); Peter G. Boag, *Environment and Experience: Settlement Culture in Nineteenth-Century Oregon* (Berkeley: University of California Press, 1992).

4. Luvina Buchanan to Nancy Hood, May 4, 1877, Luvina Buchanan Papers, LCHS. A traveling correspondent for the *Palouse Gazette* used even more vivid language to describe Paradise Valley in 1877: "We paused a moment—the sight that greeted our eyes was truly magnificent. As

far as the eye could reach over valley and rolling plain, were to be seen comfortable farm houses and broad acres of grain fields; which in the mellow light of the setting sun presented a picture alike gratifying to the artist and agriculturist" (*Palouse Gazette,* October 13, 1877).

5. See, e.g., James H. Forney to Mary E. Belknap, January 10, 1880, Belknap-Forney Papers, SC/BEL-1, LCHS. Forney notes: "This portion of Idaho and eastern Washington are receiving a large immigration, and owing to the fertile soil of the same, and its rapid development by railroads, am confident will ere long rival the Golden State in its commercial importance."

Although shifting county boundaries make precise numbers difficult to provide, the joint population of two eastern Washington territorial counties—Stevens and Spokane—grew from 734 to over 4,000 by 1880. Close to 6,000 people lived in the newly formed Whitman County. See U.S. Bureau of the Census, *Ninth Census of the United States, Statistics of Population, 1870* (Washington, D.C.: GPO, 1872); U.S. Bureau of the Census, *Tenth Census of the United States, Statistics of Population, 1880* (Washington, D.C.: GPO, 1881).

6. U.S. Bureau of the Census, *Fourteenth Census of the United States Taken in the Year 1920* (Washington, D.C.: GPO, 1921); John Fahey, *The Inland Empire: Unfolding Years, 1879–1929* (Seattle: University of Washington Press, 1986), pp. 3–21. In his first chapter, "An Influx of Strangers," Fahey traces the 1879 migration to the Palouse. The words "influx of strangers" are taken from the *Walla Walla Union,* February 16, 1878.

7. For examples of available maps, see H. H. Bancroft, *Map of Oregon, Washington, Idaho, Montana and British Columbia* (San Francisco: N.p., 1868); *Johnson's Oregon and Washington* (New York: Johnson and Ward, 1865); *Colton's Washington and Oregon* (New York: J. H. Colton, 1861); U.S. Department of the Interior, General Land Office, *Map of Public Surveys in the Territory of Washington to Accompany Report of Surveyor General* (Washington, D.C.: GPO, 1865); Daniel Lowell & Co., *Map of Nez Perces and Salmon River Gold Mines in Washington Territory* (San Francisco: Whiton, Waters, 1862).

8. For a slightly earlier description of this community, see George F. G. Stanley, ed., *Mapping the Frontier: Charles Wilson's Diary of the Survey of the 49th Parallel, 1858–1862, While Secretary of the British Boundary Commission* (Seattle: University of Washington Press, 1970), pp. 109–15, 130–41, 163–71.

9. John Esvelt, "Chinese Placer Mining on the Upper Columbia," unpublished manuscript, Northwest Room, Spokane Public Library; Robert E. Wynne, "Reaction to the Chinese in the Pacific Northwest and British Columbia, 1850–1910" (Ph.D. diss., University of Washington, 1964); Lorraine Barker Hildebrand, *Straw Huts, Sandals and Steel: The Chinese in Washington State* (Tacoma: Washington State Historical Society, 1977).

10. Other reservations and reserves were established during the 1870s and 1880s. The Colville reservation, for example, was created in 1872, Chief Moses's reservation in 1879, and the Spokane reservation in 1881. On the creation of the Coeur d'Alene reservation, see Chapter 2. Most of the Canadian reserves were set aside during the 1880s. See G. E. Shankel, "The Development of Indian Policy in British Columbia" (Ph.D. diss., University of Washington, 1945); Wilson Duff, *The Indians of British Columbia,* vol. 1 (Victoria: Provincial Museum of British Columbia, 1964); M. Gidley, *With One Sky Above Us: Life on an American Indian Reservation at the Turn of the Century* (Seattle: Putnam, 1979).

11. In addition to the sources already cited, this description of the area during the 1870s is drawn from U.S. Bureau of the Census, *Ninth Census of the United States, Population Schedules, 1870,* Idaho and Washington, RG 29; U.S. Bureau of the Census, *Tenth Census of the United States, Population Schedules, 1880,* Idaho and Washington, RG 29; Bancroft, *Map of Oregon, Washington, Idaho, Montana and British Columbia.*

12. Statement of Stephen E. Liberty, n.d., Stephen Liberty Papers, MsSC 59, EWSHS; Alexander C. McGregor, "The Economic Impact of the Mullan Road on Walla Walla, 1860–1883," *Pacific Northwest Quarterly* 65 (July 1974): 118–29.

13. U.S. Department of the Interior, General Land Office, *Map of the United States and Territories, Showing the Extent of Public Surveys, Indian and Military Reservations, Land Grant R.R.,*

Rail Roads, Canals, and Other Details Compiled from the Official Surveys of the General Land Office and Other Authentic Sources (Washington, D.C.: GPO, 1876); U.S. Department of the Interior, General Land Office, *Washington Territory* (Washington, D.C.: GPO, 1879); U.S. Department of the Interior, General Land Office, *Idaho Territory* (Washington, D.C.: GPO, 1879). For information on the U.S. rectangular survey and railroad surveys, see Lola Cazier, *Surveys and Surveyors of the Public Domain, 1785–1975* (Washington, D.C.: GPO, 1976); Hildegard Binder Johnson, *Order Upon the Land: The U.S. Rectangular Land Survey and the Upper Mississippi Country* (New York: Oxford University Press, 1976); Lowell O. Stewart, *Public Land Surveys: History, Instructions, Method* (Ames, Iowa: Collegiate Press, 1935).

14. Raymond Hull, "Editor's Foreword" in Charles Aeneas Shaw, *Tales of a Pioneer Surveyor* (Ontario: Longman Canada, 1970), pp. 6–28, is particularly clear on nineteenth-century railroad surveying methods. For a contemporary account of surveying methods, particularly triangulation, see A. D. Wilson, "Notes on the Geographical Work of the United States Geological and Geographical Survey of the Territories," *Bulletin of the United States Geological and Geographical Survey*, Vol. 3, No. 3 (Washington, D.C.: GPO, 1877), pp. 705–37. See also Canada Department of the Interior, Topographical Branch, *Manual of Instructions for the Survey of Dominion Lands*, 8th ed. (Ottawa: Government Publications Board, 1913); U.S. General Land Office, *Manual of Surveying Instructions for the Survey of the Public Lands of the United States and Private Land Claims* (Washington, D.C.: GPO, 1894).

15. In thinking about maps as texts, I have found useful Trevor J. Barnes and James S. Duncan, eds., *Writing Worlds: Discourse, Text and Metaphor in the Representation of Landscape* (London: Routledge, 1992); Denis Wood, *The Power of Maps* (New York: Guilford Press, 1992); and J. B. Harley, "Maps, Knowledge and Power," in *The Iconography of Landscape*, ed. Denis Cosgrove and Stephen Daniels (Cambridge: Cambridge University Press, 1988), pp. 277–312.

16. U.S. Congress, *Map of a Part of the Territory of Washington to Accompany Report of Surveyor General* (Olympia, Wash. Terr.: Surveyor General's Office, 1855), 34th Cong., 1st sess., Sen. Exec. Doc 1; *Map of a Part of Washington Territory Lying East of the Cascade Mountains to Accompany Report of the Surveyor General* (Olympia, Wash. Terr.: Surveyor General's Office, 1857); *Map of a Part of Washington Territory to Accompany the Report of the Surveyor General* (Olympia, Wash. Terr.: Surveyor General's Office, 1859); *Map of a Part of Washington Territory to Accompany the Report of the Surveyor General* (Olympia, Wash. Terr.: Surveyor General's Office, 1861); U.S. Congress, *Map of a Part of Washington Territory to Accompany the Report of the Surveyor General* (Olympia, Wash. Terr.: Surveyor General's Office, 1860–61), 36th Cong., 2d sess., Sen. Exec. Doc 1; *Map of Public Surveys in the Territory of Washington for the Report of Surveyor General* (Olympia, Wash. Terr.: Surveyor General's Office, 1862); U.S. Department of the Interior, General Land Office, *Map of Public Surveys in the Territory of Washington to Accompany Report of Surveyor General* (Washington, D.C.: GPO, 1865); U.S. Department of the Interior, General Land Office, *Map of Public Surveys in the Territory of Washington to Accompany Report of Surveyor General* (Washington, D.C.: GPO, 1879); U.S. Department of the Interior, General Land Office, *Map of Public Surveys in the Territory of Washington to Accompany Report of Surveyor General* (Washington, D.C.: GPO, 1883).

17. Letters home are only one example of the ways individuals worked to create new mental maps. Other words and objects such as poems, drawings, and stories also speak to the personal bonds to place these settlers created. But the letters home are more accessible to interpretation because they come at moments of personal disjuncture. In some ways, the letters home exist as liminal spaces, where the writers stand apart from their socially constructed world in order to reshape their identities. See Victor Turner, *The Ritual Process: Structure and Anti-Structure* (Chicago: Aldine, 1969); Victor Turner, *Dramas, Fields, and Metaphors: Symbolic Action in Human Society* (Ithaca: Cornell University Press, 1974). See also Kathleen M. Ashley, ed., *Victor Turner and the Construction of Cultural Criticism: Between Literature and Anthropology* (Bloomington: Indiana University Press, 1990).

18. Elizabeth Hampsten, *Read This Only to Yourself: The Private Writings of Midwestern*

Women, 1880–1910 (Bloomington: Indiana University Press, 1982). On women's "kinwork" see Micaela di Leonardo, *The Varieties of Ethnic Experience: Kinship, Class and Gender among California Italian-Americans* (Ithaca: Cornell University Press, 1984). Not all Hampsten's findings on the character of nineteenth-century women's private writings hold true in my analysis of these Pacific Northwest letters. Hampsten, whose analysis relies on a variety of women's private writings besides letters, draws a distinction between such writings and men's public published writings. She finds, for example, that men, more than women, refer to regional identity or "the kinds of unifying myths based in time and place" (p. 40). I find that this distinction is more a reflection of the public versus private nature of the writings than of gender difference.

19. James T. Lemon, *The Best Poor Man's Country: A Geographical Study of Early Southeastern Pennsylvania* (Baltimore: Johns Hopkins University Press, 1972). See also Claudia L. Bushman, *"A Good Poor Man's Wife": Being a Chronicle of Harriet Hanson Robinson and Her Family in Nineteenth-Century New England* (Hanover, N.H.: University Press of New England, 1981), esp. pp. 104–21; Stephen Aron, *How the West Was Lost: The Transformation of Kentucky from Daniel Boone to Henry Clay* (Baltimore: Johns Hopkins University Press, 1996). For studies on the importance of conceptions of place in descriptions of place, see Charles E. Osgood, George J. Suci, and Percy H. Tannenbaum, *The Measurement of Meaning* (Urbana: University of Illinois Press, 1957); David Lowenthal, *Environmental Assessment: Comparative Analysis of Four Cities*, Publications in Environmental Perception, No. 5 (New York: American Geographical Society, 1972). On the relation of language, region, and power see Pierre Bourdieu, *Language and Symbolic Power*, ed. John B. Thompson (Cambridge, Mass.: Harvard University Press, 1991).

20. William A. Craigie and James R. Hulbert, *A Dictionary of American English on Historical Principles*, 4 vols. (Chicago: University of Chicago Press, 1938–44), p. 1790; [Dallam, Ansell & Edwards], *Settlers' Guide to Homes in the Northwest, Being a Hand-Book of Spokane Falls, W.T., the Queen City of the Pacific, Its Matchless Water Power and Advantages as a Commercial Center* (Spokane Falls: Evening Review Book and Job Print, 1885), p. 66. On the nineteenth-century meanings of "poor man's," "see," and "settle," see also Mitford M. Mathews, *A Dictionary of Americanisms on Historical Principles*, 2 vols. (Chicago: University of Chicago Press, 1951), p. 1283 (poor man's), p. 1490 (see), p. 1500 (settle).

21. John Cady, "Washington Territory: What a Humboldter Thinks and Says of the Country," *Silver State* (Winnemucca, Nev.), December 19, 1879, as copied by J. Orin Oliphant, Eastern Washington University, Cheney.

22. On gendered language and the gendered experience of space, see Doreen Massey, *Space, Place, and Gender* (Minneapolis: University of Minnesota Press, 1994); Jeanne Kay, "Landscapes of Women and Men: Rethinking the Regional Historical Geography of the United States and Canada," *Journal of Historical Geography* 17, no. 4 (1991): 435–52.

23. "Letters Written Home, 1879–1880," March 13, 1881, William Henry Stoneman Papers, MS Subj, EWSHS. Diaries as well as letters home employed the same language. See, e.g., an anonymous diarist on the road to Pullman, Washington, in the Palouse country, who noted in 1892, "We started about 8 oclock for Pullman [from Colton] the wheat was fine and about as fine a country as I ever saw. . . . Pullman is a town of about 15 hundred the livelist plasce I ever saw" (1892 Diary, Cage 4279, WSU).

24. R. Hurlburt to Rhoda, August 15, 1890, Alice Roberts papers, MsSc 45, EWSHS. See also Patrick Robertson-Ross's 1872 diary: "The whole Valley of the Kootanie as well as the surrounding country is densely wooded with magnificent timber, such as would cheer the heart of an Ottawa Lumber Merchant" (Patrick Robertson-Ross Papers, E/C/R54, PABC).

25. Annie Lowden McQueen Gordon to Jessie McQueen [sister], September 1, 1887, Annie McQueen Papers, MSS 115, FtS. Although his concern is with poetic works, spatial imagery, and individual consciousness, I find the implications of Gaston Bachelard's argument about the imaginative power of the houses of one's past suggestive for this analysis (*The Poetics of Space*, trans. Marie Jolas [Boston: Beacon Press, 1969]).

26. David Robert McGinnis, "Spokane in 1883," *Spokesman-Review*, February 15, 1942, in

J. Orin Oliphant, "Early History of Spokane, Washington, Told by Contemporaries," Eastern Washington University, Cheney; Samuel McCrosky to Maggie Cochran, July 16, 1883. Samuel M. McCrosky Papers, MsSc 52, EWSHS.

27. Calvin E. Wilson to Claude Harper, March 17, 1883, C. Wilson Papers, Cage 4593, WSU.

28. Lt. Thomas W. Symons to S. E. Symons, September 28, 1879, Thomas W. Symons Papers, MsSc 98, Washington State Historical Society, Tacoma. See also Thomas W. Symons Papers, Ms ZColl., EWSHS.

29. *Letter from the Secretary of War, Transmitting in Response to Senate Resolution of April 5, 1882, a Letter from the Chief of Engineers of Yesterday's Date, and the Accompanying Copy of a Report from Lieut. T. W. Symons, Corps of Engineers, Embracing All the Information in this Department Respecting the Navigable Water of the Upper Columbia River and Its Tributaries, and of the Country Adjacent Thereto,* 47th Cong., 1st sess., Sen. Exec. Doc. 186 (1882), pp. 111, hereafter cited as *Report from Lieut. T. W. Symons,* see also Meinig, *Great Columbia Plain,* p. 264.

30. *Report from Lieut. T. W. Symons,* p. 113. The connection between the expression of an ideal and its realization in social transformation is a familiar construct in social thought: "A society is not made up merely of the mass of individuals who compose it, the ground which they occupy, the things which they use and the movements which they perform, but above all is the idea which it forms of itself." "This creation . . . is the act by which it is periodically made and remade" (Emile Durkheim, *The Elementary Forms of the Religious Life: A Study in Religious Society,* trans. Joseph Ward Swain [London: George Allen and Unwin, 1915], p. 422).

31. "Memoirs of a pioneer . . . Spokane County," Cage 4599, WSU. The emphasis is mine. See also Oral History Collection, Stevens County Historical Society, Colville; Daniel McCrae Papers, Cage 1677, WSU. Daniel McCrae, a Nova Scotian and former Nevada miner, came from Portland in 1877. As he recalled in 1920, "A friend advised me to come to the Inland Empire and I started for Spokane. . . . When I got as far as Colfax, I decided that I had come far enough and I determined to look around for a homestead and work."

32. A. E. Keats to Julia W. Lewis, January 11, 1883, Albert E. Keats Papers, MsSc 1, EWSHS; *Tenth Census, Population Schedules, 1880,* Washington, Spokane County.

33. Cady, "Washington Territory." See, for example, *Spokane Times,* August 7, 1880. Samuel Glasgow recalled the impact of his monthly community letter from Spokane Falls to his previous home, Avoca, Iowa: "Many of them answered my family letter personally. Most of them said, 'Sam, if you like it out there and stay, you will see me, before very long.' They too kept their word, and many became valuable citizens of Spokane. I was well repaid for my part in bringing them here" (Reminiscences, pp. 4, 11, Samuel Glasgow Papers, MS Sc 38, EWSHS).

34. J. Fred Hume to R. Bellamy, May 26, 1891, F. Bolton Papers, Add MSS 2084, PABC.

35. Maudie Craig to Ella Cross, March 7, 1899, Weir Papers, RHM.

36. Cady, "Washington Territory."

37. W. W. Day to Hunter, January 23, 1878, in R. L. Olson, comp., "In a Prairie Schooner by Mrs. Chester D. Ide (Lucy A. Loomis): A Diary of a Four and One-Half Month's Trip across the Plains, Under the Flapping Canvas of an Emigrant Wagon: May to September 1878," Lucy A. Ide Papers, MsSc 179, EWSHS. The number of Mondovi immigrants is derived from an analysis of the population schedules of the 1880 federal manuscript census along with the collection of letters at the Eastern Washington State Historical Society compiled by a relative, R. L. Olson.

38. D. C. Gardner to wife, December 1, 1878, James Hunter to Otis Warren, February 10, 1879, Ide Papers, EWSHS; *Tenth Census, Population Schedules, 1880,* Washington, Columbia County. This mobility within the region characterized the experience of other acquainted groups of emigrants. James Forney, a young lawyer, followed his fortunes to the area from California. He came with a group of acquaintances and friends from both his childhood hometown and his California circle. As he wrote in 1880 to Mary Belknap, a California friend who stayed behind, "Quite an exodus of Tulareans took place last summer. Capt. Wash. now in eastern Washington . . . Misses Beach and Strode are in the upper country, and Mr. Mattick and wife think on locating near here. Dr. Wells, whose brother is here, has located at Portland" (James H. Forney to Mary E. Belknap, January 10, 1880, Belknap-Forney Papers, SC/BEL-1, LCHS).

39. The quotes are taken from Josephine Dunning to Aunt Mary and Uncle Singleton Kenyon, April 20, 1880, February 6, 1881, May 22, 1881, February 24, 1882, May 17, 1884, Charles B. Dunning Papers, MsSc 186, EWSHS.

40. Alice Roberts to Ones at Home, February 24, 1889, Alice Roberts Papers, MsSc 45, EWSHS.

41. Helmer Steenberg to Helen Munson, June 25, 1905, Helmer Steenberg Papers, MsSc 79, EWSHS.

42. Dunning Papers, EWSHS; R. K. Skaife Diary, Cage 296, WSU.

43. Kate Price Grannis Oral History, Oral History Collection, LCHS.

44. Frederick P. Norbury to Nell, January 6, 1888, p. 2, Norbury Papers, Add MSS 877, PABC.

45. Maudie Craig to Ella Cross, September 8, 1899, Weir Papers, RHM.

46. W. B. Field to Alice B. Lind, August 19, 1888, W. B. Field Papers, Cage 1861, WSU.

47. Rev. S. E. Stearns, "Idaho Territory," *Baptist Home Mission Monthly* 1 (April 1879): 155, in J. Orin Oliphant, "Readings in the History of Eastern Washington," Eastern Washington University, Cheney.

48. W. H. Merrick to Mary Merrick, May 6, 1884, W. H. Merrick Papers, Cage 2011, WSU. See James N. Glover, *Reminiscences of James N. Glover* (Fairfield, Wash.: Ye Galleon Press, 1985). Glover's initial two partners gave up on the site in 1876. Browne and Cannon joined him two years later. On the history of Spokane, see also N. W. Durham, *History of the City of Spokane and Spokane Country, Washington, from Its Earliest Settlement to the Present Time*, 3 vols. (Spokane: S. J. Clarke, 1912); William Stimson, *A View of the Falls: An Illustrated History of Spokane* (Northridge, Calif.: Windsor Publications, 1985).

49. John Kendrick Truax Diary, 1883–84, October 25, 1883, J. K. Truax Papers, Cage 4213, WSU; W. H. Merrick to Mary Merrick, May 6, 1884, WSU. The dubious Truax also noted that "there [is] a fine water power here" and "there is quite a number of fine Brick Blocks going up here." Based on his study of contemporary nineteenth-century accounts of towns in the American and Canadian West, Australia, and New Zealand, David Hamer defines "three stages in the evolution of the perception of a frontier town"—from focusing on the squalid present, to seeing the present and the town's potential future of the locale, to seeing only the future (*New Towns in the New World: Images and Perceptions of the Nineteenth-Century Urban Frontier* [New York: Columbia University Press, 1990], p. 177).

50. Garner Reminiscences, edited by C. S. Kingston, Eastern Washington University, Cheney. Albert S. Johnson, traveling by train on his way back from a horse drive to Helena, went through Spokane en route to his home along Rock Creek in the Palouse. As he later recalled, he was not impressed: "When we passed Spokane all I could see, while standing on the platform at the depot, was the construction of cheap wooden buildings and the sound of the hammers building them. I noticed that very few of these new buildings were painted" (*Reminiscences of Albert S. Johnson, 1867–1950: A Pioneer Account of Early Day Experiences in Washington Territory as Told to Jerome A. Peltier* [Spokane: National Printing Co., (1950)], p. 5). Johnson moved to Spokane in 1890.

51. Henry L. Reimers, "Empire Building in the Northwest: The Story of Frank Magers, a pioneer of the Inland Empire, as related by himself, and those who knew him best," ca. 1938, Eastern Washington University, Cheney.

52. Other population statistics mark the tremendous growth. In 1888, close to seven thousand people called Spokane Falls home; two years later, in 1890, that number had risen to twelve thousand, in 1892, thirty thousand people lived in Spokane. During the 1880s letter writers and diarists were more optimistic about the future of Spokane Falls and the region. See, e.g., M. Gilbert to Mr. and Mrs. Allen Sutton, October 24, 1888, Gilbert Papers, MsSc 225, EWSHS.

53. This description of Spokane Falls during the 1880s is drawn from Sanborn-Perris Insurance Maps of Spokane Falls, 1884, 1888, Geography and Map Division, Library of Congress, Washington, D.C.; R. L. Polk Co., *Spokane Falls City Directory, 1889;* John F. Carrere, *Spokane Falls, Washington Territory and Its Tributary Country Comprising All of Eastern Washington*

and the Idaho Panhandle . . . (Spokane: City Council and Board of Trade, 1889); *Tenth Census, Population Schedules, 1880,* Washington, Spokane County.

54. Jacob J. Klein Papers, MsBiog K673, EWSHS. Klein's version of the start of the Spokane fire is one of many differing "eyewitness" accounts. It is generally accepted that the fire had its origins in the building that contained Wolfe's Lunch Counter and second-story lodgings. The building was located on the north side of Railroad Avenue, four buildings east of Lincoln Street, at 208 West Railroad Avenue.

55. Boris Eichenbaum, "The Theory of the 'Formal Method,' " in *Russian Formalist Criticism: Four Essays,* trans. Lee T. Lemon and Marion J. Reis (1926; rpt. Lincoln: University of Nebraska Press, 1974), pp. 99–139. See also Victor Erlich, *Russian Formalism: History-Doctrine* (New Haven: Yale University Press, 1981). Whereas the Russian Formalists are concerned with literary texts and tend to segregate literature from culture, my interpretation here draws on their connections of history with literary genres and extends their examination of the transformation of literary genres into the transformation of urban space and cultural memory. See also Yuri M. Lotman, *Universe of the Mind: A Semiotic Theory of Culture,* trans. Ann Shukman (Bloomington: Indiana University Press, 1990), esp. "Part Three: Cultural Memory, History and Semiotics," pp. 215–72.

56. Anna M. Stratton Diary, August 10, 1889, Anna M. Stratton Papers, MsSc 174, EWSHS. Anna Stratton was the mother-in-law of J. J. Browne.

57. Daniel Dwight Diary, August 5, 1889, Daniel H. Dwight Papers, MsSc 231, EWSHS; Joseph H. Boyd to wife, August 11, 1889, J. H. Boyd Papers, MsSc 14, EWSHS; Dwight to Susan A. Willis, August 6, 1889, Dwight Papers, EWSHS.

58. Lois Barton, ed., *One Woman's West: Recollections of the Oregon Trail and Settling the Northwest Country by Martha Gay Masterson, 1838–1916* (Eugene, Ore.: Spencer Butte Press, 1986), p. 182.

59. John Fahey has written on the business elite that came to dominate Spokane. See *The Inland Empire: The Unfolding Years, 1879–1929* (Seattle: University of Washington Press, 1986), and *Shaping Spokane: Jay P. Graves and His Times* (Seattle: University of Washington Press, 1994). The following discussion of the rebuilding of Spokane Falls draws on the work of geographers, particularly those who examine the cultural meanings invested in landscapes. See Henri Lefebvre, *La Production de l'espace; The Production of Space,* trans. Donald Nicholson-Smith (Oxford: Blackwell, 1991); Edward W. Soja, *Postmodern Geographies: The Reassertion of Space in Critical Social Theory* (New York: Verso, 1989); J. Nicholas Entrikin, *The Betweenness of Place: Towards a Geography of Modernity* (Baltimore: Johns Hopkins University Press, 1991); Doreen Massey, *Spatial Divisions of Labor: Social Structures and the Geography of Production* (New York: Methuen, 1984); Yi-Fu Tuan, *Space and Place: The Perspective of Experience* (Minneapolis: University of Minnesota Press, 1977); Allan Pred, *Making Histories and Constructing Human Geographies: The Local Transformation of Practice, Power Relations, and Consciousness* (Boulder, Colo.: Westview Press, 1990).

60. Gilbert was referring to the Johnstown Flood of that June as well as to the Pacific Northwest fires (M. Gilbert to Mr. & Mrs. Allen Sutton, August 5, 1889, Adelaide Sutton Gilbert Papers, MsSc 225, EWSHS). See also Elwood Evans and Edmond S. Meany, eds., *The State of Washington: A Brief History of the Discovery, Settlement and Organization of Washington, the "Evergreen State" as Well as a Compilation of Official Statistics Showing the Material Development of the State Up to Date* (Tacoma: World's Fair Commission of the State of Washington, 1893), p. 144. Spokane Falls had undergone a similar fire six years before. In January 1883, when the town's population had reached one thousand, a large fire on Front Street in the downtown area led to the creation of a city fire department.

61. Daniel E. Turbeville III, "The Urban Fire Hazard on the Northwest Coast Frontier: Some Implications on Building Style and Town Planning," in *The Pacific Northwest and Beyond: Essays in Honor of Howard J. Critchfield,* ed. James W. Scott (Bellingham, Wash.: Center for Pacific Northwest Studies, Western Washington University, 1980), pp. 65–76; John J. Pauly, "The Great Chicago Fire as a National Event," *American Quarterly* 36 (Winter 1984): 668–83; David Hamer,

New Towns in the New World: Images and Perceptions of the Nineteenth-Century Urban Frontier (New York: Columbia University Press, 1990), pp. 171–72; Karen Sawislak, "Smoldering City: Class, Ethnicity, and Politics in Chicago at the Time of the Great Fire, 1867–1874" (Ph.D. diss., Yale University, 1990); Edward W. Nolan, *"A Night of Terror, Devastation, Suffering and Awful Woe": The Spokane Fire of 1889* (Spokane: EWSHS, [1989]); Daniel H. Dwight to Susan A. Willis, August 6, 1889, Dwight Papers, MsSc 231, EWSHS.

Even those interested in attracting investors and rebuilding the town, who might be expected to downplay the extent of the disaster, highlighted the comparison to Chicago. One real estate brokerage promotional pamphlet, for example, boasted, "When the size of the city is taken into consideration, it was even greater than the Chicago fire" (*Spokane Falls: The Metropolis of the Inland Empire* [Spokane Falls: Hunt Dart, 1890], p. 11).

62. Kelly reminiscence, A. A. Kelly Sr. Papers, MsSc 83, EWSHS; R. L. Polk Co., *Spokane City Directory, 1893;* Jennie Boughton, *Spokane from Memory* (Spokane: N.p., 1941), p. 9. On the role of collective memories, see Dell Hymes, "Folklore's Nature and the Sun's Myth," *Journal of American Folklore* 88 (1975): 345–69; William Bascom, "Four Functions of Folklore," in *The Study of Folklore,* ed. Alan Dundes (Englewood Cliffs, N.J.: Prentice-Hall, 1965), pp. 279–98 (originally published in the *Journal of American Folklore*).

63. *Spokane Falls Review,* August 11, 1889; "Has Great Future," *Spokane Falls Review,* September 1, 1889.

64. Carl Smith, *Urban Disorder and the Shape of Belief: The Great Chicago Fire, the Haymarket Bomb, and the Model Town of Pullman* (Chicago: University of Chicago Press, 1995); Dyar, *News for an Empire; Spokesman* (Spokane), 1890–93. By May 1890, Horace T. Brown had withdrawn from the enterprise. Even with increased investment from Chicago sources, the *Spokesman* was unable to push the *Spokane Falls Review* out of business. In 1893, the two morning papers merged as the *Spokesman-Review.*

65. C. W. Clarke Diary, August 5, 23, 1889, C. W. Clarke Papers, MS 27, EWSHS; Kelly reminiscence, A. A. Kelly Papers, MsSc 83, EWSHS; Jonathan Edwards, *An Illustrated History of Spokane County, State of Washington* (San Francisco: W. H. Lever, 1900), p. 63. Carl Abbott finds a similar "sustained excitement" regarding urban growth among boosters and businessmen in the cities of the antebellum Middle West; "they lived with one foot firmly in the future" (*Boosters and Businessmen: Popular Economic Thought and Urban Growth in the Antebellum Middle West* [Westport, Conn.: Greenwood Press, 1981], p. 206).

66. *Spokane Falls Review,* August 8, 1889; John Fahey, "Million Dollar Corner: The Development of Downtown Spokane, 1890–1920," *Pacific Northwest Quarterly* 62 (April 1971): 77–85. On the different class usages of the rhetoric of "community," especially as seen through a Marxist analysis of the industrial urban process, see David Harvey, *Consciousness and the Urban Experience: Studies on the History and Theory of Capitalist Urbanization* (Baltimore: Johns Hopkins University Press, 1985), pp. 255–62, and *The Urbanization of Capital: Studies in the History and Theory of Capitalist Urbanization* (Baltimore: Johns Hopkins University Press, 1985), pp. 29–30, 145–52, 199–200.

67. Perry Kline to Richard, Dillon, Montana, August 6, 1889, Perry Kline Papers, MsSc 262, EWSHS; *Spokane Falls Review,* August 8, 1889.

68. *Spokane Falls Review,* February 6, 1890.

69. City Ordinance 323, passed August 7, approved August 9, *Spokane Falls Review,* August 10, 1889; see also *Spokane Falls Review,* August 8, 1889.

70. Draft of Speech, J. Z. Moore Papers, Box 1, MsSc 7, EWSHS. For other descriptions of the rebuilding of Spokane Falls after the fire, see 1890 Diary, Harry J. Jones Papers, MsSc 93, EWSHS; Frances Fuller Victor, *Atlantis Arisen, or Tales of a Tourist about Oregon and Washington* (Philadelphia: J. B. Lippincott, 1891). On the influence of urban sound and activity, see Richard Fauque, "For a New Semiological Approach to the City," in *The City and the Sign: An Introduction to Urban Semiotics,* ed. Mark Gottdiener and Alexandros Ph. Lagopoulos (New York: Columbia University Press, 1986), pp. 137–59.

71. *Spokane Spokesman*, March 9, 1890, p. 1; John Fahey, "When the Dutch Owned Spokane," *Pacific Northwest Quarterly* 72 (January 1981): 2–10.

72. Memoir, p. 17, F. C. Sudhoff Papers, MsZ Coll. 17, EWSHS.

73. Joe to Annie, December 19, 1889, MsSc 196, EWSHS.

74. *Spokane Falls Review*, November 21, 1889.

75. *Spokane Falls Review*, November 21, 1889; *Spokane Globe*, December 8, 1889. Jonathan Edwards, "Autobiography," Jonathan Edwards Papers, MsSc 169, EWSHS. See also Ann Fabian, *Card Sharps, Dream Books, and Bucket Shops: Gambling in 19th-Century America* (Ithaca: Cornell University Press, 1990).

76. Edmond K. Pendergast to Mary [sister], January 26, 1890, E. K. Pendergast to Father, February 14, 1890, E. K. Pendergast Papers, MsSc 1, Washington State Historical Society, Tacoma. Similar attitudes were expressed by other residents. See Guy Waring, *My Pioneer Past* (Boston: Bruce Humphries, 1936), pp. 28–29; M. Gilbert to Mr. & Mrs. Allen Sutton, December 16, 1889, Gilbert Papers, EWSHS. See also John M. Findlay, *People of Chance: Gambling in American Society from Jamestown to Las Vegas* (New York: Oxford University Press, 1986).

77. *Spokane Falls Review*, January 11, 1890, February 13, 1890; *Spokane Globe*, January 4, 1890.

78. Although the Chinese represented less than 2 percent of Spokane's population, according to 1890 statistics, they were a particular target. Newspaper accounts continually associated Chinese with vice and violence in the city. See Ren H. Rice, *Spokane in 1897: As I Saw It* ([Spokane]: N.p., 1956). See also *Spokane Review*, November 24, 1890. The anxiety expressed by these accounts during the 1890s, as Spokane coped with the aftermath of the fire, abated during the next decade. While they still defined the city's Chinese residents as exotic "others," early twentieth-century promotional writers expressed a more tolerant view as they celebrated the Chinese as a tourist draw. "The Chinese population of Spokane is one of the most interesting features of the city," explained one author. "The Chinese are industrious and inoffensive and in Spokane are represented in many lines of business, although they are chiefly employed as laundrymen or tailors" (*Raymer's Dictionary of Spokane: An Encyclopaedic-Dictionary of the State of Washington, U.S.A., in general and the City of Spokane in Particular* [Spokane: Chas. D. Raymer, 1906], p. 36). See also M. Christine Boyer, *Dreaming the Rational City: The Myth of American City Planning* (Cambridge, Mass.: MIT Press, 1983), esp. chap. 2; Constance Perin, *Everything in Its Place: Social Order and Land Use in America* (Princeton: Princeton University Press, 1977).

79. The actions of Spokane Falls business and political leaders echoed those of other late nineteenth-century western civic leaders. See Kay J. Anderson, "The Idea of Chinatown: The Power of Place and Institutional Practice in the Making of a Racial Category," *Annals, AAG* 77 (1987): 580–98; Ramon D. Chacon, "The Beginning of Racial Segregation: The Chinese in West Fresno and Chinatown's Red Light District, 1870s–1920s," *Southern California Quarterly* 70 (Winter 1988): 371–98; Ivan H. Light, "From Vice District to Tourist Attraction: The Moral Career of American Chinatowns, 1880–1940," *Pacific Historical Review* 43 (August 1974): 367–94.

80. Although western Washington experienced the majority of the territorial violence against Chinese during the 1880s, Euro-Americans in eastern Washington were no less antagonistic toward the Chinese. See Robert Edward Wynne, "Reactions to the Chinese in the Pacific Northwest and British Columbia, 1850 to 1910" (Ph.D. diss., University of Washington, 1964); James A. Halseth and Bruce A. Glasrud, "Anti-Chinese Movements in Washington, 1885–1886: A Reconsideration," in *The Northwest Mosaic: Minority Conflicts in Pacific Northwest History*, ed. James A. Halseth and Bruce A. Glasrud (Boulder, Colo.: Pruett, 1977), pp. 116–39. As a result of anti-Chinese activities, the Chinese population in Spokane Falls had dropped to four hundred by January 1889 ("Chinese New Year," *Spokane Falls Review*, January 27, 1889, quoting Wong Frank, "an exceedingly intelligent Chinaman"). The center of Chinatown was identified as Front Street between Howard and Stevens streets. In the year before the fire, the Chinese commercial district had grown beyond its one-block area on Front Street, the unimproved road that ran along the riverbanks, to three other Front Street blocks and down several north-south streets.

81. *Spokane Falls Review,* May 15, 1890; "Tents Torn Down," *Spokane Falls Review,* August 22, 1889; *Spokane Falls Review,* November 21, 1889. Sanborn-Perris Insurance Maps of Spokane Falls, 1884, 1888, 1894, Geography and Map Division, Library of Congress.

82. John Fahey, "The Million-Dollar Corner," pp. 77–85; Boyd Papers, EWSHS; Jonathan Edwards, "An Active Building Period," Edwards Papers, EWSHS. This reorganization of the city moved beyond the original town site plans and visions of James Glover (Glover, *Reminiscences*). Fahey, "When the Dutch Owned Spokane," pp. 2–10.

83. The legacy of the post-fire architecture remains with the city today. As a group of Spokane architects explained in 1974, the six-story brick structure represents "Spokane's most typical architectural features" and is "a key to the character of the city" (Roland Colliander, David Evans, John Remington, Jim Waymire, and Thomas Stave, *Spokane Sketchbook* [Seattle: University of Washington Press, 1974], p. 42). In thinking about the influence of the new architecture, I have found useful Umberto Eco, "Function and Space: Semiotics of Architecture," in *The City and the Sign,* ed. Gottdiener and Lagopoulos, pp. 55–86.

84. *Spokane Spokesman,* March 9, 1890. On Chicago architecture, see Carl W. Condit, *The Chicago School of Architecture: A History of Commercial and Public Building in the Chicago Area, 1875–1925* (Chicago: University of Chicago Press, 1964); Perry Duis, *Chicago: Creating New Traditions* (Chicago: University of Chicago Press, 1976); Frederick Baumann, *The Art of Preparing Foundations for All Kinds of Buildings, with Particular Illustration of the "Method of Isolated Piers" as Followed in Chicago* (Chicago: J. M. Wing, 1873). See also Henry Matthews, "Kirtland Cutter: Spokane's Architect," in *Spokane and the Inland Empire: An Interior Pacific Northwest Anthology,* ed. David H. Stratton (Pullman: Washington State University Press, 1991), pp. 143–77.

85. Harry H. Hook and Francis J. McGuire, *Spokane Falls Illustrated: The Metropolis of Eastern Washington* (Minneapolis: Frank H. Thresher, 1889); Alice Roberts to Ones at Home, February 24, 1889, Alice Roberts Papers, EWSHS.

86. "Two Years in Spokane College," William Emsley Jackson Papers, MsSc 180, EWSHS. As one of the Mondovi settlers, Marion Moore, recalled, "We came to Spokane and *that* was an adventure. . . . We usually stayed at the O.W.R.&R. barns . . . I never tired of staring up at the Review Building especially if the wonderful lights were on in the tower" (Marion Moore Reminiscences, Pioneer Reminiscences, Cage 4600, WSU).

87. "The City of Spokane," *Spokane Spokesman: Annual Illustrated Supplement,* January 1892, p. 29.

88. Victor, *Atlantis Arisen,* p. 366.

89. [Northwestern Industrial Exposition], *The City of Spokane Falls and Its Tributary Resources* (New York: Matthews, Northrup, 1890), p. 6; Charles W. Robinson, "Exposition Management," *Harper's Weekly* 34 (February 1, 1890): 90–91; Robert W. Rydell, *All the World's a Fair* (Chicago: University of Chicago Press, 1984); Hamer, *New Towns in the New World.*

90. [Northwestern Industrial Exposition], *City of Spokane Falls,* pp. 6, 18–33.

91. The events surrounding the exposition are described in Durham, *History of the City of Spokane and Spokane Country, Washington,* vol. 1; Lucile F. Fargo, *Spokane Story* (Minneapolis: Northwestern Press, 1957), pp. 184–86.

92. Craig Wollner, *The City Builders: One Hundred Years of Union Carpentry in Portland, Oregon, 1883–1983* (Portland: Oregon Historical Society Press, 1990); David Montgomery, *Workers' Control in America: Studies in the History of Work, Technology, and Labor Struggles* (Cambridge: Cambridge University Press, 1979). On the Spokane labor movement, see Carlos Schwantes, *Radical Heritage: Labor, Socialism, and Reform in Washington and British Columbia, 1885–1917* (Seattle: University of Washington Press, 1979), pp. 118–21; James Leroy Hunt, "A History of the Central Labor Council of Spokane, Washington" (M.A. thesis, State College of Washington, 1940); Jonathan Dembo, *Unions and Politics in Washington State, 1885–1935* (New York: Garland, 1983). On the history of the carpenters' union, see Thomas Brooks, *The Road to Dignity: A Century of Conflict* (New York: Atheneum, 1981); Walter Galenson, *The United Brotherhood of Carpenters: The First Hundred Years* (Cambridge, Mass.: Harvard University Press, 1983).

93. R. H. Schein, "Representing Urban America: 19th-Century Views of Landscape, Space, and Power," *Environment and Planning D: Society and Space* 11 (1993): 7–21. John W. Reps includes a copy of this 1890 map in *Cities of the American West: A History of Frontier Urban Planning* (Princeton: Princeton University Press, 1979), p. 388.

Schein examines urban maps as "constructed images of constructed spaces" which "embody changing 19th-century urban ideals and attitudes" and "contributed to the definition and direction of a modernizing, industrializing America" (p. 8). They are "texts which selectively transformed and legitimized particular themes in the story of 19th-century urban America" (p. 9). See also Angela Miller, "Everywhere and Nowhere: The Making of the National Landscape," *American Literary History* 4 (1992): 207–29.

94. *Spokane Falls Review,* February 6, 1890; John R. Reavis, *The City of Spokane: Its Tributary Country and Its Resources* (Spokane: Clough & Graves, 1891). From quite different perspectives, Cecelia Tichi, *Shifting Gears: Technology, Literature, Culture in Modernist America* (Chapel Hill: University of North Carolina Press, 1987), who explores the cultural pervasiveness of social and physical engineering, and William Cronon, *Nature's Metropolis: Chicago and the Great West* (New York: Norton, 1991), who examines the economic and environmental linkages among urban areas and between city and country, outline the ways late nineteenth-century concern with social and economic control became articulated in physical spaces.

The *New York Tribune,* noting the recent acquisition of Washington statehood, poked fun at the name change and Spokane's claim of self-importance in a typical ditty entitled "A Spokane Man Talks." The *Spokesman* reprinted the verse.

> "Most people don't know," quoth one from Spokane,
> "That the name of our town rhymes exactly with man.
> That in all the wide world, in towns big or small,
> In growth in ten years, Spokane leads them all;
> That it's simply Spokane—the 'Falls' don't avail,
> That word has been dropped, like the pollywog's tail.
> But the biggest mistake in the whole category,
> Is to say that Spokane is in Wash. Territory.

It may be found in Dyar, *News for an Empire,* p. 60.

95. The annual report is reported in *Spokane Globe,* December 21, 1889.

Inset: Reservations about Empire

1. For general discussions of the economic development of the region, see John Fahey, *The Inland Empire: The Unfolding Years, 1879–1929* (Seattle: University of Washington Press, 1986); William H. Kensel, "Economic History of Spokane, Washington, 1881–1910" (M.A. thesis, Washington State University, 1962); D. W. Meinig, *The Great Columbia Plain: A Historical Geography, 1805–1910* (Seattle: University of Washington Press, 1968).

2. U.S. Congress, *Report of the Industrial Commission on the Relations and Conditions of Capital and Labor Employed in the Mining Industry, Including Testimony, Review of Evidence, and Topical Digest,* vol. 12: *Capital and Labor Employed in Mining Industry,* 57th Cong., 1st sess., H. Doc. 181, 1901–2, p. 425.

3. U.S. Department of the Interior, *Annual Report of the Commissioner of Indian Affairs to the Secretary of the Interior for the Year 1889* (Washington, D.C.: GPO, 1889), p. 12.

4. See, for example, Job Harriman, *The Class War in Idaho. The Horrors of the Bull Pen. An Indictment of Combined Capital in Conspiracy with President McKinley, General Merriam and Governor Steunenberg, for Their Crimes against the Miners of the Coeur d'Alenes,* 3d ed. (New York: N.p., 1899), p. 10. See also Thomas A. Hickey, *The Story of the Bull Pen at Wardner, Idaho* (New York: National Executive Committee, Socialist Labor Party, 1900).

5. Andrew R. L. Cayton and Peter S. Onuf, *The Midwest and the Nation: Rethinking the History of an American Region* (Bloomington: Indiana University Press, 1990), p. xviii.

6. The theoretical underpinnings of the perspective taken in this section, especially the emphasis on language and discourse, draw on the scholarly literature, from a variety of disciplines, that has come to be known broadly as postmodern. Much of this literature relies on the writings of Michel Foucault, Hayden White, and Clifford Geertz. See Michel Foucault, *Power/Knowledge: Selected Interviews and Other Writings, 1972–77*, ed. Colin Gordon (New York: Pantheon, 1980); Hayden White, *Tropics of Discourse: Essays in Cultural Criticism* (Baltimore: Johns Hopkins University Press, 1978); Clifford Geertz, *The Interpretations of Cultures* (New York: Basic Books, 1973). Other works influential in shaping this section's perspective include Anthony Giddens, *Social Theory and Modern Sociology* (Stanford: Stanford University Press, 1987), esp. pp. 73–108; Benedict Anderson, *Imagined Communities: Reflections on the Origin and Spread of Nationalism* (London: Verso Editions and NLB, 1983); James Clifford, "Identity in Mashpee," in *The Predicament of Culture: Twentieth-Century Ethnography, Literature, and Art* (Cambridge, Mass.: Harvard University Press, 1988). In thinking about the historical uses of these theoretical perspectives I have found useful Lynn Hunt, *Politics, Culture, and Class in the French Revolution* (Berkeley: University of California Press, 1984).

Chapter 2. Coeur d'Alene Fences and Walls

1. U.S. Congress, *Message from the President of the United States Transmitting a Letter of the Secretary of the Interior Relative to the Purchase of a Part of the Coeur d'Alene Reservation*, 51st Cong., 1st sess., S. Ex. Doc. 14, 1889, pp. 1, 7.

2. *Spokane Falls Review*, August 5, 1887; Andrew Seltice, one of the leaders of the Coeur d'Alenes, is usually identified as chief between 1865 and 1902. According to James Teit, an ethnographer, Seltice was chief in 1858 and took part with "a large force of Coeur d'Alene" in the Spokane war, "owing to some dissatisfaction over the treaty made with Governor Stevens, which they claimed the whites had not kept." Seltice died in 1902. See James A. Teit, *The Middle Columbia Salish* (Seattle: University of Washington Publications in Anthropology, 1928), pp. 92, 117.

This mixture of peoples who lived together on the Coeur d'Alene lands was typical of nineteenth-century Native Americans in this interior Pacific Northwest area. Descriptions by missionaries, government agents, and travelers emphasize the diversity of Salish-speaking peoples. See, for example, George Gibbs, *Report of Explorations and Surveys to Ascertain the Most Practicable Route for a Railroad from the Mississippi to the Pacific Ocean* (Washington, D.C.: GPO, 1855), 1:295; Hiram Martin Chittenden and Albert Talbot Richardson, eds., *Life, Letters and Travels of Father Pierre-Jean De Smet, S.J., 1801–1873*, 4 vols. (New York: F. P. Harper, 1905), 4:1246–47.

3. U.S. Department of the Interior, *Annual Report of the Commissioner of Indian Affairs to the Secretary of the Interior for the Year 1886* (Washington, D.C.: GPO, 1886), hereafter cited as *1886 Annual Report*. Such talk was common not only in the territories of Idaho and Washington; throwing reservations open to white settlement was a central issue in the national debate over the "Indian question." During the 1870s and 1880s the federal government emphasized nonmilitary means for dealing with western Indians. President U. S. Grant's peace policy, for example, sought to "civilize" and Christianize Native Americans through the joint work of missionaries and government agents on isolated reservations. The goal, according to many reformers and politicians, was assimilation. Full assimilation into American society included private, not communal, ownership of land. By dividing up tribally owned reservations into individually owned homesteads, the government could help break down tribal ties, foster the "civilization" and "Americanization" processes, and, not incidentally, open land for non-Indian settlers. In the national debate over this proposition, enacted in 1887 as the General Allotment or Dawes Sever-

alty Act, reformers spoke of the task of "showing the Indian how to help himself" and of the inevitable flow of white western emigration. See Frederick E. Hoxie, *A Final Promise: The Campaign to Assimilate the Indians, 1880–1920* (Lincoln: University of Nebraska Press, 1984); D. S. Otis, *The Dawes Act and the Allotment of Indian Lands*, ed. Francis Paul Prucha (1934; rpt. Norman: University of Oklahoma Press, 1973); William T. Hagan, "Private Property: The Indian's Door to Civilization," *Ethnohistory* 3 (Spring 1956): 126–37. See also Wilcomb E. Washburn, *The Assault on Indian Tribalism: The General Allotment Act (Dawes Act) of 1887* (Philadelphia: J. B. Lippincott, 1977); David M. Holford, "The Subversion of the Indian Land Allotment System, 1887–1934," *Indian Historian* 8 (Spring 1975): 11–21; Henry E. Fritz, *The Movement for Indian Assimilation, 1860–1890* (Philadelphia: University of Pennsylvania Press, 1963).

4. The minutes of the meetings are available in government documents: U.S. Congress, *Message from the President of the United States Transmitting a Communication from the Secretary of the Interior, with Accompanying Papers, Relating to the Reduction of Indian Reservations*, 50th Cong., 1st sess., House Ex. Doc. 63, 1887, hereafter cited as *Reduction of Indian Reservations;* U.S. Congress, *Message from the President*, 1889. Robert Felt, the U.S. interpreter for the Colville Indian Agency, served as interpreter in 1887. But it was a relative insider, Stephen Liberty, a Euro-American married to a Coeur d'Alene, who functioned in that role during the 1889 negotiations. Born Etienne Eduard Laliberte, Liberty was a longtime resident in the region, who received allotment lands as a Coeur d'Alene.

5. U.S. Congress, *Reduction of Indian Reservations*, p. 64; Gladys A. Reichard, *Coeur d'Alene* (New York: J. J. Augustin, 1938), extract from *Handbook of American Indian Languages*, Vol. 3, pp. 614, 616. This major study of the Coeur d'Alene language was done during the 1920s and 1930s. See also Barre Toelken, "A Sense of Place and the Sacred in Native American Tradition," paper presented at Comparative Popular Culture Research Seminar on Traditional Media, East-West Communication Institute, Honolulu, Hawaii, 1975.

6. I. R. Gildea, Farmer-in-charge, to Hal J. Cole, Indian Agent, May 23, 1890, Miscellaneous Letters Received, Coeur d'Alene, Box 32, Colville Indian Agency Records, RG 75-7 Bureau of Indian Affairs, National Archives Record Center, Seattle, Wash.; hereafter cited as NARC.

7. Robert I. Burns, S.J., "The Missionary Syndrome: Crusader and Pacific Northwest Religious Expansionism," *Comparative Studies in Society and History* 30 (April 1988): 273.

8. Anthropologists offer useful models of this process of cultural transformation. See Marshall Sahlins, *Islands of History* (Chicago: University of Chicago Press, 1985); Roy Wagner, *The Invention of Culture* (Englewood Cliffs, N.J.: Prentice-Hall, 1975). For a historian who applies these concepts, see Richard White, *The Middle Ground: Indians, Empire, and Republics in the Great Lakes Region, 1650–1815* (Cambridge: Cambridge University Press, 1991), esp. pp. 50–93.

9. See Robert H. Ruby and John A. Brown, *Indians of the Pacific Northwest: A History* (Norman: University of Oklahoma Press, 1981); Vine Deloria Jr., *Indians of the Pacific Northwest from the Coming of the White Man to the Present* (Garden City, N.Y.: Doubleday, 1977). Individual tribal histories include John Fahey, *The Flatheads* (Norman: University of Oklahoma Press, 1974), and *The Kalispel Indians* (Norman: University of Oklahoma Press, 1986); Robert H. Ruby and John A. Brown, *The Spokane Indians: Children of the Sun* (Norman: University of Oklahoma Press, 1970), and *Half-Sun on the Columbia: Chief Moses and the Columbia Indians* (Norman: University of Oklahoma Press, 1965); David C. Wynecoop, *Children of the Sun: A History of the Spokane Indians* (Wellprint, Wash.: By the author, 1969).

10. It is difficult to define the social and political relations among these peoples using the language of a different time, culture, and economic system. When ethnographers or anthropologists describe the social and political organizations of the interior Salish, they reflect this problem. They search for exact words to define the flexible boundaries between loosely affiliated groups. They speak of a "composite band political system consist[ing] of unified groups of villages with permanent alliances" and point out that "overall political unification did not develop until the time of the missionaries, treaties and reservations." See Deward E. Walker Jr., *Indians of Idaho* (Moscow: University Press of Idaho, 1982), p. 100; Claude Lévi-Strauss, *The Naked*

Man, trans. John Weightman and Doreen Weightman (New York: Harper & Row, 1971), esp. pp. 355–59.

11. W. P. Winans to Col. Samuel Ross, Supt. Indian Affairs, Washington Territory, May 30, 1870, W. Park Winans Letterbook (outgoing), January 1870–September 1872, W. Park Winans Papers, Cage 147, Series I—Correspondence, Box 4, Folder 34, WSU. For early descriptions of this environment, see Pierre-Jean De Smet to Captain A. Pleasonton, May 23, 1859, in P. J. De Smet, *New Indian Sketches* (New York: P. J. Kenedy, Excelsior Catholic Publishing House, 1904), pp. 141–46.

12. Chittenden and Richardson, eds., *Life, Letters and Travels of Father Pierre-Jean De Smet,* 1:367–75; Clifford Merrill Drury, ed., *First White Women Over the Rockies: Diaries, Letters, and Biographical Sketches of the Six Women of the Oregon Mission Who Made the Overland Journey in 1836 and 1838,* 3 vols. (Glendale, Calif.: A. H. Clark, 1963–66), 2:226.

13. For Jesuit accounts of their missionary activity among the Coeur d'Alenes, see Joseph P. Donnelly, trans., *Wilderness Kingdom: Indian Life in the Rocky Mountains, 1840–1847, The Journals and Paintings of Nicolas Point, S.J.* (New York: Holt, Rinehart and Winston, 1967); "History of the Coeur d'Alene Mission to 1850," Joset Papers, Oregon Province Archives, Crosby Library, Gonzaga University, Spokane. A Coeur d'Alene oral history of the coming of the Jesuits recorded in 1954 is printed in Ella E. Clark, *Indian Legends from the Northern Rockies* (Norman: University of Oklahoma Press, 1966), pp. 133–36. See also Edward J. Kowrach and Thomas E. Connolly, eds., *Saga of the Coeur d'Alene Indians: An Account of Chief Joseph Seltice* (Fairfield, Wash.: Ye Galleon Press, 1990).

14. Christopher L. Miller, *Prophetic Worlds: Indians and Whites on the Columbia Plateau* (New Brunswick, N.J.: Rutgers University Press, 1985); Alexander Diomedi, S.J., *Sketches of Indian Life in the Pacific Northwest* (1894; rpt. Fairfield, Wash.: Ye Galleon Press, 1978), pp. 61–84; Robert F. Berkhofer, *Salvation and the Savage: An Analysis of Protestant Missions and American Indian Response, 1787–1862* (Lexington: University of Kentucky Press, 1965); Burns, "Missionary Syndrome." Although the Catholics and Protestants differed in religious beliefs and, as Berkhofer has argued, in their interactions with Native Americans, they shared basic assumptions regarding the connections between Christianizing and "civilizing."

15. Donnelly, trans., *Wilderness Kingdom,* pp. 47–48.

16. Diomedi, *Sketches of Indian Life,* p. 83.

17. The missionaries maintained their standing among the Coeur d'Alenes even after the establishment of the reservation. Administration of the Coeur d'Alene reservation was a distant affair; the Indian agent residing on the Colville Reservation in Washington Territory also had jurisdiction over the Coeur d'Alenes after 1877. Although many Indian agents complained about the impossible logistics of this situation, it was not until 1905, on the eve of allotment, that a separate Indian agent was appointed for the Coeur d'Alenes. At times an agency-appointed farmer-in-charge resided on the Idaho reserve. But largely it was the missionaries who remained the closest non-native neighbors.

18. Donnelly, trans., *Wilderness Kingdom;* Cornelius M. Buckley, *Nicolas Point, S.J.: His Life and Northwest Indian Chronicles* (Chicago: Loyola University Press, 1989); Gilbert Garraghan, *The Jesuits of the Middle United States* (New York: America Press, 1938); Edmund R. Cody, *History of the Sacred Heart Mission* (Caldwell, Ida.: Caxton Printers, 1930); Robert Ignatius Burns, *Jesuits and the Indian Wars of the Northwest* (New Haven: Yale University Press, 1966). On the impact of the Jesuit-built environment see Carroll Van West, "Acculturation by Design: Architectural Determinism and the Montana Indian Reservations, 1870–1930," *Great Plains Quarterly* 7 (Spring 1987): 91–102.

19. The voices of the native inhabitants are particularly difficult to discern. Their few recorded words come to us always in translation, or in a non-native tongue, or as rephrased or recalled by observers in government treaty sessions, oral histories, letters, and missionary writings. The writers of these sources attempted to interpret the actions of the Coeur d'Alenes. In thinking through the various meanings embedded in these texts, I have found useful Mary Louise Pratt,

"Scratches on the Face of the Country; or, What Mr. Barrow Saw in the Land of the Bushman," in *"Race," Writing, and Difference*, ed. Henry Louis Gates Jr. (Chicago: University of Chicago Press, 1986), pp. 138–62; Dennis Tedlock, *The Spoken Word and the Work of Interpretation* (Philadelphia: University of Pennsylvania Press, 1983).

20. Missionaries and government officials rarely viewed such an apparently boundaryless lifestyle with favor. Father Diomedi noted that "the first step, and also the most difficult one," on the road to Christian religion and civilization "was to induce them to abandon their roving habits." Indian agents also worked to reduce the number of bands "roaming in Northwestern Idaho." See Diomedi, *Sketches of Indian Life*, p. 62; U.S. Department of the Interior, *Annual Report of the Commissioner of Indian Affairs to the Secretary of the Interior for the Year 1874* (Washington, D.C.: GPO, 1874), hereafter cited as *1874 Annual Report*.

21. See Dolores Janiewski, "Making Women into Farmers' Wives: The Native American Experience in the Inland Northwest," in *Women and Farming: Changing Roles, Changing Structures*, ed. Wava G. Haney and Jane B. Knowles (Boulder, Colo.: Westview Press, 1988), pp. 35–49. The writings of Christine Quintasket, a Colville woman, describe the ways interior Salish combined economic and social practices in the late nineteenth century (Jay Miller, ed., *Mourning Dove: A Salishan Autobiography* [Lincoln: University of Nebraska Press, 1990]).

22. Diomedi, *Sketches of Indian Life*, pp. 79, 63; U.S. Congress, *Reduction of Indian Reservations*, p. 36. The commission also remarked on other signs of "civilization": "The Indians are industrious, thrifty, provident, and good traders. They wear their hair short, and dress in citizen's dress from head to foot. They are polite, good-natured, and ambitious to excel, and to do in all things as white men do, except to adopt their vices." Likewise, in his first year as Indian agent, Albert Anderson found the Coeur d'Alenes "further advanced in civilization, and in better condition financially, than any other tribe connected with this agency. They are well supplied with all kinds of farming implements, from a plow to thrashing machines, of which latter they now have thirteen in operation, purchased by themselves with their own money." For examples of Coeur d'Alene dealings with the larger regional community, see U.S. Department of the Interior, *Annual Report of the Commissioner of Indian Affairs to the Secretary of the Interior for the Year 1879* (Washington, D.C.: GPO, 1879), p. 144, hereafter cited as *1879 Annual Report*; U.S. Department of the Interior, *Annual Report of the Commissioner of Indian Affairs to the Secretary of the Interior for the Year 1880* (Washington, D.C.: GPO, 1880), pp. 184–85; U.S. Department of the Interior, *Annual Report of the Commissioner of Indian Affairs to the Secretary of the Interior for the Year 1882* (Washington, D.C.: GPO, 1882), p. 154, hereafter cited as *1882 Annual Report*.

23. U.S. Congress, *Reduction of Indian Reservations*, p. 36; U.S. Department of the Interior, *Annual Report of the Commissioner of Indian Affairs to the Secretary of the Interior for the Year 1885* (Washington, D.C.: GPO, 1885), hereafter cited as *1885 Annual Report*.

24. As one visiting commission reported their demands, "The Coeur d'Alenes . . . agreed to relinquish their claim to Northern Idaho, on the condition that the Government supply them with stock and farming implements, and to remain upon the reservation, provided its boundaries should be changed so as to include the Coeur d'Alene mission and some farming-lands in the valley of the Lotah or Hangman's Creek" (*1874 Annual Report*, pp. 57–58).

25. U.S. Congress, *Letter from the Acting Secretary of the Interior, Transmitting in Response to Senate Resolution, March 30, 1886, Report upon the Claims of Certain Indians for Compensation for Lands*, 49th Cong., 1st sess., S. Ex. Doc. 122, pp. 11–12. See also Diomedi, *Sketches of Indian Life*, p. 81; Indophile [Lawrence Benedict Palladino, S.J.], *The Coeur d'Alene Reservation* (Montana: St. Ignatius Print, 1886).

26. *1879 Annual Report*, p. 144. James O'Neil's last name sometimes appears as O'Neill.

27. Ibid.

28. U.S. Department of the Interior, *Annual Report of the Commissioner of Indian Affairs to the Secretary of the Interior for the Year 1873* (Washington, D.C.: GPO, 1873), pp. 157, 160–61; Burns, *Jesuits and the Indian Wars*, pp. 96–114; Jack Dozier, "Coeur d'Alene Country: The Creation of the Coeur d'Alene Reservation in Northern Idaho," *Idaho Yesterdays* 6 (Fall 1962): 2–7.

29. Andrew Seltice et al. to John J. Simms, U.S. Indian Agent, Colville Agency, October 21, 1883, Miscellaneous Letters Received, Coeur d'Alene, 1880–84, Box 32, RG 75-7, NARC; *1874 Annual Report*, p. 58; U.S. Department of the Interior, *Report of the Commissioner of General Land Office to the Secretary of the Interior for the Year 1869* (Washington, D.C.: GPO, 1870), p. 346; "Reports of Agents in Washington Territory," in U.S. Department of the Interior, *Annual Report of the Commissioner of Indian Affairs to the Secretary of the Interior for the Year 1884* (Washington, D.C.: GPO, 1884), p. 159, hereafter cited as *1884 Annual Report*. For an overview, see Jack Dozier, "History of the Coeur d'Alene Indians to 1900" (M.A. thesis, University of Idaho, 1961); Ross R. Cotroneo and Jack Dozier, "A Time of Disintegration: The Coeur d'Alenes and the Dawes Act," *Western Historical Quarterly* 5 (October 1974): 405–19.

30. "The Coeur d'Alene Indians. Why Their Reservation Should Not Be Thrown Open," *Coeur d'Alene Sun*, April 6, 1886, p. 1; John Mullan to Rev. Joseph Cataldo, December 9, 1886, Pacific Northwest Tribes Missions Collection of the Oregon Province Archives of Society of Jesus, Microfilm, roll 16.

31. U.S. Congress, *Letter from the Secretary of the Interior Transmitting, in Response to Senate Resolution of January 25, 1888, Information about the Coeur d'Alene Indian Reservation, in Idaho*, 50th Cong., 1st sess., S. Ex. Doc. 76, 1887–88, p. 6; James O'Neil to Sidney D. Waters, July 26, 1884, Miscellaneous Letters Received, Coeur d'Alene, Box 32, Colville Indian Agency Records, RG 75-7, NARC; *1884 Annual Report; 1885 Annual Report; 1886 Annual Report*. See also Diomedi, *Sketches of Indian Life*, pp. 66, 68; H. Price, Commissioner of Indian Affairs (CIA), to Waters, March 20, 1884, May 21, 1884, Letters Received from the CIA, Box 18a; Atkins, CIA, to Gwydir, June 1, 1887, April 19, 1888, R. V. Bell, Acting CIA, to Cole, October 1, 1890, Letters Received from the CIA, Box 19a; William R. Carlin, Col., 4th Infantry, Fort Sherman, Idaho, to Gwydir, June 28, 1887, Holmes to Gwydir, July 17, 1887, Miscellaneous Letters Received, Box 32, Colville Indian Agency Records, RG 75-7, NARC.

32. Rickard D. Gwydir, U.S. Indian Agent, Colville, Wash., to Hon. Commissioner of Indian Affairs J. D. C. Atkins, Washington D.C., September 22, 1888, Colville Indian Agency Papers, Cage 2014, WSU; Robert Flett petition, September 14, 1888, Miscellaneous Letters Received, Coeur d'Alene, Box 32, Colville Indian Agency Records, RG 75-7, NARC. See J. Orin Oliphant, "Encroachments of Cattlemen on Indian Reservations in the Pacific Northwest, 1870–1890," *Agricultural History* 24 (January 1950): 42–58; Gwydir to Atkins, August 19, 1887, Miscellaneous Letters Received, Coeur d'Alene, Box 32, Colville Indian Agency Records, RG 75-7, NARC.

33. *Report of the Governor of Idaho to the Secretary of the Interior* (Washington, D.C., GPO, 1889), p. 339. According to the *Railroad Gazette*, May 18, 1888, the Northern Pacific leased this roadbed from the Washington and Idaho Railway Company in 1888.

34. "Report of Timber Trespass, Spokane Falls, Washington, July 14, 1890," *Records of Bureau of Indian Affairs*, National Archives, as noted in William N. Bischoff, "The Coeur d'Alene Country, 1805–1892: An Historical Sketch," Docket 81, C1 Ex 138, May 1956, Indian Claims Commission Reports, pp. 53–54, reprinted as *Interior Salish and Eastern Washington Indians I*, comp. and ed. David Agee Horr (New York: Garland, 1974), pp. 264–65. The mills were operated by J. Sexton (Hangman's Creek) and a Portland firm, Hoffman and Bates (Trout Creek).

35. Z. J. Hatch to J. N. Dolph, Portland, Oregon, April 26, 1884, *Records of the Bureau of Indian Affairs*, National Archives, as noted in Bischoff, "Coeur d'Alene Country."

36. Gwydir to Atkins, July 19, 1887, Colville Indian Agency Papers, WSU.

37. U.S. Congress, *Letter from the Secretary of the Interior, 1888*, p. 6; Gildea to Cole, March 8, 14, 18, 23, 1891, August 7, 1891, Miscellaneous Letters Received, Coeur d'Alene, Box 33, Colville Indian Agency Records, RG 75-7, NARC.

38. Gwydir to Atkins, July 19, 1887, Colville Indian Agency Papers, WSU; J. Holmes to Gwydir, June 28, 1887, Seltice et al. to Gwydir, June 4, 1888, Gildea to Cole, June 22, 1890, Miscellaneous Letters Received, Coeur d'Alene, Box 32, Colville Indian Agency Records, RG 75-7, NARC.

39. L. Harrison, Acting Commissioner, General Land Office, Washington, D.C., to William A. Chandler, U.S. Surveyor General, Boise, Idaho, March 10, 1884, John Mullan to Rev. Joseph

Cataldo, October 19, 1885, Mullan to Cataldo, n.d. [1884], Seltice to Hon. W. S. Holman, October 20, 1885, Pacific Northwest Tribes Missions Collection of the Oregon Province Archives of the Society of Jesus, Microfilm, roll 16; U.S. Congress, *Letter from the Acting Secretary of the Interior, Transmitting a Response to Senate Resolution, March 30, 1886, Report upon the Claims of Certain Indians for Compensation for Lands,* 46th Cong., 1st sess., S. Ex. Doc. 122, 1886, p. 10.

40. J. P. Sweeney, Additional Farmer, Colville Agency, to Major S. D. Waters, U.S. Indian Agent, Colville Agency, June 25, 1885, Miscellaneous Letters Received, 1885, Box 35, Colville Indian Agency Records, RG 75-7, NARC.

41. Contemporary and later accounts of interior Salish social and political customs describe the power of band leaders. See S. A. Chalfant and W. Bischoff, *Interior Salish and Eastern Washington* (New York: Garland, 1974); Jeffrey C. Reichwein, *Emergence of Native American Nationalism in the Columbia Plateau* (New York: Garland, 1990). "Under the recognized law and custom of the tribe, the chief of the tribe had power to make and promulgate its laws and had power to determine who should constitute the members of the tribe" (Statement of Stephen Liberty, Stephen Liberty Papers, EWSHS).

42. *Spokan Times,* April 28, 1881.

43. Waters to Price, November 29, 1884, Colville Agency Records, WSU; U.S. Department of the Interior, *Annual Report of the Commissioner of Indian Affairs to the Secretary of the Interior for the Year 1881* (Washington, D.C.: GPO, 1881), p. 158, hereafter cited as *1881 Annual Report.*

44. H. Price, Commissioner of Indian Affairs, to Sydney D. Waters, November 24, 1883, General Records, Box 18a, Colville Indian Agency Records, RG 75-7, NARC; Sydney Waters, U.S. Indian Agent, to H. Price, Commissioner of Indian Affairs, November 29, 1884, Colville Indian Agency Papers, WSU.

45. Ruby and Brown, *Spokane Indians;* Chalfant and Bischoff, *Interior Salish and Eastern Washington;* Reichwein, *Emergence of Native American Nationalism in the Columbia Plateau; 1881 Annual Report.*

46. Waters to Price, November 19, 1884, Colville Indian Agency Papers, WSU.

47. Simms had also offered this suggestion in his annual reports to the commissioner of Indian affairs. See *1881 Annual Report,* p. 158; *1882 Annual Report,* p. 153; U.S. Department of the Interior, *Annual Report of the Commissioner of Indian Affairs to the Secretary of the Interior for the Year 1883* (Washington, D.C.: GPO, 1883), p. 142.

48. W. Park Winans to Selucius Garfielde, July, 15, 1872, Box 4, W. Park Winans Papers, WSU, quoted in Ruby and Brown, *Spokane Indians,* p. 157; A. Seltice and others to Sydney D. Waters, U.S. Indian Agent, April 20, 1884, Miscellaneous Letters Received, 1880–84, Coeur d'Alene, Box 34, Colville Indian Agency Records, RG 75-7, NARC; *1886 Annual Report,* p. 232. The agent continued: "They pass their time in gambling and drinking whisky and are a curse to themselves and to every one else with whom they come in contact."

49. Gibbs, *Reports of Explorations and Surveys* 1:414.

50. A. Seltice and others to Waters, April 20, 1884; Holmes to Gwydir, July 17, 1887, Miscellaneous Letters Received, Coeur d'Alene, Box 32, Seltice to Chief Lot, Spokane Reserve, May 1, 1891, J. J. Walsh to Cole, May 14, 1893, Miscellaneous Letters Received, Coeur d'Alene, Box 33, Geo. F. Steele, Carpenter, DeSmet, Idaho, to Major Geo. H. Newman, Indian Agent, February 21, 1897, Miscellaneous Letters Received, Coeur d'Alene, Box 34, Colville Indian Agency Records, RG 75-7, NARC.

51. S. E. Liberty to Waters, July 23, 1885, Miscellaneous Letters Received, Coeur d'Alene, Box 32, Colville Indian Agency Records, RG 75-7, NARC.

52. A. B. Upshaw, acting commissioner, to Moore, October 23, 1886, and Petition against Liberty et al., June 14, 1898, RG 75, NARC. In the early 1900s, when the reservation was dismantled under the provisions of the Dawes Severalty Act and the Coeur d'Alenes were forced under protest to take homestead allotments, Euro-American settlers near the reservation noted with dismay that the four "squawmen" and their descendants had received a total of sixty-six of the allotments. See Charles O. Worley to Commissioner of Indian Affairs, July 8, 1907, Official

Letters sent from the Coeur d'Alene Superintendent, 1905–14, Box 1–2, and Patents in Fee/Deeds, Box 82, North Idaho Indian Agency Papers, RG 75–19, NARC.

53. Stephen Liberty papers, EWSHS.

54. Andrew Seltice and others to Anderson, February 8, 1902, Miscellaneous Letters Received, Coeur d'Alene, Box 34, Colville Indian Agency Records, RG 75–7, NARC. As a November 10, 1907, article in the *Spokesman-Review* pointed out in reference to the Colville and Spokane reservation allotment process, "a strain of Indian blood is a valuable asset at present, and it is wonderful how many white skins have turned red lately."

55. U.S. Congress, *Reduction of Indian Reservations*, pp. 32, 61.

56. U.S. Congress, *Reduction of Indian Reservations*, pp. 32, 33, 34; "Proceedings of the Northwest Indian Commission Held at Spokane Falls Commencing March 7, 1887, and Ending March 17, 1887," EWSHS.

57. J. J. Walsh to Hal Cole, July 5, 1893, Box 22, Colville Indian Agency Records, RG 75–7, NARC.

58. Idaho, *Session Laws, 1888–89*, 74–75, 80–81.

59. U.S. Congress, *Letter from the Secretary of the Interior*, 1887–88, p. 6.

60. U.S. Congress, *Message from the President*, 1889, p. 6.

61. U.S. Department of the Interior, *Annual Report of the Commissioner of Indian Affairs to the Secretary of the Interior for the Year 1889* (Washington, D.C.: GPO, 1889), p. 12.

62. Gwydir to Atkins, September 22, 1888, July 19, 1887, Colville Indian Agency Papers, WSU. Gwydir, "as an Agent for the *Indians*," was also strongly opposed "to granting many priviliges to whites on the reservation." John Walters, for example, wished to "run a boarding house on the reserve," and W. A. Bennett asked "for permission to camp thereon" (Gwydir to Atkins, September 22, 1888).

63. [Palladino], *Coeur d'Alene Reservation*. See also [Lawrence B. Palladino, S.J.], *Our Friends the Coeur d'Aleine Indians* (Montana: St. Ignatius Print, 1886); Palladino, *Indian and White in the Northwest* (Baltimore: J. Murphy, 1894); Wilfred P. Schoenberg, S.J., *Jesuit Mission Presses in the Pacific Northwest: A History and Bibliography of Imprints, 1876–1899* (Portland: Champoeg Press, 1957).

64. Myra Eells to Herbert Welsh, Corresponding Secretary, Indian Rights Association, January 3, 1894, Clifford M. Drury Collection, MS 17, EWSHS. Eells, living at that time on the Skokomish reservation, referred primarily to Washington Indians in his letter. "Although I have not been among all the Indians in the State, I have been among those who have progressed the most, as the citizen Indians, the Yakimas and others." Eells, the son of the early Spokane missionary Cushing Eells, had been born in Washington Territory. Father Diomedi's objections to taking land in severalty were many. "The best remedy," according to Diomedi, "is to leave to the Indians as much land as is necessary for their own use and their stock, and let them have sufficient time to acquire the habits of civilization" (Diomedi, *Sketches of Indian Life*, pp. 83–84).

65. See Hoxie, *A Final Promise;* Francis Paul Prucha, *Indian Policy in the United States: Historical Essays* (Lincoln: University of Nebraska Press, 1981), esp. pp. 180–97, 229–62.

66. Franz Boas, *The Mind of Primitive Man* (New York: Macmillan, 1911), p. 102.

67. Ronald P. Rohner, comp. and ed., *The Ethnography of Franz Boas: Letters and Diaries of Franz Boas Written on the Northwest Coast from 1886 to 1931* (Chicago: University of Chicago Press, 1969), pp. 139, 196; James A. Teit, "The Salishan Tribes of the Western Plateaus," ed. Franz Boas, *Forty-Fifth Annual Report of the Bureau of Ethnology to the Secretary of the Smithsonian Institution, 1927–1928* (Washington, D.C.: GPO, 1930). Between 1900 and 1910 James Teit's activities were financed privately by Homer E. Sargent. He also worked under the auspices of Anthropological Section of the Geographical Survey of Canada and the American Museum of Natural History of New York.

68. See, for example, A. G. Tonner to Anderson, November 15, 1902, April 29, 1903, Letters Received from the Commissioner of Indian Affairs, Box 19a, Colville Indian Agency Records, RG 75–7, NARC. Other area reservations were opened before the Coeur d'Alene. Allotments were

completed in January 1900 for the Colville reservation, and 1.5 million acres were opened for settlement and entry (U.S. Department of the Interior, *Annual Reports of the Department of the Interior for the Fiscal Year Ended June 30, 1913, U.S. Office of Indian Affairs, Part I, Report of Commissioner and the Appendixes* [Washington, D.C.: GPO, 1914], p. 101, hereafter cited as *1913 Annual Report.*)

69. U.S. Department of the Interior, *Annual Reports of the Department of the Interior for the Fiscal Year Ended June 30, 1903, U.S. Office of Indian Affairs, Part I, Report of Commissioner and the Appendixes* (Washington, D.C.: GPO, 1904), p. 332, hereafter cited as *1903 Annual Report.*

70. "Reports Concerning Indians in Washington," in U.S. Department of the Interior, *Annual Reports of the Department of the Interior for the Fiscal Year Ended June 30, 1904, U.S. Office of Indian Affairs, Part I, Report of Commissioner and the Appendixes* (Washington, D.C.: GPO, 1905), p. 350; Charles J. Kappler, *Indian Affairs: Laws and Treaties* (Washington, D.C.: GPO, 1904), 2:53. There are other examples. In 1908 the Woodlawn Cemetery Association of St. Marie's purchased 40 acres, and in the same year 8,000 acres were purchased by the secretary of the interior near Chatcolet and Benewah lakes and later given to Idaho for a park. In 1909, 640 acres were acquired by the Board of Regents of the University of Idaho.

71. "Reports Concerning Indians in Washington," *1903 Annual Report,* p. 331.

72. On Boas see Ronald P. Rohner and Evelyn C. Rohner, "Franz Boas and the Development of North American Ethnology and Ethnography," in *Ethnography of Franz Boas,* comp. and ed. Rohner, pp. xiii–xxx; Melville J. Herskovits, *Franz Boas: The Science of Man in the Making* (Clifton, N.J.: Augustus M. Kelley, 1973); Boas, *Mind of Primitive Man.*

73. See George W. Stocking Jr., ed., *Observers Observed: Essays on Ethnographic Fieldwork,* vol. 1, *History of Anthropology* (Madison: University of Wisconsin Press, 1983); James Clifford, "On Ethnographic Self-Fashioning: Conrad and Malinowski," in *Reconstructing Individualism: Autonomy, Individuality and the Self in Western Thought,* ed. Thomas C. Heller, Morton Sosna, and David E. Wellbery (Stanford: Stanford University Press, 1986), pp. 140–62. As Clifford suggests, "The omissions and commissions of ethnographies, their particular shadings of 'subjective' and 'objective,' their paradigms of cultural coherence and temporal process, their modes of authority, irony, allegory, and belief—all these have changed and are changing" (p. 142).

74. Teit, "Salishan Tribes," pp. 126.

75. James Clifford, "Introduction: Partial Truths," in *Writing Culture: The Poetics and Politics of Ethnography,* ed. James Clifford and George E. Marcus (Berkeley: University of California Press, 1986), p. 17. Although they would likely disagree with these conclusions, my argument here is also based on reading Tedlock, *Spoken Word and the Work of Interpretation,* and Dell Hymes, *"In Vain I Tried to Tell You": Essays in Native American Ethnopoetics* (Philadelphia: University of Pennsylania Press, 1981).

76. Teit, "Salishan Tribes," p. 147.

77. Franz Boas, ed., *Folk-Tales of Salishan and Sahaptin Tribes,* collected by James A. Teit, Marian K. Gould, Livingston Farrand, and Herbert J. Spinden (Lancaster, Pa.: American Folklore Society, 1917), pp. 123–24, 119–28. See Walter J. Ong, *Orality and Literacy: The Technologizing of the Word* (New York: Methuen, 1982); Franz Boas, "Mythology and Folk-Tales of the North American Indians," in *Race, Language and Culture* (New York: Macmillan, 1940), originally published in *Journal of American Folk-Lore* 27 (1914): 374–410; Gladys A. Reichard, *An Analysis of Coeur D'Alene Indian Myths* (Philadelphia: American Folklore Society, 1947).

Dell Hymes, among others, questions the authenticity of such tales. At the linguistic level at which Hymes and Tedlock operate, these collected tales *are* suspect. Indeed, as accounts of the "primitive" Indian myths that Boas and Teit intended to collect, they also fall short. But as social documents that reveal cultural conflicts on the eve of allotment they have much to say. Teit's informants speak out through his collection to offer explanations and descriptions of the past that tell as much about the present reservation situation. Boas may have warned against such "secondary interpretations," but it is just such secondary interpretations that are of interest here.

See Boas, *Mind of Primitive Man;* or Franz Boas, "Psychological Problems in Anthropology," *American Journal of Psychology* 21 (1910): 371–84, reprinted in George W. Stocking Jr., ed., *The Shaping of American Anthropology, 1883–1911: A Franz Boas Reader* (New York: Basic Books, 1974), pp. 243–54; Hymes, *"In Vain I Tried to Tell You";* Tedlock, *Spoken Word and the Work of Interpretation;* James C. Scott, *Domination and the Arts of Resistance: Hidden Transcripts* (New Haven: Yale University Press, 1990), esp. pp. 152–54.

78. U.S. Congress, *Letter from the Secretary of the Interior, 1888,* p. 6. See also Gwydir to Atkins, August 19, 1887, Colville Indian Agency Papers, WSU: "I have recently visited the Coeur d'Alene Reservation and while they held a full and well attended council with the Indians in regard to taking their bonds in severalty and they voted unanimously not to take their bonds otherwise than they now hold them. That is to say, each family already have a separate tract which it claims, the tracts varying in quantities from forty to two hundred acres."

79. 34 Stat. L., Chap. 3504, pp. 325, 335–38; 104,077 acres remained in Coeur d'Alene hands.

80. Cotroneo and Dozier, "A Time of Disintegration," pp. 410–11. The 638 included 56 Spokanes living on the reservation and 66 individuals identified as members of the Stephen Liberty, Julian Boutelier, Joseph Peavy, and Patrick Nixon families. On the impact of the Dawes Act, see Richard White, *The Roots of Dependence: Subsistence, Environment, and Social Change among the Choctaws, Pawnees, and Navajos* (Lincoln: University of Nebraska Press, 1983); Leonard A. Carlson, *Indians, Bureaucrats, and Land: The Dawes Act and the Decline of Indian Farming* (Westport, Conn.: Greenwood Press, 1981); Thomas R. Cox, "Tribal Leadership in Transition: Chief Peter Moctelme of the Coeur d'Alenes," *Idaho Yesterdays* 23 (Spring 1979): 2–9.

81. *1913 Annual Report,* p. 101; Great Northern Railway, *Opening of the Flathead, Coeur d'Alene and Spokane Indian Reservations* (N.p.: N.p., [1909]); 219,767 acres were distributed out of a possible 224,410.

82. John Eikum Oral History, Oral History Collection, LCHS. Eikum is confusing the openings of the Pacific Northwest reservations. President Taft proclaimed the lands of the Flathead, Coeur d'Alene, and Spokane reservations open for homestead application in 1909. Applications received between July 15 and August 5, 1909, were entered into a lottery to determine the order of land choice. After September 1, 1910, any unclaimed lands could be entered under the provisions of the Homestead Laws (Great Northern Railway, *Opening of the Flathead, Coeur d'Alene and Spokane Indian Reservations,* pp. 2–5; Lawrence F. Schmeckebier, *The Office of Indian Affairs* [Baltimore: Johns Hopkins Press, 1927], pp. 105–00). The Coeur d'Alene lottery system was patterned after one used at the recent opening of the Colville reservation. See also Jack Dozier, "The Coeur d'Alene Land Rush, 1909–10," *Pacific Northwest Quarterly* 53 (October 1962): 145–50.

83. See, e.g., Minnie Louise Bailey to Mr. and Mrs. G. W. Bailey, January 24, 1910, George Cecil Bailey Papers, 1990, A II B 1/3, UW.

84. John Eikum Oral History, LCHS. Lottery participants were not, of course, the only new settlers. In Plummer and other new town sites merchants and others provided support services. For a description of Plummer during this period, see letter from Mr. and Mrs. LeRoy Willard read by Glen Baughman, No. 78–71, Oral History Collection, Eastern Washington University, Cheney; Karl Wetter, ed., *Tales of Early Plummer* (Plummer, Ida.: Plummer High School, 1962).

85. J. P. Kinney, *A Continent Lost—A Continent Won: Indian Land Tenure in America* (Baltimore: Johns Hopkins University Press, 1937), p. 266; U.S. Congress, House Res. 807, 56th Cong., 2d sess., 1910. See also correspondence in Miles Poindexter Papers, No. 3828, Boxes 67, 68, UW.

86. Minnie Louise Bailey to Mr. and Mrs. G. W. Bailey, May 1, 1910, Bailey Papers, 1990, UW. For a similar rose-colored perspective see the reminiscence by J. Russell Roberts, "Growing Up on the Last Frontier: A Minaloosa Valley Boyhood," *Idaho Yesterdays* 26 (Summer 1982): 2–8.

87. Frank King Oral History, 25, Black Oral History Collection, CT 2, WSU. See also Mr. and Mrs. William King Oral History, 27, Black Oral History Collection, WSU.

Chapter 3. Coeur d'Alene Mining Debates

1. "Well Pleased Indians," *Spokane Weekly Review,* April 28, 1892, pp. 6, 8. The Coeur d'Alenes received $1,130 individual shares. A local settler, Charles O. Brown, also commented on the allocation, noting in 1893, "Some two years ago these Indians [Coeur d'Alenes] sold the northern or timbered part of their reservation to the U.S. for 550,000 dollars and as there are only 500 Indians of all ages in this tribe and the money was divided per capita they got in some families as much as 14,000 dollars. They have fine horses and carriages but I suspect the church got a good slice" (1893 Diary, Charles Odell Brown Papers, MSS 88, Department of Special Collections, University of Idaho Library, Moscow).

2. Vernon Jensen, *Heritage of Conflict: Labor Relations in the Nonferrous Metals Industry up to 1930* (Ithaca: Cornell University Press, 1968); Melvyn Dubofsky, "The Origins of Western Working Class Radicalism, 1890–1905," in *Workers in the Industrial Revolution: Recent Studies of Labor in the United States and Europe,* ed. Peter N. Stearns and Daniel J. Walkowitz (New Brunswick, N.J.: Transaction Books, 1974); Robert Wayne Smith, *The Coeur d'Alene Mining War of 1892* (Corvallis: Oregon State College, 1961); Richard E. Lingenfelter, *The Hardrock Miners: A History of the Mining Labor Movement in the American West, 1863–1893* (Berkeley: University of California, 1974); Mark Wyman, *Hard-Rock Epic: Western Miners and the Industrial Revolution, 1860–1910* (Berkeley: University of California Press, 1979); Thomas Carpenter, "Labor Conflict in the Mining Industry of the Coeur d'Alenes, 1892 and 1899" (Ph.D. diss., New York University, 1973); Patricia Hart and Ivar Nelson, *Mining Town: The Photographic Record of T. N. Barnard and Nellie Stockbridge from the Coeur d'Alenes* (Seattle: University of Washington Press; Boise: Idaho State Historical Society, 1984).

3. "Our Trade," *Coeur d'Alene Miner* (Wallace, Ida.), January 1, 1891.

4. *Coeur d'Alene Press* (Coeur d'Alene, Ida.), February 20, 1892, p. 4. For similar expressions from other "tributary" areas, see *The Palouse Country* (Pullman, Wash.: N.p., [1910]).

5. On these 1860s mining strikes see John Willis Christian, "The Kootenay Gold Rush: The Placer Decade, 1863–1872" (M.A. thesis, Washington State University, 1967); Harold Albert York, "The History of the Placer Mining Era in the State of Idaho" (M.A. thesis, University of Oregon, 1939); William J. Trimble, *Mining Advance into the Inland Empire* (Madison: Bulletin of the University of Wisconsin, 1914).

6. W. Hudson Kensel, "Inland Empire Mining and the Growth of Spokane, 1883–1905," *Pacific Northwest Quarterly* 60 (April 1969): 84–97; John Fahey, *Inland Empire: D. C. Corbin and Spokane* (Seattle: University of Washington Press, 1965), and *Ballyhoo Bonanza: Charles Sweeny and the Idaho Mines* (Seattle: University of Washington Press, 1971); James Wardner, *James Wardner of Wardner, Idaho* (New York: Anglo-American Publishing Co., 1910); John Fahey, "The Milwaukee-Youngstown Connection: Midwestern Investors and the Coeur d'Alene Mines," *Pacific Northwest Quarterly* 81 (April 1990): 42–49.

7. Alan Derickson, *Workers' Health, Workers' Democracy: The Western Miners' Struggle, 1891–1925* (Ithaca: Cornell University Press, 1988), pp. 86–100; "A Miners' Hospital," *Coeur d'Alene Miner,* March 7, 1891; Carlos A. Schwantes, *Radical Heritage: Labor, Socialism, and Reform in Washington and British Columbia, 1885–1917* (Seattle: University of Washington Press, 1979); Schwantes, "The Concept of a Wage Workers' Frontier: A Framework for Future Research," *Western Historical Quarterly* 18 (January 1987): 39–55; Wyman, *Hard Rock Epic.* For an example of the district attitude toward Chinese, see "A Chinese Excursion," *Coeur d'Alene Miner,* June 18, 1892, about the expulsion of forty-eight Chinese residents and businessmen from nearby Bonner's Ferry, Idaho.

8. John Fahey, "Coeur d'Alene Confederacy," *Idaho Yesterdays* 12 (1968): 2–7; Clark C. Spence, *Mining Engineers and the American West: The Lace-Boot Brigade, 1849–1933* (New Haven: Yale University Press, 1970).

9. "Letter from Sweeney," *Coeur d'Alene Miner* (Wallace, Ida.), April 2, 1892, p. 5.

10. The Northern Pacific and the Union Pacific, which operated the ninety-one miles of rail-

road tracks in the district, had been increasing their shipping rates each year. Charles Sweeney, owner of the Last Chance mine, announced the MOA plan to shut down the mines to force the railroad companies to lower their freight rates (Richard G. Magnuson, *Coeur d'Alene Diary: The First Ten Years of Hardrock Mining in North Idaho* [Portland: Metropolitan Press, 1968], pp. 152, 168; Fahey, *Ballyhoo Bonanza*, pp. 73–74).

11. Edward Chase Kirkland, *Dream and Thought in the Business Community, 1860–1900* (Ithaca: Cornell University Press, 1956), esp. pp. 1–28; Richard H. Peterson, *The Bonanza Kings: The Social Origins and Business Behavior of Western Mining Entrepreneurs, 1870–1900* (Lincoln: University of Nebraska Press, 1971).

12. In an effort to focus on the contemporary debate, the discussion that follows relies on the words written during the years of mining strife. Reminiscences and memoirs are also part of the ongoing debate, particularly from the side of the mine owners. See John Hays Hammond, *The Autobiography of John Hays Hammond*, 2 vols. (New York: Farrar & Rinehart, 1935); Flora Colman, *I'd Live It Over* (New York: Farrar & Rinehart, [1941]); William Stoll, *Silver Strike* (Boston: Little, Brown, 1932); Wardner, *James Wardner;* John F. MacLane, *A Sagebrush Lawyer* (New York: Pandick Press, 1953); "Albert Burch" in T. A. Rickard, *Interviews with Mining Engineers* (San Francisco: Mining and Scientific Press, 1922).

13. On northern Idaho and eastern Washington newspapers see Ralph E. Dyar, *News for an Empire: The Story of the Spokesman-Review* (Caldwell, Ida.: Caxton Printers, 1952); David James Vergobbi, "Hybrid Journalism: Bridging the Frontier/Commercial Cusp on the Coeur d'Alene Mining Frontier" (Ph.D. diss., University of Washington, 1992). The district newspapers also included the *Wallace Press* (later the *Coeur d'Alene American*), *Coeur d'Alene Miner* (Wallace), *Mullan Tribune, Coeur d'Alene Sun* (Murray), *Wardner News,* and *Coeur d'Alene Statesman* (Osburn). Although complete runs of all these papers are no longer available, the Idaho State Historical Society, Boise, and University of Idaho Library, Moscow, have the most extensive sets.

14. Existing diaries and letters written by Coeur d'Alene miners also record their concerns with work conditions, frequent unemployment, and wages. See, for example, the letters of Richard Thomas printed in A. C. Todd, "Cousin Jack in Idaho," *Idaho Yesterdays* 8 (Winter 1964–65): 2–11. Kent C. Ryden, *Mapping the Invisible Landscape: Folklore, Writing, and the Sense of Place* (Iowa City: University of Iowa Press, 1993), traces the sense of place still exhibited through the oral history narratives of twentieth-century Coeur d'Alene mining district residents.

15. *Spokane Spokesman,* March 31, 1892.

16. *Spokane Spokesman,* April 1, 1892. The miners' union vigorously opposed such characterizations of their actions. See the union reply to the mine owners in *Coeur d'Alene Miner,* April 2, 1892.

17. *Mullan Tribune,* April 2, 1892. Punctuation as in original. Making a clear distinction between Spokane and Coeur d'Alene, the same issue castigated "the mine owners who inculcated so many lies into a small a space at their last meeting in Spokane. The mis statements were so glaring as to make their authors objects of ridicule and contempt with all fair minded, thinking people in the Coeur d'Alene."

18. *Coeur d'Alene Barbarian.* David Vergobbi details this "war of words and labor" as an example of a "hybrid journalism"—a "vital bridge between frontier and commercial/market press eras"—"that reflected its transitional wage worker environment" ("Hybrid Journalism," pp. 2, 4).

19. William Joseph Gaboury, "From Statehouse to Bullpen: Idaho Populism and the Coeur d'Alene Troubles of the 1890s," *Pacific Northwest Quarterly* 58 (January 1967): 14–22; Gaboury, *Dissension in the Rockies: A History of Idaho Populism* (New York: Garland, 1988); *Mullan Tribune,* May 4, 1892. The connections between the Populists and labor unions in the Pacific Northwest are also noted by Schwantes, *Radical Heritage.* In July 1892, the Washington Populists, meeting in Ellensburg, passed a plank in support of the striking miners: "We extend our heartiest sympathy to the locked out men of Coeur d'Alene and Homestead, and we will send to them financial aid in their struggle with monopoly and plutocracy." See Thomas W. Riddle, *The Old*

Radicalism: John R. Rogers and the Populist Movement in Washington (New York: Garland, 1991), p. 122; *Seattle Post-Intelligencer*, July 26, 1892. The Populist perspective infuses the work of Thomas Carpenter, who argues that "the miners regulated their society through mass participation to provide equal economic opportunity for all whose luck and labor could endure" ("Labor Conflict in the Mining Industry").

20. *Wallace Press*, April 30, 1892; *Spokane Weekly Review*, March 31, 1892. The resolutions were reprinted in most of the regional newspapers. See, e.g., *Mullan Tribune*, April 2, 1892; *Spokane Spokesman*, March 27, 1892; *Spokane Review*, June 9, 1892.

21. U.S. Congress, *Proceedings before the Committee on Military Affairs of the House of Representatives in Relation to the Coeur d'Alene Labor Troubles* (Washington, D.C.: GPO, 1900), p. 852, hereafter cited as *Proceedings before the Committee on Military Affairs*.

22. *Spokane Spokesman*, March 31, 1892.

23. Pioneer, "The Wage War," *Wallace Press*, June 11, 1892. David R. Roediger, *The Wages of Whiteness: Race and the Making of the American Working Class* (New York: Verso, 1991), examines the development of white working-class racism before 1877. Although his assertion that the white working class forged its identity in opposition to blacks holds true for the rhetoric of the Coeur d'Alene miners, the evidence from the Coeur d'Alene mining district of the 1890s also suggests that such a dialectic rhetoric ran into difficulties in a working environment where racial and ethnic distinctions did not fit into neat categories. In his related study, Alexander Saxton, *The Rise and Fall of the White Republic: Class Politics and Mass Culture in Nineteenth-Century America* (New York: Verso, 1990), argues that in the West, Chinese replaced blacks in white supremacist ideology (esp. pp. 310–13).

24. *Coeur d'Alene Barbarian*, April 9, 1892; *Wallace Press*, April 23, 1892.

25. See, for example, the *Mullan Tribune*, March 19, 1892; *Coeur d'Alene Miner*, March 26, 1892. On the use of the Spokane daily papers, see *Wallace Press*, April 9, 1892; "Come Let Us Reason Together," *Coeur d'Alene Miner*, April 2, 1892.

26. *Spokane Weekly Review*, March 31, 1892, p. 11; *Coeur d'Alene Barbarian*, April 2, 1892; *Coeur d'Alene Statesman* (Osborn), June 6, 1892. In response, the union statement started, "As miners we are not gifted with the literary abilities of the hired attorneys of the Mine Owners' association." The Central Miners' Union of the Coeur d'Alenes' official statement was widely printed. See *Spokane Review*, March 27, 1892; *Coeur d'Alene Miner*, April 2, 1892.

27. *Spokane Spokesman*, May 12, 1892.

28. *Wallace Press*, May 14, 1892.

29. *Coeur d'Alene Mining & Concentrating Company v. Wardner's Miners' Union*, RG21, National Archives Records Center, Seattle, Wash. See also *Coeur d'Alene Miner*, May 14, 21, June 11, July 16, 1882; Monique C. Lillard, "The Federal Court in Idaho, 1889–1907: The Appointment and Tenure of James H. Beatty, Idaho's First Federal District Court Judge," *Western Legal History* 2 (Winter–Spring 1989): 35–78.

30. Charles Siringo, *Riata and Spurs* (Boston: Houghton Mifflin, 1927), *Two Evil Isms: Pinkertonism and Anarchism* (Chicago: CAS, 1915), pp. 36–42, and *A Texas Cowboy* (Chicago: M. Umbdenstock, 1885); *Coeur d'Alene Miner*, September 24, 1892.

31. *Coeur d'Alene American*, July 23, 1892.

32. *Spokane Review*; *Coeur d'Alene Miner*; *Spokesman*. See also George Edgar French, "The Coeur d'Alene Riots of 1892," *Overland Monthly* 26 (July 1895): 32–49.

33. Although talking was initially forbidden in the bull pens, restrictions soon eased.

34. William Haywood, *Bill Haywood's Book: The Autobiography of Big Bill Haywood* (New York: International Publishers, 1929), pp. 62–63.

35. The decline in silver prices was felt throughout the region. In January 1894, a regional businessman, J. C. Eaton, noted, "Spokane is the worst off of any city of its size in the United States. She is adjacent to the best Silver-Lead countries in the world. viz: Slocan Country B.C. & the Coeur d'Alenes in Idaho, but silver is not in it now" (J. C. Eaton to F. G. Jaques, January 7, 1894, Spokane, OR Northwest File, Vault, Northwest Room, Spokane Public Library).

36. Coeur d'Alene Miners' Union, "Resolutions," 1899, Idaho State Historical Society, Boise; *Mullan Mirror,* June 10, 1899. The *Spokane Review* and the *Spokesman* had joined in 1893.

37. *Spokane Review,* June 12, 1892; *Spokane Spokesman,* July 28, 1892. Although they deal with different times and classic texts, I have found Joyce Appleby, *Capitalism and a New Social Order: The Republican Vision of the 1790s* (New York: New York University Press, 1984), and Richard Tuck, *Natural Rights Theories: Their Origin and Development* (Cambridge: Cambridge University Press, 1979), useful in thinking about the historical groundings of the language of rights, liberty, and civic responsibility.

38. U.S. Congress, *Report of the Industrial Commission on the Relations and Conditions of Capital and Labor Employed in the Mining Industry, Including Testimony, Review of Evidence, and Topical Digest,* vol. 12: *Capital and Labor Employed in Mining Industry,* 57th Cong., 1st sess., H. Doc. 181, 1901–2, p. 494, hereafter cited as *Report of the Industrial Commission.*

39. *Report of the Industrial Commission,* 12:xcviii, 425, 414.

40. *Proceedings before the Committee on Military Affairs,* p. 546. See David Montgomery, *The Fall of the House of Labor* (Cambridge: Cambridge University Press, 1987), for the equation that late nineteenth-century workers made between race and work.

41. Mary Ellen Rowe, "The Early History of Fort George Wright: Black Infantrymen and Theodore Roosevelt in Spokane," *Pacific Northwest Quarterly* 80 (July 1989), 91–100; Rowe, "Fort George Wright, Washington, 1894–1912: A Case Study in Civilian-Military Relations before the First World War" (M.A. thesis, University of Washington, 1980); Arlen L. Fowler, *The Black Infantry in the West, 1869–1891* (Westport, Conn.: Greenwood, 1971). Fort George Wright had been established as one of the "many schemes proposed" by Spokane businessmen "to attract new capital and business to the city" after the devastating fire and panic of 1893.

42. May Arkwright Hutton, *Coeur d'Alenes, or A Tale of Modern Inquisition in Idaho* (Denver: App Engraving and Printing for May Arkwright Hutton, 1900), p. 233; *Proceedings before the Committee on Military Affairs,* pp. 325, 372; Job Harriman, *The Class War in Idaho. The Horrors of the Bull Pen. An Indictment of Combined Capital in Conspiracy with President McKinley, General Merriam and Governor Steunenberg, for Their Crimes against the Miners of the Coeur d'Alenes,* 3d ed. (New York: N.p., 1899). For other examples, see *Report of the Industrial Commission,* 12:420, 432, 433; *Spokesman-Review,* May 2, 3, 4, 11, 13, 1899; U.S. Congress, *Coeur d'Alene Labor Troubles. Investigation of Conduct of Army in Idaho Riots,* 56th Cong. 1st sess., H. Report 1999, 1899–1900, esp. pp. 73, 125.

43. *Mullan Mirror,* June 10, 1899. At the 1892 Spokane labor rally in support of the Coeur d'Alene miners, along with speeches and songs the crowd heard a poem entitled "The Miner's Wife." The stanzas described a hunted band of Coeur d'Alene union men hiding out in the Idaho mountains who are saved from starvation by "a faithful woman" who enters the wilds to bring them food. "If man is waiting, our women are here, God bless the miner's wife," ends the final verse (*Spokane Spokesman,* July 28, 1892).

44. *Spokesman-Review,* June 12, 1899.

45. Hutton, *The Coeur d'Alenes,* p. 10.

46. Mary (Hallock) Foote to C. C. Buel, Esq., Assistant Editor, *Century Magazine,* [January 1893], Foote Collection, Huntington Library, San Marino, Calif.; Mary Hallock Foote, "Coeur d'Alene," *Century Magazine* 47 (February 1894): 502–14, (March 1894): 722–31, (April 1894): 895–908; 48 (May 1894): 102–15. Foote's serialized story was later distributed in book form as Mary Hallock Foote, *Coeur d'Alene* (New York: Houghton Mifflin; Cambridge, Mass.: Riverside Press, 1894). See also Mary (Hallock) Foote to Mr. Johnson, *Century Magazine,* February 2, 1891, Foote to Buel, *Century Magazine,* February 26, 1893, [Mary (Hallock) Foote], [Notes on Miners War in Idaho, 1892], Foote Collection; Rodman W. Paul, ed., *A Victorian Gentlewoman in the Far West: The Reminiscences of Mary Hallock Foote* (San Marino, Calif.: Huntington Library, 1972).

47. Foote, writing in 1893 and 1894, retells the events of 1892; Hutton, writing in 1900, comments on the 1892 events but speaks more directly to the 1899 disputes. A comparison of

these two romantic accounts of Coeur d'Alene mining troubles also suggests the constraints on women's role in late nineteenth-century public discourse.

48. See Mary Hallock Foote to Helena de Kay Gilder, February 20, March 27, 1893, Box 68, James D. Hague Collection, Huntington Library, San Marino, Calif.; copies of letters from the Mary Hallock Foote Collection, Stanford University Library, Palo Alto, Calif. As Rodman Paul notes: "Already a part of the genteel tradition when she first went west, her [Foote's] continued reliance on the Gilders, who were the embodiment of eastern culture, kept her subject to what would today be called the viewpoint of the Eastern Establishment, at a time when she was becoming known as a leading writer and illustrator of scenes that were regarded as being 'authentically western' " (*A Victorian Gentlewoman in the Far West*, p. 9).

49. Foote to Buel, [January 1893], Foote Collection; Foote, *Coeur d'Alene*, p. 46; Foote, "Coeur d'Alene," p. 512.

50. Hutton, *The Coeur d'Alenes*, pp. 9, 173–76. The Huttons later moved out of the working-class world of northern Idaho. As investors in the successful Hercules Mine, they moved to Spokane, where May Hutton became active in a variety of civic activities. She led a flamboyant eastern Washington campaign for women's suffrage. See John Fahey, *The Days of the Hercules* (Moscow: University Press of Idaho, 1978); Benjamin H. Kizer, "May Arkwright Hutton," *Pacific Northwest Quarterly* 57 (April 1966): 49–56; Patricia Voeller Horner, "May Arkwright Hutton: Suffragist and Politician," in *Women in Pacific Northwest History: An Anthology*, ed. Karen J. Blair (Seattle: University of Washington Press, 1988), pp. 25–42.

51. Stanley Stewart Phipps, "From Bull Pen to Bargaining Table: The Tumultuous Struggle of the Coeur d'Alene Miners for the Right to Organize, 1887–1942" (Ph.D. diss., University of Idaho. 1983).

Inset. Empire Building

1. Spokane Chamber of Commerce, *What You Will Enjoy in Spokane* (Spokane: Spokane Chamber of Commerce, 1915), pp. 8–9; R. E. Bigelow, "Tourist Travel," *Annual Meeting, Spokane Chamber of Commerce* (Spokane: N.p., 1915), p. 5; "Hostess for a City," *Spokesman-Review*, May 18, 1958.

2. *Market Facts about the Spokane Country and the Five Major Markets of the Pacific Northwest* (Spokane: [Spokane Chamber of Commerce], 1927); Spokane Chamber of Commerce Papers, MS 1, EWSHS; *The Scenic Lure of Spokane and the Great Inland Empire of the Pacific Northwest* (Spokane: Spokane & Inland Empire, 1924).

3. James A. Ward, *Railroads and the Character of America, 1820–1877* (Knoxville: University of Tennessee Press, 1986); Leo Marx, *The Machine in the Garden: Technology and the Pastoral Idea in America* (New York: Oxford University Press, 1964); John R. Stilgoe, *Metropolitan Corridor: Railroads and the American Scene* (New Haven: Yale University Press, 1983); William Cronon, *Nature's Metropolis: Chicago and the Great West* (New York: Norton, 1991); Carlos A. Schwantes, *Railroad Signatures across the Pacific Northwest* (Seattle: University of Washington Press, 1993). M. M. Mattison hyperbolically expressed this perspective in his 1908 *Pacific Monthly* article "Rail Transportation in Washington": "The pioneer railroads had to bring the people who furnished the traffic; had to open up the state's first coal mines; set the pace in lumber operation, point out the way to apply irrigation principles, donate manufacturing sites to encourage the building of coast seaports, build and maintain the first line of grain warehouses, exploit the possibilities of foreign trade and give financial encouragement to the first struggling shippers. Then, in order that nothing in the way of paternalism might be overlooked, the earlier railroads took complete charge of the state's legislative efforts and even indicated where the streets in the larger cities should run so as not to interfere with railroad terminals" (quoted in Schwantes, *Railroad Signatures*, p. 13).

4. John Fahey, *Shaping Spokane: Jay P. Graves and His Times* (Seattle: University of Wash-

ington Press, 1994). The Spokane and Inland Empire Railroad Company operated both the interurban Spokane and Inland Empire Railway and Spokane city traction lines. Its financial story can be traced in part through *Annual Report of the Spokane & Inland Empire Railroad Company*, 11 vols. (Spokane: Shaw & Borden, 1907–17); *Spokane & Inland Empire Railroad Company, First and Refunding Mortgage Five Per Cent Twenty Year Gold Bonds, Protective Agreement* (N.p., 1918).

5. William Deverell, *Railroad Crossing: Californians and the Railroad, 1850–1910* (Berkeley: University of California Press, 1994), explores similar contestations in California.

6. *Spokesman-Review* (Spokane), August 2, 1909; also quoted in Schwantes, *Railroad Signatures*, p. 174.

Chapter 4. Expansion and Promotion

1. L. Ella Hewitt, "Memories of Spokane," *Spokesman-Review*, April 23, 1950; John Brinkerhoff Jackson, *American Space: The Centennial Years, 1865–1876* (New York: Norton, 1972), pp. 231–40; John G. Cawelti, "America on Display: The World's Fairs of 1876, 1893, 1933," in *The Age of Industrialism in America: Essays in Social Structure and Cultural Values*, ed. Frederic Cople Jaher (New York: Free Press, 1968), pp. 317–63.

2. Hewitt, "Memories of Spokane."

3. *Walla Walla Union*, May 5, 1877; Richard Slotkin, *The Fatal Environment: The Myth of the Frontier in the Age of Industrialization, 1800–1890* (New York: Atheneum, 1985), pp. 3–5.

4. The Spokane Falls Fourth of July celebrations continued to be significant events for the homesteaders in the region through the 1870s and 1880s. Their influence is particularly noticeable in local histories and oral lore. See, for example, the account in Alice V. Campbell, *A Short History of Rosalia, Whitman County* [N.p.: N.p., 1930], p. 5: "The first Fourth of July celebration in the Palouse country was held in Spokane Falls in 1879, and pioneers of Rosalia tell of the pleasure anticipated. But, a few days before came rain, and snow which 'dampened' but did not 'squelch' their patriotism, as most of them attended. It was necessary that they go the day before as it took a whole day by team to make the trip which we now make in less than an hour by auto."

5. Prospectors drawn to the Pacific Northwest by the 1883 Coeur d'Alene gold strikes had uncovered a wealth of veins not only gold but silver, copper, lead, zinc, and quartz—in the Kootenay Mountains of southeastern British Columbia. Along Kootenay Lake that year they staked claims that eventually developed into the Ainsworth silver-lead district. In 1886 copper and silver outcroppings on Toad Mountain led to the establishment of the Silver King Mine. The rich lodes of Red Mountain near Trail Creek were uncovered in 1889. Two years later, discoveries of silver, lead, and zinc opened up the Slocan region. In 1892 finds uncovered in the East Kootenays led to the development of the Sullivan mines. The standard accounts of the Kootenay mining boom are William J. Trimble, *The Mining Advance into the Inland Empire*, Bulletin of the University of Wisconsin No. 638, History Series 3, no. 2 (Madison: University of Wisconsin, 1914); Fred J. Smyth, *Tales of the Kootenays with Historical Sketches by the Author and Others* (1937; rpt. Vancouver: J. J. Douglas, 1977); F. W. Howay, W. N. Sage, and H. F. Angus, *British Columbia and the United States: The North Pacific Slope from Fur Trade to Aviation* (Toronto: Ryerson Press, 1942), pp. 264–98. See also Martin Robin, *The Rush for Spoils: The Company Province, 1871–1933* (Toronto: McClelland and Stewart, 1972), pp. 16–48; Margaret A. Ormsby, *British Columbia: A History* (Vancouver: Macmillans, 1958), pp. 315–17; and Albert Metin, *La Colombie britannique: Etude sur la colonisation au Canada* (Paris: A. Colin, 1908), pp. 241–77. More recent studies include Jeremy Mouat, *Roaring Days: Rossland's Mines and the History of British Columbia* (Vancouver: University of British Columbia Press, 1995).

6. Although no separate population statistics were kept for Moyie or the Kootenays at this time, personal accounts and more general census records agree that the American presence in

the Kootenays was strong. See John Spencer Church, "Mining Companies in the West Kootenay and Boundary Regions of British Columbia, 1890–1900—Capital Formation and Financial Operations" (M.A. thesis, University of British Columbia, 1961), pp. 14–15. On the changing population of the area, see Stanley H. Scott, "The Origins of Kootenay Society, 1890–1930," in *Northwest Perspectives: Essays on the Culture of the Pacific Northwest*, ed. and comp. Edwin R. Bingham and Glen A. Love (Seattle: University of Washington Press, 1979), pp. 78–96.

7. Carlos A. Schwantes, *Radical Heritage: Labor, Socialism, and Reform in Washington and British Columbia, 1885–1917* (Seattle: University of Washington Press, 1979), p. 115. See also Church, "Mining Companies in the West Kootenay and Boundary Regions."

8. Smyth, *Tales of the Kootenays*, p. 156.

9. Cawelti, "America on Display," p. 319. For examples of recent work in this field, see Umberto Eco, V. V. Ivanov, and Monica Rector, *Carnival!* ed. Thomas A. Sebeok (Berlin: Mouton, 1984); Frank E. Manning, *The Celebration of Society: Perspectives on Contemporary Cultural Performance* (Bowling Green, Ohio: Bowling Green University Popular Press, 1983); Alessandro Falassi, ed., *Time Out of Time: Essays on the Festival* (Albuquerque: University of New Mexico Press, 1987).

The work of Victor Turner on the ritual process has been particularly influential in symbolic anthropology. See Turner, *The Ritual Process: Structure and Anti-Structure* (London: Routledge & Kegan Paul, 1969), and *Dramas, Fields, and Metaphors: Symbolic Action in Human Society* (Ithaca: Cornell University Press, 1974). For specific applications, see Turner and Edward M. Bruner, eds., *The Anthropology of Experience* (Urbana: University of Illinois Press, 1986). For overviews of this literature, see Joseph R. Gusfield and Jerzy Michalowicz, "Secular Symbolism: Studies of Ritual, Ceremony, and the Symbolic Order in Modern Life," *Annual Review of Sociology* 10 (1984): 417–35.

10. In thinking about the relations among those who create and participate in public celebrations, especially in regard to political and ideological power struggles, I have found useful Susan G. Davis, *Parades and Power: Street Theatre in Nineteenth-Century Philadelphia* (Berkeley: University of California Press, 1986); Eric Hobsbawm, "The Invention of Tradition," in Hobsbawm and Terence Ranger, eds., *The Invention of Tradition* (Cambridge: Cambridge University Press, 1982), pp. 1–14.

11. Roy Rosenzweig, *Eight Hours for What We Will: Workers and Leisure in an Industrial City, 1870–1920* (Cambridge: Cambridge University Press, 1983), pp. 65–90, 153–68; William H. Cohn, "A National Celebration: The Fourth of July in American History," *Cultures* 3, no. 1 (1976): 141–56.

12. Jeffrey C. Alexander, *Actions and Its Environments: Toward a New Synthesis* (New York: Columbia University Press, 1988), pp. 301–33.

13. Bruce Lincoln, *Discourse and the Construction of Society: Comparative Studies of Myth, Ritual, and Classification* (New York: Oxford University Press, 1989); Mikhail Bakhtin, *Rabelais and His World*, trans. Helene Iswolsky (Bloomington: Indiana University Press, 1984); Bakhtin, *Speech Genres and Other Late Essays*, trans. Vern W. McGee, ed. Caryl Emerson and Michael Holquist (Austin: University of Texas Press, 1986). As Bakhtin's analysis of carnivals suggests, these self-presentations might be seen as a type of "carnivalized literature" that use elaborate and excessive prose to compete for cultural authority. My reading of Bakhtin has been guided by Katerina Clark and Michael Holquist, *Mikhail Bakhtin* (Cambridge, Mass.: Belknap Press of Harvard University Press, 1984); Dominick LaCapra, "Bakhtin, Marxism, and the Carnivalesque," in *Rethinking Intellectual History: Texts, Contexts, Language* (Ithaca: Cornell University Press, 1983), pp. 291–324; Peter Burke, "Bakhtin for Historians," *Social History* 13 (1988): 85–90; Renate Lachmann, "Bakhtin and Carnival: Culture as Counter-Culture," trans. Raoul Eshelman and Marc Davis, *Cultural Critique*, no. 11 (Winter 1988–89): 115–52.

14. The political boundary issue had been settled in 1846; see Norman A. Graebner, *Empire on the Pacific: A Study in American Continental Expansion* (New York: Ronald Press, 1955). On the creation of borderland communities, studies of the Mexico–United States border offer instructive comparisons; see Oscar J. Martinez, *Troublesome Border* (Tucson: University of Ari-

zona Press, 1988); Gloria Anzaldua, *Borderlands/La Frontera: The New Mestiza* (San Francisco: Aunt Lute Books, 1987); Patricia Nelson Limerick, "The Adventures of the Frontier in the Twentieth Century," in *The Frontier in American Culture*, ed. James R. Grossman (Berkeley: University of California Press; Chicago: Newbery Library, 1994), pp. 66–102.

15. For a contemporary example, see Barry Wellman, Peter J. Darrington, and Alan Hall, "Networks as Personal Communities," in *Social Structures: A Network Approach*, ed. Barry Wellman and S. D. Berkowitz (Cambridge: Cambridge University Press, 1988), pp. 130–84.

16. Stanley Jones Oral History, Interviewer Les Walker, Vancouver, B.C., 1958, RHM. See also E. Spraggett Reminiscences, 1930, E/E/SP7, PABC. "We never had any trouble on the boundary line then," recalled Spraggett, "there was no question of Canadian side or American; we drove across from each side with whatever we had and there was no question of customs." Customs officers were assigned to a couple of border locations in 1893, but travelers habitually used routes that bypassed custom stations.

17. Young Man Reminiscences, Add MSS 177, File 13, Selkirk Regional Archives, Selkirk College, Castlegar, British Columbia.

18. Robert Buchanan Graham Oral History, Interviewer J. M. Cameron, 1956, RHM; Peter Chapman, *Where the Lardeau River Flows*, Sound Heritage Series no. 32 (Victoria: Provincial Archives of British Columbia, 1981), pp. 12–13; Mouat, *Roaring Days*, esp. pp. 20–21.

19. Spraggett Reminiscences, PABC; Maria Drope House to Candace [Drope], April 6, 1908, Ft. Steele, House Papers, MSS 90, FtS. On the importance of correspondence in sustaining kinship ties and influencing migration patterns, see Dorothy O. Johansen, "A Working Hypothesis for the Study of Migrations," *Pacific Historical Review* 36 (February 1967): 1–12. Johansen suggests that "the first settlers determine the character of a community and by communicating their value satisfactions or dissatisfactions to potential migrants, they, in effect, 'select' the migrants who will follow and thereby perpetuate the character of the differentiated community" (pp. 11–12). See also Elizabeth Hampsten, *"Read This Only to Yourself": The Private Writings of Midwestern Women, 1880–1910* (Bloomington: Indiana University Press, 1982); Micaela di Leonardo, *The Varieties of Ethnic Experiences: Kinship, Class, and Gender among California Italian-Americans* (Ithaca: Cornell University Press, 1984).

20. Smyth, *Tales of the Kootenays*, p. 36; Nation to Laura Turton Nation, November 29, 1900, Moyie, British Columbia, Harold Turton Nation Papers, MSS 293, FtS.

21. Spraggett Reminiscences, PABC; Carrie Allen Oral History, Oral History Collection, Stevens County Historical Society, Colville, Wash.

22. Clarke Bros. to W. D. Middaugh, Esq., Nelson, British Columbia, May 30, 1893, Charles W. Clarke Papers, MG 36, University of Idaho Library, Moscow. Outlining their attributes, they explained, "We are experienced in this line; familiar with the frontier and its ways. . . . Mr. C. W. Clarke is a correspondent of the Spokane REVIEW."

23. Clifford Stewart to British Columbia Land Commissioner, October 22, November 24, 1903, Box 217, Folder 2112, British Columbia Land Department Files, Canadian Pacific Railroad Papers, GAI; M. Wendell to "Papa," November 8, 1909, Murray, B.C., M. Wendell Papers, uncataloged, FtS; Clara Graham Papers, Add MSS 197, File 13, Selkirk Regional Archives, Selkirk College, Castlegar, B.C.; C. ["Ed"] Tiegart to James Tiegart, March 9, [1890], Tiegart Family Papers, MSS 178, FtS.

24. Diaries for 1916, 1917, and 1919, John Andrew Forin Papers, Add MSS 741, PABC; Archie Coombs Oral History, RHM; Margaret Graham, " 'Tobacco Plains' Once Upon a Time," GAI.

25. *Advance* (Midway, B.C.), October 2, 1899; Smyth, *Tales of the Kootenays*, p. 25; W. C. Stayt to William Whyte, 2nd Vice President, Canadian Pacific Railway, December 16, 1905, and January 4, 1906, Box 212, Folder 2069, Canadian Pacific Railway Papers, GAI.

26. Diary for 1903, John Dean Papers, Add MSS 5, PABC; "Platform Reception Committee" Pass, Ephemera Collection, Huntington Library, San Marino, Calif. Roosevelt visited Spokane on May 26, 1903.

27. Edgar Jamieson Reminiscences, Nelson Museum, Nelson, B.C.; Mouat, *Roaring Days*, pp. 23–46.

28. *Visit Spokane—the Empire City!* [Spokane; N.p., 1919]; *Spokane, the City Beautiful: A Souvenir of Spokane, Washington and the Inland Empire* (Spokane: N.p., 1906); *Spokane and the Inland Empire: The Land of Mighty Rivers and Giant Waterfalls, Great Lakes, Rugged Mountains with Vast Mineral Storehouses, Grand Forests, and Immense Wheat Fields* (Buffalo, N.Y.: W. G. Mac Farlane; Spokane: F. B. Wright, [1903]).

29. Charles W. Clarke 1886 Diary, entries for January 17 and 7, 1886, Charles W. Clarke Papers, MS27, EWSHS; Roy H. Clarke Papers, MS14, EWSHS. The Clarke brothers did eventually abandon the ranch, known as the Knolls, in 1889. See Charles W. Clarke 1889 Diary.

30. Charles W. Clarke, "Carbonair: The Adventure of Two Brave Boy 'Forty-Niners,' " *Youth's Companion* 69 (March 14, 1895): 127–28, "Armajo," *Youth's Companion* 66 (February 16, 23, and March 2, 9, 16, 23, 1893): 81–82, 93–94, 109–10, 121–22, 133–34, 145–46, "Klat-awa," *Youth's Companion* 60 (June 23, 1887): 273–74; and "Keequilly," *Youth's Companion* 68 (March 22, 1894): 130–31; Daniel T. Rodgers, *The Work Ethic in Industrial America, 1850–1920* (Chicago: University of Chicago Press, 1978), pp. 125–52. The prolific Clarke also published his children's stories in other periodicals, often under a pseudonym. See, for example, Wood Ruff Clarke, "Max," *Christian Advocate Supplement,* April 7, 1887, pp. 234–35.

31. Clarke, "Klat-awa," pp. 273–74, quotes on p. 274.

32. Charles W. Clarke Papers, EWSHS.

33. "Advertising" Scrapbook, File 32, Box 3, Charles Clarke Papers, EWSHS; Roderick Nash, *Wilderness and the American Mind,* 3d ed. (New Haven: Yale University Press, 1982); Lee Clark Mitchell, *Witnesses to a Vanishing America: The Nineteenth-Century Response* (Princeton: Princeton University Press, 1981); Ann Vincent Fabian, "Rascals and Gentlemen: The Meaning of American Gambling" (Ph.D. diss., Yale University, 1982).

34. Charles Clarke, as a Republican, sought local political offices at the Kootenai County level. He followed local Populist Party activities as well and hoped for a fusion between local Republicans and Populists in the election of 1894. See 1894 Diary, Charles Clarke Papers, EWSHS.

35. On the Clarke brothers' move west and reflections on their lack of success in certain ventures, see Charles W. Clarke, Mt. Lookout, Ohio, to Robert E. Clarke, Spokane, March 15, 1885, pp. 6–7, Roy Clarke Papers, EWSHS: "We all unitedly accepted this change and must endure its results; and the burden of liability hits us all. You charge on Geo a large responsibility for our cattle project because of his tremendous enthusiasm in '83. He, on the other hand, might deem you primarily accountable, because from your series of trips West and your persistent advocacy of that field as superior for money making, sprang the original influence which led us Westward; subsequently enforced by your acceptance of this Very enterprise in '83. And either of you might place grave weight on me, because of my restlessness in the Bracket business, my readiness for change, and the important factor my correspondence became in formenting and forwarding our consolidated transfer West."

36. *An Illustrated History of North Idaho Embracing Nez Perces, Idaho, Latah, Kootenai and Shoshone Counties, State of Idaho* (N.p.: Western Historical Publishing Co., 1903), pp. 804–6, 829–30; Hiram T. French, *History of Idaho: A Narrative Account of Its Historical Progress, Its People and Its Principal Interests,* vol. 1 (Chicago: Lewis, 1914), pp. 188–89.

37. Charles and Robert Clarke entered into an agreement with Post: town lots in exchange for advertisements and circulars, and other lots if and when manufacturers moved to Post Falls. See "Copy of Agreement between Fred Post and Clarke Bros. relating to water power," March 16, 1889, Box 3, Roy Clarke Papers, EWSHS.

38. Clarke Brothers, "The Great Northwest. Free Sites for Manufacturers. Free Water Power. Low Prices to All at Post Falls, Idaho," March 1889; "A Sound Investment," March 1888; "Advertising" Scrapbook, Charles Clarke Papers, EWSHS. The shared language included the following: "As a town-site this place challenges the continent for beauty combined with utility." According to Clarke's prose, Post Falls (and Spokane Falls) "commands an immense and fertile agricultural region. It is the natural distributing center for . . . mining districts. It controls a vase area of

timber, accessible both by rail and river. *Its water power is the best on the continent, excelling that of Minneapolis in volume, frontage, and regularity.* Moreover this region is in the direct path of immigration."

39. See Charles W. Clarke 1890 Diary, pp. 26, 29, 36, 38, 40, and "Advertising" Scrapbook, Charles W. Clarke Papers, EWSHS; *Spokane Falls Review*, August 5, 1890; *Northwest Magazine*, April 1890, pp. 33–34, April 1891, p. 9; Clarke Bros. to Charles Henry, March 29, 1890, Clarke Bros. to *Northwest Magazine*, April 21, 1890, and Scrapbook, 1889–93, MG36, Charles W. Clarke Papers, University of Idaho Library, Moscow.

40. *Spokane Falls Review*, August 5, 1890, pp. 11, 7; Sanborn Fire Insurance Co., Post Falls, Idaho, Maps, 1890.

41. Charles Clarke to Robert Clarke, June 23, 1892, Roy Clarke Papers, EWSHS. The years 1889 and 1890 were Clarke Bros. Real Estate Company's most successful ones. Sales dropped off precipitously by 1891 as the Coeur d'Alene reservation excitement abated. The 1893 depression also contributed to the end of the Clarkes' Post Falls ventures. See 1894 Diary, Charles Clarke Papers, EWSHS.

42. Northwest Homeseeker and Investor, *The Inland Empire and What It Comprehends: Together with a Sketch of the Principal Cities and Surrounding Country That Should Be Seen by Every Visitor to the Lewis and Clark Exposition at Portland* (Spokane: Hutchinson and Bronson, 1905), p. 27. The following interpretation is based on a survey of available promotional literature and maps. Substantial bodies of material are located in the Northern Pacific Railroad Pamphlet Collection at the Beinecke Rare Book and Manuscript Library, Yale University, New Haven, Conn.; the Great Northern Railway and Northern Pacific Railroad collections at the Minnesota Historical Society, St. Paul; and the Canadian Pacific Railroad Collection at the Glenbow-Alberta Institute, Calgary. Scattered holdings are also available at other archives such as those at the Eastern Washington State Historical Society, Spokane; Washington State University Library, Pullman; Eastern Washington University Library, Cheney; University of Washington Libraries, Seattle; Spokane Public Library; Sterling Library, Yale University, New Haven, Conn.; University of Wyoming Library, Laramie; Bancroft Library, University of California, Berkeley; Huntington Library, San Marino, Calif., and Latah County Historical Society, Moscow, Idaho.

43. *Catechism of the Inland Empire and the Pacific Northwest: Resources, Opportunities, Advantages* (Spokane: N.p., [1911]); Spokane Falls Chamber of Commerce, *An Ideal Country. The Great Inland Empire and Spokane Falls, Its Metropolis* (Spokane Falls: Snow & Willcox Printers, [1891]); *Spokane Falls. Its Banking, Commercial and Manufacturing Interests* (Spokane: *Daily Chronicle*, 1889), p. 1.

44. See, e.g., Edward Lange, *Birdseye View Map of Yakima Valley and Central Washington* (N.p.: [Legh R. Freeman], 1907); Sandpoint Commercial Club, *Sandpoint, Idaho, Center of the Underdeveloped Northwest* (N.p., 1915); [P. B. Johnson], *The Pacific Northwest: A Concise and Accurate Description of the Geography, Soil, Climate, Resources and Industries of Washington Territory, Northern Oregon and Idaho* ([Walla Walla, Wash.: *Walla Walla Union*], 1884); Frank J. Parker, comp. and ed., *Washington Territory! The Present and Prospective Future of the Upper Columbia Country, Embracing the Counties of Walla Walla, Whitman, Spokane and Stevens, with a Detailed Description of Northern Idaho* (Walla Walla, W.T.: Statesman Book and Job Office, 1881).

45. William Cronon, *Nature's Metropolis: Chicago and the Great West* (New York: Norton, 1991), pp. 41–46; David Hamer, *New Towns in the New World: Images and Perceptions of the Nineteenth-Century Urban Frontier* (New York: Columbia University Press, 1990), pp. 230–33.

46. "The New Spokane," *Spokane Falls Review*, August 5, 1890.

47. Spokane Falls Chamber of Commerce, *An Ideal Country; Northwest Magazine*, October 1883, p. 8; C. B. Carlisle, *Spokane Country as It Is. Solid Facts and Actual Results. For the Information of Immigrants and Others*, 2d ed. (Portland: Himes the Printer, 1883), p. 4; [Dallam, Ansell & Edwards], *Settlers' Guide to Homes in the Northwest, Being a Hand-Book of Spokane Falls, W.T., the Queen City of the Pacific, Its Matchless Water Power and Advantages as a Com-*

mercial Center (Spokane Falls: Evening Review Book and Job Print, 1885). See also E. A. Bryan, "Washington for the Immigrant: Frank Advice to Homeseekers," *Pacific Monthly* 19 (April 1908): 390–97. Bryan wrote: "The intending immigrant may obtain valuable information from the 'Chambers of Commerce' or 'Commercial Clubs' which are to be found in almost every city or town. So glowing and so unusual do many of the things which are set forth in these publications seem to the Easterner that he is likely to think them false. So far as my observation goes they are true and well authenticated statements of fact. He would not be a wise reader, however, who would not guess that the best examples are given and the failures and drawbacks omitted. One sees what is possible under good conditions to the thrifty and energetic. Nowhere in the world does wealth come merely from the wish. Here, as everywhere, it requires skill, energy, economy and sound judgment to succeed. I have no hesitancy in asserting, however, that the field of opportunity to the man endowed with these virtues is remarkably good. The State College of Agriculture and the Experimental Station, with which I have been connected for fifteen years, have not only been an important factor in the development of the state, but they will, as in the past, give unbiased advice to the settler if his specific case is stated. They have the development of every part of the state equally at heart and no private ends to gain. They do not wish to encourage any settlers but the best to come to Washington, and they wish to guard the settler against mistakes" (pp. 396–97).

48. [Dallam, Ansell & Edwards], *Settlers' Guide to Homes in the Northwest;* Spokane Falls Chamber of Commerce, *An Ideal Country,* pp. 1–2.

49. Harry H. Hook and Francis J. McGuire, *Spokane Falls Illustrated. The Metropolis of Eastern Washington. A History of the Early Settlement and the Spokane Falls of To-Day . . .* (Minneapolis: F. L. Thresher, 1889).

50. John R. Reavis, "Spokane and Its Country," *Northwest Magazine,* June 1892, p. 27.

51. *A Race for Empire and Other True Tales of the Northwest* (Spokane: *Morning Spokesman-Review,* 1896); *Spokane Falls. Its Banking, Commercial and Manufacturing Interests.*

52. Reavis, "Spokane and Its Country," pp. 19, 17, 22; [Dallam, Ansell & Edwards], *Settlers' Guide to Homes in the Northwest,* p. 10; *Spokane: The Heart of the Inland Empire* (Spokane: E. P. Charlton, 1909); *Northwest Magazine,* April 1890, pp. 33–34.

53. Robert V. M. Schawl wrote several pamphlets promoting the uses of advertising. Schawl, *Nature's Energy. Who Pays for Advertising?* itself was advertised in Schawl, *Wise and Otherwise: A Secret of Successful Advertising,* Vertical File, Northwest Room, Spokane Public Library. Quotations are from this advertisement for the former pamphlet.

54. *Eighth Annual Report of the Spokane Chamber of Commerce* (Spokane: Shaw & Borden, 1905), pp. 6–7; *City of Spokane Falls and Its Tributary Resources, Issued by the Northwestern Industrial Exposition, Spokane Falls, Washington, October 1st to November 1st 1890* (Buffalo, N.Y.: Matthews, Northrup, 1890); *Pacific Monthly* 18 (December 1907), advertising section; Ben Burgunder, "What Part Shall We Take in the Lewis & Clarke Exposition?" Burgunder Papers, MsSc 110, EWSHS. For examples of exposition-related publications, see the map printed for the World's Columbian Exposition held in Chicago: C. H. Amerine, *Spokane, the Greatest Railroad Center of the Pacific Coast, with Statistical Data Pertaining to It's Growth and the Resources of It's Surrounding Country* (Spokane: Chamber of Commerce, 1893); *The Inland Empire and What It Comprehends; On the Lewis and Clark Trail. Illustrated. Supplemented by Concise and Valuable Information Concerning Portland's Great Centennial. Compliments of the Citizens of Spokane, Wash.* [Chicago: Rand, McNally, 1905]. On Spokane as a convention city, see Spokane Chamber of Commerce, Publicity Committee, *What You Will Enjoy in Spokane on Your Western Tour* (Spokane: McKee Printing Co., 1915); Spokane Chamber of Commerce, Travel Service Bureau, *Miss Spokane Invites You* (Spokane: N.p., [1915]); Davenport Hotel, Spokane, *Miss Spokane Welcomes You to One of America's Exceptional Hotels* [Spokane: N.p., 1915].

55. See Oregon Immigration Board, *The New Empire, Oregon, Washington, Idaho: Its Resources, Climate, Present Development and Its Advantages as a Place of Residence and Field for Investment . . .* (Portland: Ellis & Sons, 1888), p. 73; Union Pacific Railway, Passenger Depart-

ment, *The Oregon Short Line Country. A Description of Oregon, Southeastern Washington and Idaho* . . . (Omaha: The Republican, Printers, 1885); P[atrick] Donan, *The Columbia River Empire: Some Hurried Glimpses of a Region Where All Glories of Scene, All Charms of Climate and All Riches of Resources Meet and Shake Hands* (Portland: Passenger Department of the Oregon Railroad & Navigation Co., 1898).

56. Reminiscences, p. 3, Samuel Glasgow Papers, MS Sc 38, EWSHS. See, for one later exception, Northern Pacific Railway Co., *Spokane and the Inland Empire* [St. Paul: N.p., 1916]. R. A. Laird, "Spokane and the Inland Empire," *Union Pacific Magazine,* September 1922, was written by the head of the Spokane Chamber of Commerce.

57. Henry J. Winsor, Bureau of Information, Northern Pacific Railroad Company (NPRR), to Paul Schultze, General Land Agent, NPRR, Portland, Oregon, February 10, 1883, Windsor Letterbooks, Land Department, Northern Pacific Railroad Company Papers, 9.E.11.10F, Division of Archives and Manuscripts, Minnesota Historical Society, St. Paul. See Canadian Pacific Railway Papers, GAI; E. J. Hart, "See This World before the Next: Tourism and the CPR," in *The CPR West: The Iron Road and the Making of a Nation,* ed. Hugh A. Dempsey (Vancouver: Douglas & McIntyre, 1984), pp. 151–69; *Northwest Magazine* 2 (July 1884): 11–16.

58. R. M. Newport, General Land Agent, Northern Pacific Railroad Company, *The Golden Northwest: Northern Pacific Railroad Lands* (St. Paul: Pioneer Press, [1881]); Northern Pacific Railroad Company, *The Pacific Northwest. Facts Relating to the History, Topography, Climate, Soil, Agriculture . . . etc. of Oregon and Washington Territory . . .* (New York: [E. W. Sackett & Rankin], 1882), also published under variant titles by other publishers in 1882 and 1883; Siegfried Mickelson, "Promotional Activities of the Northern Pacific Railroad, 1870–1902" (M.A. thesis, University of Minnesota, 1940); Chicago and North Western Railway, *The Northwestern Pacific Coast Regions: Oregon, Washington Territory and British Columbia* (Chicago: John Anderson, 1884); Passenger Department, Chicago and North Western Railway, *The Pacific Northwest: A Description of the Natural Resources, Scenic Features and Commercial Advantages of Oregon, Washington and Idaho,* 4th ed. (Chicago: Poole Bros., 1907); Great Northern Railway, *To the Scenic Northwest* (N.p.: N.p., [1909]).

On the promotional activities of the Northern Pacific and others, see Arthur J. Brown, "The Promotion of Emigration to Washington, 1854–1909," *Pacific Northwest Quarterly* 36 (January 1945): 3–17; Ross R. Cotroneo, "Western Land Marketing by the Northern Pacific Railway," *Pacific Historical Review* 37 (August 1968): 299–320; James B. Hedges, "The Colonization Work of the Northern Pacific Railroad," *Mississippi Valley Historical Review* 13 (December 1926): 311–42; James B. Hedges, "Promotion of Immigration to the Pacific Northwest by the Railroads," *Mississippi Valley Historical Review* 15 (September 1928): 183–203.

59. "Our North-West Corner," *Scribner's,* May 1985, in Great Northern Railway Company, Advertising and Publicity Department, Magazine and Newspaper Advertisements, 1884–1970 (microfilm), Division of Archives and Manuscripts, Minnesota Historical Society, St. Paul; Great Northern Railway, *The Truth about the Palouse Country: Eastern Washington and Northern Idaho* (N.p.: N.p., 1910); Northern Pacific Railroad Company, *Homeseekers: How and Where to Secure a Home* (St. Paul: The Department, [1895–96]), p. 23.

60. "Follows the Kootenai River," *Harper's Weekly,* June 5, 1897, in Great Northern Railway Company, Magazine and Newspaper Advertisements, 1884–1970. Carlos Schwantes finds a sharp contrast between the images of Washington and British Columbia in general promotional writing during this period. In the indigenous promotional literature of the Inland Empire region, however, such a distinction did not exist. See Schwantes, *Radical Heritage,* pp. 3–11.

61. D. W. Meinig, *The Great Columbia Plain: A Historical Geography, 1805–1910* (Seattle: University of Washington Press, 1968), pp. 3–4.

62. See, e.g., Huber and Hough, *Dillman's Map Showing Spokane Falls as the Great Railroad Center of the New Northwest* (Spokane Falls: Crocker, 1890); "Map of the Inland Empire of the Northwest, Tributary to Spokane," in *Spokane of 1900,* ed. H. N. Stockton and Clarence E. Weaver ([Spokane]: Northwest Illustrating Co., 1900), p. 31.

63. Great Northern Railway, *An Atlas of the Northwest with Maps of the United States and the World* (Chicago: Rand McNally, [1896]), p. 1. See also Northern Pacific Railroad Company, *Sectional Map Showing the Lands of the Northern Pacific Railroad Company in Eastern Washington and Northern Idaho with Condensed Information Relating to the Northern Pacific Country* [Buffalo, N.Y.: Matthews, Northrup, 1884], other versions published in 1887 and 1890; "County Map of Washington and the Inland Empire Region," in *Eastern Washington and Northern Idaho* (N.p.: Northern Pacific Railway, 1910).

64. Day Allen Willey, "Our Inland Empire," *Moody's Magazine* 6 (November 1908): 348. From Willey's perspective, railroads played a key role in the future of the region: "With the construction of the railroads what is known as the Inland Empire of Eastern Oregon and Washington was placed in touch with the rest of the world" (pp. 343–44).

65. See, e.g., Great Northern Railway, *Pacific Coast Conventions, 1902* (St. Paul: Pioneer Press, 1902); Great Northern Railway, *Western Trips for Eastern People* (N.p.: N.p., [1914]). On tourism, see Dean MacCannell, *The Tourist: A New Theory of the Leisure Class* (New York: Schocken Books, 1976); Earl Pomeroy, *In Search of the Golden West: The Tourist in Western America* (New York: Knopf, 1957).

Recent studies on modern tourism in Third World nations suggest some interesting parallels. See Valene L. Smith, ed., *Hosts and Guests: The Anthropology of Tourism* ([Philadelphia]: University of Pennsylvania Press, 1977); Pierre Rossel, ed., *Tourism: Manufacturing the Exotic* (Copenhagen: International Work Group for Indigenous Affairs, 1988); Special Issue, "Tourism and Behavior," *Studies in Third World Societies* 5 (September 1978); Special Issue, "Tourism and Economic Change," *Studies in Third World Societies* 6 (December 1978).

66. Spokane Chamber of Commerce, *What You Will Enjoy in Spokane*, pp. 8–9. See also *Spokane, a Modern City* (Spokane: Chamber of Commerce, [1905]); *Spokane: A Tale of a Modern City* (Spokane: Inland Printing Co., 1908); *The Spokane Country: You Can Make a Barrel of Money Growing Apples in the Spokane Country* (Spokane: Chamber of Commerce, [1908]).

67. Elizabeth B. Custer, *"Boots and Saddles"; or, Life in Dakota with General Custer* (New York: Harper Brothers, 1885), *Tenting on the Plains; or, General Custer in Kansas and Texas* (New York: C. L. Webster, 1887), and *Following the Guidon* (New York: Harper & Brothers, 1899). Although there is an extensive literature on George Armstrong Custer, the secondary work on Elizabeth Bacon Custer is sparse; see Shirley A. Leckie, *Elizabeth Bacon Custer and the Making of a Myth* (Norman: University of Oklahoma Press, 1993), and Lawrence A. Frost, *General Custer's Libbie* (Seattle: Superior, 1976).

68. Elizabeth B. Custer, "An Out-of-the-Way 'Outing,' " *Harper's Weekly* 35 (July 18, 1891): 534–35.

69. [Thomas H. Ryan], *An Open Door to a Magnificent Country* (New York: Spokane Falls and Northern Railway Co., Albert B. King, Printer, 1890), pp. 12, 18, 7–10.

70. Elizabeth Bacon Custer 1890 Diary, Elizabeth Bacon Custer Papers, Monroe County Historical Commission Archives, Monroe County Historical Society, Monroe, Mich.

71. Custer, "An Out-of-the-Way 'Outing,' " pp. 534, 535.

72. *Kettle Falls Pioneer* (Kettle Falls, Wash.), September 3, 1891. See also William S. Lewis and Naojiro Murakami, eds., *Ranald MacDonald: The Narrative of His Early Life on the Columbia under the Hudson's Bay Company's Regime; of His Experiences in the Pacific Whale Fishery; and of His Great Adventure to Japan; with a Sketch of His Later Life on the Western Frontier, 1824–1894* (Spokane: Inland-American Printing Co. for the Eastern Washington State Historical Society, 1923), pp. 23–70, 265.

73. Judge Malcolm McLeod to Ranald MacDonald, [April 1–11, 1893], November 8, 1893, Jacob A. Meyers Collection, Huntington Library, San Marino, Calif.; Lewis and Murakami, eds., *Ranald McDonald*. See also Jean Murray Cole, *Exile in the Wilderness: The Biography of Chief Factor, Archibald McDonald, 1790–1853* (Ontario: Burns & MacEachern, 1979). Although his experience provided a fuller understanding of Japan than that of his contemporaries, MacDonald was far from the "expert" on Japan and the Japanese that he claimed to be. Indeed, the

Japanese who may have read his account could easily have been just as outraged by MacDonald's portrait of their lives as MacDonald was by Custer's portrait.

74. Eva Emery Dye, *MacDonald of Oregon: A Tale of Two Shores* (Chicago: A. C. McClurg, 1906), p. v, *The Conquest: The True Story of Lewis and Clark* (Chicago: A. C. McClurg, 1902), and *McLoughlin and Old Oregon: A Chronicle* (Chicago: A. C. McClurg, 1900). According to Dye, "In his last years, Ranald McDonald desired me to write the story of his life" (Dye, *MacDonald of Oregon*, p. vi). (Although Ranald MacDonald spelled his last name MacDonald, his father's name was usually spelled as McDonald.)

75. Charles W. Freeman to Walter Van Arsdale, February 2, 1909, D. Kaye Papers, MSS 200, FtS.

Chapter 5. Outsiders in the Palouse

1. My thinking about the ideas and behaviors of late nineteenth-century and early twentieth-century farmers has been influenced by Ann Fabian, *Card Sharps, Dream Books and Bucket Shops: Gambling in 19th-Century America* (Ithaca: Cornell University Press, 1990), pp. 153–202; Jane Marie Pederson, *Between Memory and Reality: Family and Community in Rural Wisconsin, 1870–1970* (Madison: University of Wisconsin Press, 1992); and Mary Neth, *Preserving the Family Farm: Women, Community and the Foundations of Agribusiness in the Midwest, 1900–1940* (Baltimore: Johns Hopkins Press, 1995).

2. James J. Hill, *Highways of Progress* (New York: Doubleday, Page, 1910), pp. 141, 153. Many of the essays and speeches in this volume, including "The Northwest," were previously published in the *World's Work*.

3. Hill to Jacob R. Schiff, August 30, 1891, Letterbooks, James J. Hill Papers, JJH. See also Howard L. Dickman, "James Jerome Hill and the Agricultural Development of the Northwest" (Ph.D. diss., University of Michigan, 1977). For overviews of Hill's life, see the authorized biography, Joseph G. Pyle, *The Life of James J. Hill*, 2 vols. (Garden City, N.Y.: Doubleday, Page, 1916–17); and the more recent Albro Martin, *James J. Hill and the Opening of the Northwest* (New York: Oxford University Press, 1976).

4. James J. Hill to John Kennedy, July 30, 1898, p. 2, Letterbooks, James J. Hill Papers, JJH; see also Hill to A. R. Ledoux, July 28, 1898, Letterbooks, James J. Hill Papers, JJH; John Fahey, *Inland Empire: D. C. Corbin and Spokane* (Seattle: University of Washington Press, 1965). On the role of the Great Northern Railway in the Pacific Northwest railroad struggles, see the classic Robert Edgar Riegal, *The Story of the Western Railroads* (New York: Macmillan, 1926); William J. Wilgus, *The Railway Interrelations of the United States and Canada* (New Haven: Yale University Press, 1937); and the company history, Ralph W. Hidy, Muriel E. Hidy, and Roy V. Scott with Don L. Hofsommer, *The Great Northern Railway: A History* (Boston: Harvard Business School Press, 1988).

5. Hill, *Highways of Progress*, pp. 153–55.

6. D. W. Meinig, *The Great Columbia Plain: A Historical Geography, 1805–1910* (Seattle: University of Washington Press, 1968), pp. 241–83. Fahey, "The Railroads: Beneficent, Malignant, Fickle," in *The Inland Empire: Unfolding Years, 1879–1929* (Seattle: University of Washington Press, 1986), pp. 22–47, is a particularly clear overview of the relations between the regional farmers and the railroads.

7. John A. Walker to James J. Hill, April 20, 1901, General Correspondence, James J. Hill Papers, JJH.

8. *Spokesman-Review*, July 2, 30, 1902. On the 1902 meetings see *Spokesman-Review*, July 2, 30, and August 3, 4, 5, 6, 7, 1902; *Colfax Gazette*, August 8, 1902; *Seattle Post-Intelligencer*, August 5, 6, 1902; *Seattle Times*, August 6, 10, 1902; Alexander Campbell MacGregor, *Counting Sheep: From Open Range to Agribusiness on the Columbia Plateau* (Seattle: University of Washington Press, 1982), p. 105; Clippings Scrapbook No. 1, James J. Hill Papers, JJH.

9. *Spokesman-Review,* August 5, 6, 1902; *Seattle Times,* August 10, 1902.

10. Hill to Frank H. Williams, May 18, 1902, Letterbooks, James J. Hill Papers, JJH. See also N. W. Durham, *History of the City of Spokane and Spokane Country, Washington, from Its Earliest Settlement to the Present Time,* Vol. 1 (Spokane: S. J. Clarke, 1912), pp. 513–14.

11. Meinig, *Great Columbia Plain,* p. 374. See also notes on the conference meetings in *Spokesman-Review,* August 6, 1902.

12. "Lived Here Once," *Spokesman-Review,* August 7, 1902, p. 10.

13. See W. N. Carter, *Harry Tracy, the Desperate Western Outlaw: A Fascinating Account of the Famous Bandit's Stupendous Adventures and Daring Deeds* (Chicago: Laird & Lee, 1902); W. B. Hennessy, *Tracy the Bandit, or, The Romantic Life and Crimes of a Twentieth-Century Desperado* (Chicago: M. A. Donahue, 1902); Harry Hawkeye, *Tracy, the Outlaw King of Bandits: A Narrative of the Thrilling Adventures of the Most Daring and Resourceful Bandit Ever Recorded in the Criminal Annals of the World* (Baltimore: Ottenheimer, 1908).

14. Thomas Burke to Hill, August 13, 1902, General Correspondence, James J. Hill Papers, JJH.

15. Parts of the freight rate story are told in Douglas Smart, "Spokane's Battle for Freight Rates," *Pacific Northwest Quarterly* 45 (January 1954): 19–22; Durham, *History of the City of Spokane,* 1:595–604; Glenn Chesney Quiett, *They Built the West: An Epic of Rails and Cities* (New York: D. Appleton-Century, 1934), pp. 496–541; Albro Martin, "Hill or Harriman—What Difference Did It Make to Spokane?" in *Spokane and the Inland Empire: An Interior Pacific Northwest Anthology,* ed. David H. Stratton (Pullman: Washington State University Press, 1991), pp. 109–21. See also "Inland Empire Loses Rate Case," *Spokesman-Review,* January 24, 1919; Charles Edward Russell, "The Heart of the Railroad Problem, Part Two—The Story of the Great Inland Empire and How It was 'Built Up' by Freight Rates," *Hampton's Magazine* 22 (May 1909): 592–604.

16. Hugo Richard Meyer, *Government Regulations of Railway Rates* (New York: Macmillan, 1905), p. 393.

17. U.S. Congress, *Regulation of Railway Rates: Hearings before the Committee on Interstate Commerce, United States Senate in Special Session, Pursuant to Senate Resolution No. 288, 58th Congress, 3d Session, May 18, 1905-May 23, 1905,* vol. 4 (Washington, D.C.: GPO, 1906), pp. 2913–41.

18. The Adams family investments in Spokane, Washington, and Idaho are discussed briefly in Arthur F. Beringause, *Brooks Adams: A Biography* (New York: Knopf, 1985), pp. 214, 267, 290; Edward Chase Kirkland, *Charles Francis Adams, Jr., 1835–1915: The Patrician at Bay* (Cambridge, Mass.: Harvard University Press, 1965), pp. 74, 78; Paul C. Nagel, "A West That Failed: The Dream of Charles Francis Adams II," *Western Historical Quarterly* 18 (October 1987): 397–407. John Fahey traces some of the Adams's Spokane financial transactions in *Shaping Spokane: Jay P. Graves and His Times* (Seattle: University of Washington Press, 1994), pp. 40–41, 47–50. The Adams brothers disagreed over these western real estate investments, especially after their large losses during the Panic of 1873; Brooks worked to divest the family's fortunes from the West.

19. Brooks Adams, *The Law of Civilization and Decay: An Essay on History* (New York: Macmillan, 1897), *America's Economic Supremacy* (New York: Macmillan, 1900), *The New Empire* (New York: Macmillan, 1902). On various interpretations of Brooks Adams's character, writings, and thought, see Daniel Aaron, *Men of Good Hope: A Story of American Progressives* (New York: Oxford University Press, 1951), pp. 245–81; Timothy Paul Donovan, *Henry Adams and Brooks Adams: The Education of Two American Historians* (Norman: University of Oklahoma Press, 1961); Thornton Anderson, *Brooks Adams: Constructive Conservative* (Ithaca: Cornell University Press, 1951); Beringause, *Brooks Adams;* Paul C. Nagel, *Descent from Glory: Four Generations of the John Adams Family* (New York: Oxford University Press, 1983).

20. Brooks Adams, *Railways as Public Agents: A Study in Sovereignty* (Boston: Plimpton Press, 1910); Quiett, *They Built the West,* pp. 528–34.

21. On the "logic of capitalism," see William Cronon, *Nature's Metropolis: Chicago and the Great West* (New York: Norton, 1991), pp. 81–93.

22. Brooks Adams, *Interstate Commerce Commission. No. 819. City of Spokane et al. v. Northern Pacific Railway et al. Brief for Complainants* (Boston: Addison C. Getchell & Son, 1907), hereafter cited as Adams, *Brief for Complainants*; Adams, *Interstate Commerce Commission. No. 819. City of Spokane et al. v. Northern Pacific Railway et al., and Pacific Coast Jobbers' and Manufacturers' Association et al., Interveners. Supplemental Brief for Complainants* (Boston: Addison C. Getchell & Son, 1907). See Theodore Roosevelt to ICC, October 23, 1906, in Elting E. Morrison, ed., *The Letters of Theodore Roosevelt*, vol. 5 (Cambridge, Mass.: Harvard University Press, 1952), pp. 464–65, and discussion of Adams–Theodore Roosevelt correspondence in Beringause, *Brooks Adams*, pp. 284–85.

23. Adams, *Brief for Complainants*, pp. 117, 61; Logan G. McPherson, *Railroad Freight Rates in Relation to the Industry and Commerce in the United States* (New York: Henry Holt, 1909), p. 367; *Before the Interstate Commerce Commission. City of Spokane . . . vs. Northern Pacific Railway Company . . . Reply Brief of Petitioners and Complainants* (Spokane: Inland Printing, 1907).

24. In 1909, the ICC decided in favor of Spokane's 1906 complaint and proposed a new rate schedule. Several events—primarily, hearings on a counterproposal by the railroads, congressional debate over the amendment of ICC's long and short haul clause, and the railroads' appeal to the Supreme Court—postponed the implementation of the terminal rates for Spokane until 1918.

25. Russell, "The Heart of the Railroad Problem," p. 596. Charles Edward Russell republished his *Hampton's Magazine* articles as "The Romance of the Inland Empire" and "The Greatest Melon Patch in the World" in *Stories of the Great Railroads* (Chicago: Charles H. Kerr, 1912), pp. 33–56.

26. Frank Parsons, *The Heart of the Railroad Problem: The History of Railway Discrimination in the United States, the Chief Efforts at Control and the Remedies Proposed, with Hints from Other Countries* (Boston: Little, Brown, 1906), p. 213. For other examples of contemporary studies of railway rates that present Spokane and the Inland Empire in this light, see Robert James McFall, *Railway Monopoly and Rate Regulation*, Columbia University Studies in History, Economics and Public Law, vol. 69, no. 1 (New York: Columbia University, Longmans, Green, 1916); Albert N. Merritt, *Federal Regulation of Railway Rates* (Boston: Houghton, Mifflin, Cambridge, Mass.: Riverside Press, 1907).

27. Adams, *Railways as Public Agents*. "What would Spokane be to-day had she been fairly treated for the last ten years and not discriminated against by the railroads? What would she be to-day if she had enjoyed terminal rates for the last seven or even five years? What will she be five years from now if she shall continuously, during that period be put and kept on an equality with her neighbors?" (Quiett, *They Built the West*, p. 532).

28. Zane Grey, *The Desert of Wheat* (New York: Harper & Brothers, 1919); MacGregor, *Counting Sheep*, pp. 189–90. The novel was originally published in serial form in *Country Gentleman: A Journal for the Farm, the Garden and the Fireside* 83 (May 4, 1918-July 20, 1918). As a group, the farmers clearly identified themselves as Inland Empire residents. See the speeches at regional conventions such as H. C. Sampson, "Why I Believe in the Pacific Northwest," *Proceedings of the Eleventh Annual Convention of the Washington State Grain Growers, Shippers and Millers Association, Pullman, Washington, Jan. 2, 3, & 4, 1917* ([Pullman: N.p., 1917]), pp. 16–21.

29. Grey, *Desert of Wheat*, p. 2; Zane Grey, "What the Desert Means to Me," *American Magazine* 93 (November 1924): 7.

30. Grey, *Desert of Wheat*, p. 37; *Desert of Wheat* manuscript, Zane Grey Papers, Manuscript Division, Library of Congress, Washington, D.C. The newspaper clippings—with few editorial changes—are pasted into manuscript pages.

31. F. D. Heald and H. M. Woolman, "Bunt or Stinking Smut of Wheat," *Bulletin, Washington*

Agricultural Experiment Station 122 ([1917]): 1–23; *Desert of Wheat* manuscript, Grey Papers; McGregor, *Counting Sheep*, p. 188. Established in 1892, the Agricultural College, Experiment Station, and School of Science of the State of Washington (now Washington State University) along with the agricultural experiment station at the University of Idaho in nearby Moscow, published circulars and bulletins, and their agents traveled throughout the region to farmers' institutes and on railroad demonstration trains to communicate their results to farmers. See Wayne D. Rasmussen, "A Century of Farming in the Inland Empire," in Stratton, ed., *Spokane and the Inland Empire*, pp. 33–51; Hegnauer manuscript, esp. chap. 20, Cage 27, Leonard Hegnauer Papers, WSU.

32. Fahey, *Inland Empire: Unfolding Years*, pp. 64–65; Melvyn Dubofsky, *We Shall Be All: A History of the Industrial Workers of the World*, 2d ed. (Urbana: University of Illinois Press, 1988); Paul Frederick Brissenden, *The I.W.W.: A Study of American Syndicalism* (New York: Columbia University, 1919).

33. Carlos A. Schwantes, *Radical Heritage: Labor, Socialism, and Reform in Washington and British Columbia, 1885–1917* (Seattle: University of Washington Press, 1979), p. 214; Latah County Protection Association Records, MG 40, University of Idaho, Moscow. On the organization of the protective leagues, see also *Spokesman-Review*, July 1, 10, 20, August 6, 18, 1917, March 21, 1918.

34. *Spokesman-Review*, August 16, 18, 20, 21, 28, 29, 1917; Carlos A. Schwantes, "Making the World Unsafe for Democracy," *Montana, the Magazine of Western History* 31 (Winter 1981): 18–29. See also *Spokesman-Review*, March 19, June 6, 20, December 28, 1918, May 9, October 22, 1919.

35. Latah County Protective Association Papers; "Colfax to Arm against I.W.W.," *Spokesman-Review*, February 8, 1918; Edwin T. Coman to Henry Rising, March 21, 1918, Henry Rising Papers, MsSC 119, EWSHS. For other examples, see "Citizens of Ione Drive Out I.W.W.," *Spokesman-Review*, January 1, 1918; "Will Use Club on Idaho I.W.W.," *Spokesman-Review*, March 12, 1918; "Twelve I.W.W. Declared Guilty," *Spokesman-Review*, May 31, 1918; "New I.W.W. Office Raided," *Spokesman-Review*, January 24, 1919.

On the World War I–era treatment of the IWW in the Pacific Northwest, see Hugh T. Lovin, "Idaho and the 'Reds,' 1919–1926," *Pacific Northwest Quarterly* 69 (July 1978): 107–15, and "Moses Alexander and the Idaho Lumber Strike of 1917: The Wartime Ordeal of a Progressive," *Pacific Northwest Quarterly* 66 (July 1975): 115–22; Robert L. Tyler, *Rebels of the Woods: The I.W.W. in the Pacific Northwest* (Eugene: University of Oregon Books, 1967); Carl F. Reuss, "The Farm Labor Problem in Washington, 1917–18," *Pacific Northwest Quarterly* 34 (October 1943): 339–52.

36. Christine Bold, for example, considers *The Desert of Wheat* one of Grey's best (*Selling the Wild West: Popular Western Fiction, 1860–1960* [Bloomington: Indiana University Press, 1987], pp. 87–88). For the New York critics' responses to the novel see, e.g., "A 'Movie' of the Northwest," *New York Evening Post*, March 1, 1919, Book Section, p. 8; "The Desert of Wheat," *New York Review of Books*, January 26, 1919, pp. 34–35; "Zane Grey's Fresh Novel of Our Northwest Is One Long Fight," *New York World*, January 26, 1919, p. 4E. On Grey's attempt to break out of the formula western market, see Bold, *Selling the Wild West*, pp. 79–91; Cynthia S. Hamilton, *Western and Hard-Boiled Detective Fiction in America: From High Noon to Midnight* (Iowa City: University of Iowa Press, 1987), pp. 71–93; Frank Gruber, *Zane Grey* (New York: World, 1970).

Conclusion. Ghost Region

1. Marshall Sahlins, *Islands of History* (Chicago: University of Chicago Press, 1985), p. viii. The essays collected in this volume explore the theoretical implications of the Cook encounter. See also Sahlins, *Historical Metaphors and Mythical Realities: Structure in the Early History of the Sandwich Islands Kingdom* (Ann Arbor: University of Michigan Press, 1981); Howard Lamar

and Leonard Thompson, eds., *The Frontier in History: North America and Southern Africa Compared* (New Haven: Yale University Press, 1981), p. 7; and Mary Louise Pratt, *Imperial Eyes: Travel Writing and Transculturation* (London: Routledge, 1992), pp. 6–7, on contact zones.

2. David M. Wrobel, "Beyond the Frontier-Region Dichotomy," *Pacific Historical Review* 65 (August 1996): 401–29; Clyde A. Milner II, "The View from Wisdom: Four Layers of History and Regional Identity," in *Under an Open Sky: Rethinking America's Western Past*, ed. William Cronon, George Miles, and Jay Gitlin (New York: Norton, 1992), pp. 203–22; Elliott West, *The Way West: Essays on the Central Plains* (Albuquerque: University of New Mexico Press, 1995), pp. 127–66; Patricia Nelson Limerick, "Region and Reason," in *All Over the Map: Rethinking American Regions*, ed. Edward L. Ayers et al. (Baltimore: Johns Hopkins University Press, 1996), pp. 83–104; Nancy Shoemaker, "Regions as Categories of Analysis," *Perspectives* 34 (November 1996): 7–8, 10.

3. John Hutchinson and Anthony D. Smith, eds., *Nationalism* (Oxford: Oxford University Press, 1994). Although I would not deny the power of the state or the pervasive presence of the federal government in the West, my emphasis here is on the ways in which regionalism intersects with nationalism.

4. Homi K. Bhabha, "Introduction: Narrating the Nation," in *Nation and Narration*, ed. Bhabha (London: Routledge, 1990), p. 4; Jan Penrose and Peter Jackson, "Conclusion: Identity and the Politics of Difference," in *Constructions of Race, Place and Nation*, ed. Jackson and Penrose (Minneapolis: University of Minnesota Press, 1993), pp. 202–9. See also E. J. Hobsbawn, *Nations and Nationalism since 1780: Programme, Myth, Reality* (Cambridge: Cambridge University Press, 1990); Ernest Gellner, *Nations and Nationalism* (Ithaca: Cornell University Press, 1983); Liah Greenfeld, *Nationalism: Five Roads to Modernity* (Cambridge, Mass.: Harvard University Press, 1992); Benedict Anderson, *Imagined Communities: Reflections on the Origins and Spread of Nationalism*, rev. ed. (London: Verso, 1991).

INDEX

Katherine G. Morrissey
is Assistant Professor of History
at the University of Arizona.